MY ANCE~~STOR~~
WAS
A MERCHANT SEAMAN

HOW CAN I FIND OUT MORE ABOUT HIM?

Christopher T and Michael J Watts

2002

Published by
Society of Genealogists Enterprises Limited
14 Charterhouse Buildings
Goswell Road
London EC1M 7BA
Company Number 3899591

Society of Genealogists Enterprises Limited is a wholly owned subsidiary of
Society of Genealogists, a registered charity, no 233701

First edition 1986
Re-printed, with addendum, 1991
Second edition 2002
© Christopher T and Michael J Watts

ISBN 1 903462 51 7

British Library Cataloguing in Publication Data
A CIP Catalogue record for this book is available from the British Library

ACKNOWLEDGEMENTS

The authors wish to express their gratitude to all the custodians of the records described in this book for the assistance they have rendered over the years. Particular mention must be made of:

* Colleagues at the Public Record Office, especially Kelvin Smith, Rod Ward-Horner, Sarah Collins, John Carr, and William Spencer.
* The staff at the National Maritime Museum, past and present, especially Clive Powell, Alan Giddings, Kiri Ross-Jones and Liza Verity.
* Joanne Smith of Southampton Archives Service and Neil Staples of the Registry of Shipping and Seamen.

We also wish to thank the many individuals who have drawn our attention to particular records or provided information about them. Enquiries received by post, by e-mail, from internet groups, from our own and our professional research and from queries posed at the enquiry desks at the PRO at Kew have all contributed in their way. The names of many of these individuals are unknown to us, so it would be invidious to try to name those whom we do know thereby ignoring those whom we do not. To all of them we are grateful.

We are grateful to Peter Owens, organiser of the CLIP project, for providing an updated list of crew list holdings at various record offices.

We are grateful to Marjorie Moore for reading the draft and offering valuable suggestions and to Sue Lumas for editorial improvements.

Whilst the authors acknowledge assistance given, any errors are ours alone. We would be grateful to hear of any omissions or errors, and about any other useful records not included here.

We are grateful to Geraldine Charles for her permission to use some material from the draft of her book *India and the Far East: A Genealogists Guide*.

Transcripts and facsimiles of Crown copyright records appear by permission of the Controller of HM Stationery Office. Permission to reuse portions of text and illustrations generated whilst in the employ of the PRO and hence Crown Copyright is acknowledged. Transcripts of records preserved in the National Maritime Museum are included by permission of the Trustees of the National Maritime Museum. The transcript of a Retirement Notice from *About Ourselves* is included with the permission of the Peninsular & Oriental Steam Navigation Company. The transcript of Frank Emms' Certificate of Discharge is included with the permission of its owner, his great-granddaughter, Miss Lindsay M. Emms.

About the Authors

Christopher and **Michael Watts** are family historians with 30 years of experience using these records to trace the seafaring activities of their own ancestors. Both are well-known in the family history world, having been active in, and serving on committees of, Family History Societies.

Chris originally trained and worked as a research chemist, but for the past two decades or more has worked as an analyst in the defence electronics industry; since 1997 he has been a part-time Reader Adviser at the Public Record Office. Michael has worked as a nuclear engineer and as a lecturer in mechanical engineering at the University of Manchester.

Both took the opportunity of early retirement and have been continuing their studies both for themselves and, on a professional basis, for others. They are well known, especially in the world of family history, for their books and articles, and lectures in the UK, USA and Australia. They have written, or contributed, to several books including *My Ancestor was in the British Army* and *Records of Merchant Shipping and Seaman*. The first edition of *My Ancestor was a Merchant Seaman* was in print for over 12 years and became recognised as the authoritative work on the subject both for academic and family historians.

CONTENTS

INTRODUCTION

Background

The British have always had a reputation as a seafaring nation, being reliant on this form of transport for trade and for communication with their far-flung empire.

Mainland Britain has almost 2500 miles of coastline, and it is impossible to be more than some 60 to 70 miles from the sea. Such a distance would be considered by any of our ancestors to be no more than a couple of days walking. Against this backdrop, it would therefore be somewhat surprising if a British family did not, at some time, have a connection with the sea or one of its allied trades. Indeed when we set out, many years ago, to trace details of one of our seafaring ancestors we were not to suspect that, in the course of this research, we would uncover details of a dozen other relatives who also had a connection with the sea.

As with any other genealogical research, the searcher should not expect to find records compiled specifically with his interests in mind. Central government was not for the most part, until perhaps the mid-18th century, interested in the welfare of seamen. Consequently it had no interest in compiling records of them. The searcher must therefore turn to records compiled for other purposes, which may incidentally refer to seamen. There are many such records concerned with topics such as the control of trade, taxation on imports and exports by central government; the pursuit and settlement of disputes in the law courts; interaction between the military and merchant arms of the seafaring community and the registration of ships, their insurance and that of their cargoes.

This represents quite a range of possible sources. In this book we set out to survey these sources, albeit briefly, giving details of where to find them, indicating to whom they apply, and providing some examples of their contents. Here we are concerned solely with the merchant seaman; it is true that individuals can and did move between the merchant navy and the Royal Navy. Anybody interested in the Royal Navy should refer to the PRO's Readers' Guide by Dr. Nicholas Rodger[1]. Similarly this book does not concern itself with seamen in the employ of the East India Company, although some mention of it is made in a short section later in this book. Anybody interested in the topic should read the Society of Genealogists' book[2] (currently in press), and the article by Terrick Fitzhugh[3] and then consult the Oriental and India Office Collections at the British Library (often referred to by its former name of the India Office Library) who hold copious material[4].

Getting started

Perhaps the most difficult stage in tracing details of a possible seafaring ancestor is deciding just where to start. The initial clue may well be rather vague - and the searcher may not know whether his ancestor saw service in the military (i.e. the Royal Navy) or the mercantile (i.e. merchant navy). That is not to say that individuals did not see service in both. The Royal Navy, in earlier years, pressed merchant seamen, and others too, into its ranks. And both officers and sailors certainly saw service as merchant seaman after leaving the Royal Navy. What is important is that the records of the two communities are quite distinct and so initially you may need to search in both sets of records.

The second important fact is to determine whether your ancestor was an officer or not. The records of both the Royal Navy and the merchant navy are quite distinctly divided in this fashion. So again your search will be greatly reduced once you have determined this.

It may be tempting to use descriptions of, or used by, your ancestor to help categorise his service. These can be helpful, but should only be used as a tentative indication. The first of these is the use of the word 'boat'. I was once asked whether I thought that an individual had sailed on a particular vessel as crew or passenger. I was shown a postcard of a large ocean-going liner on which the traveller had written 'this is the boat that took us to Canada'. A seafarer would never have referred to a vessel large enough to cross the Atlantic (in any era) as a boat - unless, of course, it was a submarine; he would have called it a ship!

The second term that may, and I stress may, help is the use of the words 'sailor', 'seamen' and 'mariner'. A mariner would most likely have been a merchant seaman. I would have suggested that somebody describing himself as a sailor would most probably have served in the Royal Navy; and that a seaman would have served in the merchant navy. But that distinction is not by any means absolute, especially so if it is being used by non-seafarer. And, confusingly, the terms ordinary seaman and able seaman are used both by the Royal Navy and the merchant navy to denote a seafarer's competence.

Some terms may help you determine whether your ancestor had been an officer or not; but again these need to be used cautiously. Master is the term used in the merchant navy to describe the captain of a ship. But it is also used by the Royal Navy to describe the individual (a warrant, not a commissioned, officer until 1808) who had responsibility for navigation of the vessel.

Captain, though, is perhaps the most confusing of terms. It can, of course, describe officers from the army or the Royal Marines - i.e. non-seafarers. But also it may be a senior Royal Navy officer with that rank - usually referred to as a post Captain. It is also used, within the Royal Navy, as a courtesy title for any more-junior officer who has command of vessel. It is also used, within the Royal Navy, to describe the particular job assigned to a senior sailor - e.g. captain of the foretop has responsibility for some of the sails and rigging aboard a Royal Navy sailing vessel. Lastly, but perhaps not finally, captain is used as a title when addressing the master of a merchant vessel.

In short these words may guide your initial searching, but don't take their meaning too literally until the records have revealed the facts. You may need to search all four categories of material (Royal Navy/Merchant Navy; Officer/Rating) before the truth comes to light. At least one category can be easily ruled in, or out, namely that of Royal Navy officer. The *Navy List* published since 1814 (with a private publication of similar title from 1782 to 1817) lists all Royal Navy officers and there is a printed work *Commissioned Sea Officers of the Royal Navy 1660-1815*[5] that will serve this purpose. But, and there is always a but, a number of ranks that we now consider as officers were not so in days gone by.

There is one further complication if your ancestor served in Indian waters - he could have been in one of the East India Company's navies. A very brief outline of these is given in a later section.

Some warnings!

When describing records we have tried always to name the repository where the originals are held. If we have inadvertently overlooked this then check Appendix 2; in the majority of cases it will be the Public Record Office (PRO).

Where records have been described as in the process of transfer to the PRO then it is essential that you enquire before making a visit since the transfer process may take some considerable time during which the material will be unavailable.

Some material (in particular at the PRO and the National Maritime Museum (NMM)) may be outhoused so, unless you are sure, enquire before you make a special visit.

The Registrar-General of Shipping and Seamen kept on changing his mind as to how to arrange material where the surname began with Mc. In some record series (e.g. Register of Seamen, Series II, Part 1) they will be found under the letter M; in others (e.g. Register of Seamen, Series II, Part 2) under the letter following the Mc prefix (e.g. McDonald under D). So be prepared to check both.

3

TRADE AND TAXATION

Introduction

Two of the major concerns of central government over the centuries have been the control of trade, and the levying of tax on imports and exports. As one might expect this has resulted in the generation of significant quantities of records, which can provide useful information for the family historian. The four that we shall consider here are the Port Books, the Shipping Returns, the records of the Customs and State Papers.

Port Books

Since the time of Edward I (1272) central government has exerted a measure of control over shipping for tax purposes. The records that resulted from this include Receipts of duty paid on imports and exports, Information on the examination of cargoes in the coasting trade and the Issuing of bonds for unloading in ports of the realm.

These documents normally mention the merchants involved and the name of the master of the ship. Typically the information they will contain will be:

- Name of ship and its master
- Name of the merchants
- Description of goods
- Duty paid (if an import or an export, but none was due for coastal trading)
- Places to/from which shipment is made.

For example:

Ilfracombe (Coastal), Midsummer 1733 - Xmas 1733   E 190/999/10
23^d August 1733 In the *Friends Adventure* of Ilfracombe, Cha: Wittingham ma^r from Neath. Twenty chalders of Coal, 5 baggs stockins, and 8 bundles of Flaxxen.   Per Cocq^r.

These documents are to found at the PRO in the following series:

E 122	Custom Accounts	Edward I (1272) - 1565
E 190	Port Books	1565 - 1798
	(Note: Port Books for London, 1696-1795, have been destroyed)	
E 209	Coast Bonds	Elizabeth I (1558) - George III (1820)

The documents are arranged by port (smaller ports being listed under a larger nearby 'head' port) into coastal and overseas; each book normally covers one year. Series E 209 has not yet been sorted or listed. A number of finding aids for series E 190 and E 122 have been published by the PRO[6] and the List and Index Society[7]. Some early material from these records has been published[8] a good description of these records is given in R. W. K. Hinton's book.

Port books sometimes also list passengers if they were travelling together with dutiable goods; J. C. Hotten lists those to America[9].

Equivalent material (Customs Accounts) related to movement of ships in and out of Scottish ports is to be found at the National Archives of Scotland in series referenced E.71 (up to 1640), E.72 (1661-1696) and E.504 (1742-1830); these are arranged by ports. The master of the ship is given but no names of crew or passengers are listed.

Shipping Returns

Similar information, to that found in the Port Books, on the movement of ships inwards and outwards from colonial ports, can be found in both the Board of Trade and Naval Officers' Shipping Returns. These are to be found in a wide variety of series preserved at the PRO, the most important of which are listed below; further material may also be found amongst the various series of Colonial Office correspondence.

Board of Trade Shipping Returns for:

CO 5/508-511	America - Carolina, South	1716-1765
CO 5/573	- Florida, East	1765-1769
CO 5/709-710	- Georgia	1764-1767
CO 5/749-750	- Maryland	1689-1765
CO 5/848-851	- Massachusetts	1686-1762
CO 5/967-969	- New Hampshire	1723-1769
CO 5 /1035-1036	- New Jersey	1722-1764
CO 5/1222-1229	- New York	1713-1799
CO 5/1441-1450	- Virginia	1699-1770
CO 10/2	Antigua and Montserrat	1784-1814
	(See CO 157/1 for 1704-1720)	
CO 27/12-15	Bahamas	1721-1815
CO 33/13-26	Barbados	1678-1819
CO 41/6-12	Bermuda	1715-1820
CO 47/80-83	Upper Canada - Quebec	1786-1814
	- St. John's	1786-1795

CO 66/4	Curacao	1808-1818
CO 76/4-8	Dominica	1763-1819
CO 95/1-2	Gibraltar	1804-6, 1825
CO 106/1-8	Grenada	1764-1816
CO 110/23-24	Guadeloupe	1810-1812
CO 116/17	Guiana, British (Demerara)	1808-1809
CO 128/1	Honduras, British	1807-1812
CO 142/13-29	Jamaica	1680-1818
CO 157/1	Leeward Islands (incl. Montserrat)	1683-1787
CO 166/6-7	Martinique	1809-1814
CO 187/1-2	Nevis	1704-1729
	(See CO 157/1 for 1683-1715)	
CO 193/1-2	New Brunswick	1786-1815
CO 221/28-33	Nova Scotia	1730-1820
CO 221/34-35	Cape Breton	1785-1815
CO 231/2	Prince Edward Island	1807-1809
CO 243/1	St. Christopher	1704-1787
	(See CO 157/1 for 1685-1787)	
CO 259/1	St. Thomas	1808-1815
CO 265/1-2	St. Vincent	1763-1812
CO 278/7-9	Surinam	1804-1816
CO 290/1-3	Tobago	1766-1825
CO 317/1	Virgin Islands	1784-1786

Other similar material can be found in:

BT 6   Miscellanea (1697-1850) include Shipping Returns for:

/186	Jamaica	1781
/188	St. Vincent Island	1784-1788
/188	Norfolk, Virginia	1801
/190	Quebec	1887-1894
HO 76/1-2	Naval Officers' returns - Vessels cleared inwards and outwards at Colonial Ports	1791-1797

T 1   Treasury Board Papers (1557-1920) include:

/430	Shipping Lists - Nova Scotia	1764
/435	Shipping Lists - Annapolis, Maryland	1764
/512	Naval Office Shipping Returns for Antigua, St. Christopher, Nevis and Montserrat	1774-1775
/523	Customs & Excise Returns of ships arriving from and leaving for North America	1775-1776

T 64	Miscellanea, Various (1547-1930) include:	
	Ships entered and cleared	
/47-50	- Barbados	1710-1829
/82	- St. John's, Newfoundland	1770
/84	- Halifax, Nova Scotia	1749-1753
/251-252	Shipping Returns - Scotland	1771-1785
/273-289	Colonies (incl. Shipping & Trade Returns)	1680-1867

A typical entry reads:

A List of all Ships and Vessels which have cleared Outwards in Potomac in Virginia ...

When cleared	*Nov. 10 [1741]*
Vessel's Name	*Cumberland*
Master's Name	*Gerrard Robinson*
Type of ship	*Rd H {= Round Hull}*
Tons	*140*
Guns	*10*
Men	*1*
Where and when built	*Ravenglass, 1735*
When and where Registered	*Whitehaven, Dec 13 1740*
Owner's Name, of what place	*Sir James Lowther*
The General Cargoe - Quantity of	
Tob[acco] H[ogs]h[ea]ds	*338*
Staves	*7000*
Feet of Plank	*600*
Where bound	*Whitehaven*
Where and when bond given	*Whitehaven, 16 Feb 1740*

**Colonial Office: America & West Indies Original Correspondence etc:
Shipping Returns, South Potomac & Accomack Districts, 1735-1736 CO 5/1445**

Some of the Naval Officers' Shipping Lists, related to North America and the West Indies have been published on microfilm[10].

Customs

The records of the Board of Customs and Excise contain much material of potential interest to the family historian. They go back to the late 17th century, though the headquarters records, 1671-1814, were destroyed by fire. Preserved, at the PRO, are the remnants of the headquarters records plus those of the various outports.

The quantity and scope of material is vast, and a comprehensive guide[11] to it was produced by Edward Carson, a former Librarian of the Customs and Excise, in whose custody the records were prior to transfer to the PRO. There is also a useful article in the *Genealogists' Magazine*[12] , albeit a little out of date now.

For those interested in Customs Officers, there are a series of Establishment Books, which can be used to trace a man's career:

CUST 18	Establishments, Series I	1675-1813
CUST 19	Establishments, Series II	1814-1829
CUST 20	Salary Books and Establishments (Ireland)	1682-1826
CUST 21	Miscellaneous Books	1715-1857
	(include Establishments at Bermuda,	
	British Guiana and West Indies c.1806)	
CUST 39	Establishment: Staff Lists	1671-1922
CUST 40	Establishment: General	1818-1926

The series lists for CUST 18 to CUST 21 have been published in *List and Index Society, Vol. 20*[13].

Establishment Books for the separate Scottish Board of Customs, which operated from 1707 to 1829, are to be found at the National Archives of Scotland in series CE.3 and CE.12. These quarterly lists, which are arranged by port, include all Customs officials except junior clerks and the crews of cutters (although masters and mates are named). Salaries paid to Customs officers are recorded in series E.502. Those Customs officers on the establishment in 1752 and 1755 are listed in GD.1/372/1 and RH.2/8/102 respectively.

Those interested in seamen, ships' masters and owners will find the outport records, and in particular the Outport Letter Books, most useful. These contain copies of the correspondence sent by the local Customs officials to the Board in London; the corresponding replies have been lost though. The content of this material is very varied covering all aspects of the duties of the Customs and Excise. A typical entry might be:

Outport Letter Books: Great Yarmouth	CUST 97/59
No. 297	4 December 1838

Letter of complaint from the Tide Surveyor complaining about the conduct of James Watts, master of the steam tug *Accommodation* of this port. Watts refused to bring ship to proper station for boarding by Revenue. Watts has been working in this capacity for 3 years. Customs Officer fines him £100.

These volumes are arranged by port, and most volumes contain a good index.

CUST 50 - 102	Outport Records for ports in England and Wales	late 17th cent. - mid 20th cent.
CUST 104	Outport Records, Isle of Man	1820-1970
CUST 105	Outport Records, Channel Isles	1806-1965
CUST 113	Outport Records, Ireland	1679-1849

Reference will be found, in these Outport Letter Books, to the sending in of copies of Apprentices' Indentures that are now in BT 151 and BT 152; these are described later with the records of the Registrar General of Shipping and Seamen. However the Customs records do not seem to contain the early copies of those indentures that should have been retained locally. But some Registers of Apprentices, usually from the late 1800s, seem to have been kept by local Customs Houses. Occasionally these may be found here, e.g.

CUST 69/224	Bideford	1857-1880
CUST 67/81	Fowey	1825-1925
CUST 57/28	Littlehampton	1856-1897
CUST 56/89	Newhaven	1893-1908
CUST 52/112	Ramsgate	1893-1908
CUST 91/121	Scarborough	1884-1894
CUST 68/185	Scilly Isles	1857-1878
CUST 64/205	Teignmouth	1853-1893

More often though, where they survive, they are to be found at the appropriate County Record Office.

Also to be found locally, again normally now at County Record Offices, are Shipping Registers; these are described with the other Registers of Shipping that they complement.

Early Crew Lists (Muster Books) are sometimes found amongst the Outport Letter Books; for example those for Scarborough ships, 1754-1765, are in CUST 91/112 and for Plymouth, 1776-1780 in CUST 66/227 and it is possible that further ones still await discovery. These are further mentioned later with the records of the Registrar General of Shipping and Seamen.

The payment of bounties to the crews of Scottish ships engaged in whaling and herring fishing may reveal useful information; these include:

E.508/47/8-130/8	Vouchers for bounties: whale-fishing	1750-1825
E.502/48-130	Customs cash accounts related to	1750-1825
	Vouchers for bounties: whale-fishing	
E.508/49/9-96/9	Vouchers for bounties: herring-fishing	1752-1796
E.502	Customs cash accounts related to	1752-1796
	Vouchers for bounties: herring-fishing	

From these one should be able to determine the names of the crew, the ship, its owners and port. These records are at the National Archives of Scotland.

State Papers

The various series of State Papers, Domestic and Foreign may contain information incidentally about ships and seafarers, but locating references, if any should exist, to any particular individual, ship or incident will depend greatly on luck and perseverance. But the recently published CD-ROM of the *Calendar of State Papers, Colonial, North America and West Indies*[14] does make such a search great deal easier. Otherwise the best starting point is the over 200 volumes of Calendars to the Domestic, Foreign and Colonial Papers, ranging from the reign of Henry VIII to that of George III. These calendars often contain sufficient information from the original document making recourse to the original papers often unnecessary.

Series *SP 35 (State Papers Domestic, George I, 1714-1727)* and *SP 36 (State Papers Domestic, George II, 1727-1760)* have had extended lists compiled which contain indexes to persons, places and ships.

Amongst the *State Papers Domestic, Addenda, Edward VI to James I (1547-1625) (SP 15)* is to be found a 'Register of merchant ships in England, with the names of their masters' compiled by Thomas Colshill, surveyor of the Port of London dated 1572 (SP 15/22).

In the 1620s to 1640s, surveys of maritime resources were made on a parish-by-parish basis; these survive mostly at the PRO amongst the State Papers, Domestic. The detail within the returns does vary, but they often include lists of names of mariners together with their ages; lists of ships are also given with the names of their owners and masters. The most comprehensive returns are probably those for Devon and Cornwall and these, compiled from records in SP 16 and associated sources elsewhere, have been published by the Devon and Cornwall Record Society[15]. The bibliography in this publication gives a number of other useful sources of information both at a local and national level.

Counties for which similar material is believed to survive at the PRO, mostly amongst the *State Papers Domestic, Charles I (SP 16 and SP 17)* are:

Bristol	SP 16/39/50 and 138/4
Chester	SP 16/33/120
Cornwall	SP 16/33/69-70, 34/104, 34/107, 135/5
Devon	SP 16/34/98, 34/101 and 34/103
Dartmouth:	SP 16/34/99
South Devon:	*The Duke of Buckingham's Survey of Mariners and Ships,* 1619 (Pepys Library, Magdalene College, Cambridge. Ref: PL 2122)
Dorset	SP 16/138/11
Hampshire	SP 16/32/72 and 132/34
Isle of Wight	SP 16/33/3 and 132/20
Kent	SP 16/34/109-111 and 132/19, SP 14/140/64-69, 142/39 and 142/52
Hastings:	SP 16/142/24-5
Lancaster with Liverpool	SP 16/36/1
Lincoln	SP 16/33/129 and 138/60-61
London	SP 16/135/4 and 135/38
Norfolk	SP 16/34/1
Northumberland	SP 16/34/42
North Wales	SP 16/31/56 and 35/12

MILITARY CONNECTIONS

Introduction

Until the introduction of Continuous Service, in 1856, sailors in the Royal Navy were signed on for a single voyage. In theory, when the ship returned to the UK, they were discharged. As both the Royal Navy and the Merchant Navy were drawing on the same pool of labour to man their ships, we would expect to find Admiralty records containing information related to merchant seamen. This interaction was reinforced by the fact that the Royal Navy could, and indeed still does, draw on the resources of the Merchant Navy to assist it in time of war.

As a result of this there are at least five sets of Admiralty records that can yield information about merchant seamen, namely: Letters of Marque; Mediterranean Passes; Receiver of Sixpences; Registers of Protection from being Pressed; and Royal Naval Reserve service records. The first four of these are described below; the Royal Naval Reserve is described later in the section on War Service and Medals. All these records, unless otherwise indicated, are held at the PRO.

Letters of Marque

During times of war, the Admiralty made use of armed merchantmen against enemy shipping. Letters of Marque are the authority, granted by the Admiralty, to the commander of a vessel to act as a privateer and harass enemy shipping.

Records exist covering the period 1549-1815, but most apply to the late 1700s and early 1800s. The series of relevance are:

ADM 7	Admiralty and Secretariat Miscellanea include /317-332, 649 Registers of Letters of Marque, 1777-1815	1563-1947
DEL 2	Delegates Causes Papers	c.1600-1834
HCA 25	Letters of Marque, Bonds etc.	1549-1815
HCA 26	Letters of Marque, Declarations	1689-1814
PC 5	Plantation Books include Warrants for Letters of Marque	1678-1806

HCA 26 contains the Declarations, made in the High Court of Admiralty, by each commander giving the name of ship, number of guns, number of crew, and names of owners and principal officers. These Declarations are indexed, by ship's name for the period 1793-1814. Declarations related to America, France and Spain have been published on microfilm with an introductory booklet and index[16]. HCA 25 contains Bonds for observance of the articles or instructions; these are signed by sureties; a few bonds are to be found in DEL 2. The series lists are arranged by year and nationality of the enemy; the series lists for HCA 25 and HCA 26 have been reprinted in *List and Index Society, Vol. 27*[17].

These records may be of use in finding information about owners, commanders and principal officers.

Mediterranean Passes

In addition to the Letters of Marque, mentioned above, ADM 7 contains a series of Mediterranean Pass Registers and Indexes (ADM 7/73-164, 630) covering the period 1662-1850. These were issued to provide English ships with protection against attack by the Corsairs of the Barbary Coast of North Africa; they are available on microfilm[18].

A typical entry from the Pass Book for 1818-1811 (ADM 7/124) includes:

Number of Pass	*7958*
Date of Certificate	*1807 May 23*
Nature	*Snow*
Ship's Name	*Nancy*
Of what place	*Dublin*
Burthen	*157*
Guns	*2*
At what place	*London*
Master's Name	*Rob Moreton*
Men - British / Foreign	*2 / 6*
Built	*British*
Whether bound directly from the place the pass was recorded at	*Malta*

Letters relating to Mediterranean Passes (1730-1816) are to be found in ADM 2/1319-1325.

Receiver of Sixpences

When originally founded, Greenwich Hospital was supposed to be for the benefit of merchant seamen as well as the Royal Navy. To help finance the hospital a levy was made of sixpence a month that was deducted from each merchant seaman's wages. Despite this, there is no evidence that merchant seamen actually benefited from the facilities provided by that institution; these seem to have been reserved for Royal Navy personnel. This was a point of major discontent amongst the merchant seafaring community. The levy was raised in 1834 to 2 shillings for a master or owner and one shilling for a seaman; the fund, then known as the Seamen's Fund, was wound up in 1851.

The records of the receiver for the Thames survive in *ADM 68 (Greenwich Hospital, Various Accounts and Ledgers)*; pieces 194 - 219 covering the period 1725-1830. They are arranged chronologically, but include an Index of Masters (/219), for the period 1745-1752, and an Index of Ships' names. A typical entry from ADM 68/210 reads:

Receiver of Sixpences Annual Accounts (1805-1818)	ADM 68/210
Date (when paid the 6d per man)	*29th Jan 1806*
Where last paid	*London*
Ship or Vessel's name	*Hester*
Of What place	*Yarm°*
Of What Burthen (tons)	*135*
No. of men usually sailed with	*8*
Master's Name	*Wm Bristow*
Whence Arrived or what Trade	*Riga*
To what time last paid	*15 Aug 1805*
Time of first Man's entry	*16 Aug 1805*
Time of last Man's discharge	*29 Jan 1806*
No of Months for a man	*36*
Monies rec^d.	*£0-18-0*

The dates given may be used to guide a search through these records to trace the voyages of a ship or its master. Sometimes the entry under the heading 'To what time last paid' the term '1 Paymt' (i.e. first payment) is given indicating no previous (recent) payment for this ship.

The Index of Masters (ADM 68/219) is quite informative in itself, e.g.

No. of men	*15*
Time of entry	*23 Nov 1746*
Commander's name	*Wade, Saml*
Ship's name	Greyhound
Of what place	*Yarmouth*
Whence	*Kinsale*
When cleared	22
When paid	*22 Dec^r*

The date on which the levy was paid was usually a week or two after entering the river.

Whilst most of the surviving records relate to the Thames, three volumes for the port of Exeter (1800-1820 and 1832-1851) are to be found in BT 167/38-40. Also in the same series, under the heading 'Seamen's Fund Registers' (BT 167/41-52) is some material, described as 'Ships Books' and 'Alphabetical Lists of Ships', for the period 1837-1851, that may possibly relate to the receipt of monies at other ports. The entries in these volumes are arranged alphabetically by ship's names and record ship's name, master's name, port, tons, men paid from, paid to and number (of men?).

Further details about these records may be found in articles by Dr. Nicholas Rodger[19] and by Ralph Davis[20].

Register of Protection from being Pressed

During war the Royal Navy resorted to the Press to man its ships, but various categories of men were, theoretically, exempt. For instance an Act of 1739 defines protected persons as: all those under eighteen and over fifty-five; foreigners; volunteers after two years service; harpooners, line managers, boat steerers engaged in the Greenland fishery, but not the Newfoundland fishery; herring fishers on the east coast during the season. But Christopher Lloyd[21] questions to what degree these protections were actually honoured in practice.

ADM 7 (Admiralty and Secretariat Miscellanea) contain *Registers of Protection from being Pressed*, pieces 363-400 covering the period 1702-1828. A typical entry therein reads:

Register of Protection from being Pressed, Fishermen and Coastal Trade: Persons under Age (1803-1816)			ADM 7/391
Date of Examination	Reason for Protection	Man's Name	[Date of Birth*] [Date of becoming of age (= 18)*]
26 Dec 1804	Over Age	Robert Thorne	
13 March	Under Age	W. Fry	19 July 1790 19 July 1808

* Note: The meaning of the last two columns is our interpretation.

The documents are arranged chronologically and are not indexed.

Repatriation of shipwrecked mariners

For the period 1729 to 1826, records survive giving details of payments to masters of merchant ships for giving passage home to shipwrecked mariners and other distressed British subjects. These survive, at the PRO, in records series *ADM 30 Navy Board: Navy Pay Office: Various Registers*. Pieces 22, 24 and 25 are chronological registers; the last two (covering the period 1816-1826) include indexes to masters' names. Piece 23 is correspondence between 1729 and 1815. The registers record the master's name, the ship's name , the number of men brought home, from what place, when put on board and when and where landed.

LEGAL DISPUTES

Introduction

Records of legal disputes have long been recognised as a fruitful area for research by the family historian. The High Court of Admiralty is the court where matters relating to the high seas were brought. Although the High Court of Admiralty was probably set up in the time of Edward III, it was initially mostly concerned with matters of piracy and spoil. Up to 1525, general high seas matters were dealt with by the Chancery Court. Much has already been written on the records of the Chancery Court[22,23,24,25], and we will not duplicate it here. Appeals from the Instance Court of the High Court of Admiralty were, until 1833, to the High Court of Delegates and thereafter to the King in Council and subsequently to the Judicial Committee of the Privy Council.

All these records are preserved at the PRO. Potential searchers are warned that most of the records of the High Court of Admiralty and the High Court of Delegates are, until 1733, in Latin although depositions may be in English. This, combined with the fact that there are very few satisfactory indexes, makes these records very difficult to use. Material about ships and individual seafarers of all classes is certainly to be found here but locating anything about a specific individual or ship must be considered as serendipity.

Certain prerogative jurisdictions did also exist and records of such courts might be found locally. For instance the Tyne & Wear Record Office hold the records of the Newcastle Admiralty Court from 1664-1756.

The material described above does not apply to Scotland that has its own laws and courts quite separate from those of England. A brief outline of the records relevant to Scotland is included at the end of this chapter.

High Court of Admiralty

The High Court of Admiralty was concerned with cases involving piracy, privateering, ships and merchandise on the high seas and overseas. Its jurisdiction was subdivided into two parts, Ordinary or Instance, and Prize Courts. The Instance Court, which is of most interest to us, dealt with Civil, Criminal and Admiralty Droits matters; droits being rights or perquisites such as proceeds arising from the seizure of wrecks. Either of the first two, civil and criminal, matters may be of interest to the family historian. The List and Index Society have published many of the PRO series lists for this material[26].

Instance Court

The records of the Instance Court include proceedings over wages, over collisions and about commercial disputes. Clearly they may make mention of anybody who went to sea, or had an interest in the sea. The following series may contain material of interest:

HCA 3	Acts	1524-1786
HCA 13	Examinations and Answers	1536-1826
HCA 15	Instance Papers, Early	1629-1778
HCA 16	Instance Papers, Series I	1772-1806
HCA 17	Instance Papers, Series II	1807-1839
HCA 18	Instance Papers, Series III	1840-1859
HCA 19	Instance Papers, Series IV	1860-1876
HCA 20	Instance Papers, Series V	1875-1943
HCA 24	Libels etc.	1519-1814
HCA 27	Minute Books (Instance)	1860-1924
HCA 30	Miscellanea	1531-1888

The *Instance Papers (HCA 15 - HCA 20)* and *Libels etc (HCA 24)* contain the original files relating to instance cases and are thus the main source of information; HCA 15 also contains some prize papers. The *Minute Books (HCA 27)* contain brief notes on each case and, up to 1918, each volume is indexed by ship's name. *Miscellanea (HCA 30)* include many subsidiary documents and is well worth exploring. Earlier instance papers may be found in *Acts (HCA 3)*, which consist of Act Books and minutes or drafts of acts, and *Examinations and Answers (HCA 13)*.

In addition the series *Oyer and Terminer Records 1535-1834 (HCA 1)*, contain proceedings for crimes, including piracy, committed on the high seas.

Prize Court

The series of *Prize Papers (HCA 32)* contains a miscellany of material concerning ships captured as prizes in time of war that could yield something useful. Included there are allegations, claims, attestations, commissions, affidavits and exhibits such as ships' papers and intercepted letters. It is arranged alphabetically by ship's name, and the series list also gives the master's name.

Examinations and Answers (HCA 13) also refer to the Prize Court and contain depositions of witnesses and examinations taken on commission and thus may be very useful. Examinations are statements or depositions made by the accused or by a witness. An answer is the counter-statement made in reply to a complainant's bill of charges.

The series *Monitions (HCA 31)* may also contain something of interest. Monitions were part of the summons process, giving notice of the seizure of a ship as a prize and warning those interested to appear before the Court to show cause why the ship should not be condemned as a lawful prize.

HCA 13	Examinations and Answers (Prize)	1536-1826
HCA 31	Monitions (Prize)	1664-1815
HCA 32	Prize Papers	1661-1855

High Court of Delegates

Appeals from the Instance Court of the High Court of Admiralty were to the High Court of Delegates. After that Court was abolished in February 1833, appeal was to the King in Council and subsequently the Judicial Committee of the Privy Council. The *Assignation Books of the King's (Queen's) Proctor (TS 15)* contain notes of proceedings in Appeals (1827-1873) from Admiralty Instance and Prize Courts and from Vice-Admiralty Courts; and in prize cases during the Russian War, 1854.

The following series may contain information about seamen and seafaring activities:

DEL 1	Processes	1609-1834
DEL 2	Cause and Miscellaneous Papers	c.1600-1834
DEL 7	Bound Volumes of Printed Appeal Cases	1796-1834
DEL 8	Miscellanea	1536-1866
DEL 9	Muniment Books	1652-1859
DEL 10	Testamentary Exhibits	1636-1857

Indexes to some records in these series, covering the 19th century, are in *Miscellaneous Lists and Indexes (DEL 11)*.

Scotland

In Scotland, the High Court of Admiralty, a quite separate court from that of England, had jurisdiction in all maritime and seafaring cases, both criminal and civil, until 1830. The key series of records that may assist, which are now held at the National Archives of Scotland[27], are the Decreets and Processes; these are to be found in AC.7, AC.8, AC.9, AC.10, and AC.15. If your ancestor committed a crime at sea, between 1705 and 1830, details may be found in AC.16 - but the court in fact heard few such cases. Such guides as are available may be consulted in the reading rooms.

REGISTRATION OF MERCHANT SEAMEN

Introduction

The first Register of Seamen was actually instituted in 1696 under the Act for the Increase and Encouragement of Seamen. But, as registration was voluntary, it met with little success and the act was repealed in 1710. Unfortunately for us no records of those registering seem to have survived.

The Ship Owners' Society (London General Shipowners' Society[28]) did actually set up a Merchant Seamen's Registry in 1817 but it was short-lived, lasting until 1826 or thereabouts. Occasionally a certificate issued to one of the 1,731 men that did register is discovered in private hands, but no central register has been discovered. Minute books of the society, dating from 1816, do survive with General Council of British Shipping - but no records of individual registrations survive there and the minute books do not mention individual seamen.

In the mid-18th century central government began to introduce measures to control the Merchant Navy of Britain and its Colonies. The purpose of this was twofold, firstly to improve seamen's conditions and perhaps more importantly to help man the Royal Navy in time of war. The reasons, for our purposes, are unimportant. It is sufficient to say that this movement resulted in copious quantities of records, which survive today mostly at the PRO. For those interested in knowing more about the records and the history behind their generation, there is a very useful article by Dr. Nicholas Cox[29].

Following the passing of the 1835 Merchant Shipping Act, masters of ships were required to file Agreements and Crew Lists with the new Register Office of Merchant Seamen (the forerunner of the Registrar General of Shipping and Seamen (RGSS)). The Act had provided for the registration of seamen in order to create a means of manning the Navy in time of war, and to meet this need the Registrar attempted to create an index of seamen from the crew lists. The indexes and registers so produced are the key to tracing an ordinary seaman during the period 1835-1857; they give details of the seaman himself and a cross-reference to the crew lists filed for his voyages.

It should be noted that the Registrar, in creating these indexes and registers, had an extremely difficult task in identifying individual seamen; many were illiterate, or made illegible signatures or gave false names. Also some masters seemed more concerned with meeting the legal requirement of filing a return than with the accuracy of its contents. When searching the registers, possible errors in transcription should be borne in mind.

Register of Seamen, Series I, 1835-1836

The first series of registers consists of a mere five volumes, in which seamen are arranged alphabetically; *Register of Seamen, Series I (BT 120).* A typical entry reads:

No.	Name	Age	Place of Birth	Quality	Ship belonging to	How disposed of
	Th					
2766	*Thompson .M.*	*23*	*Pidl.*		*Jemima Kincardie of Stole*	
2767	*Thomas George*	*20*	*Swansea*		*Isle Hilyar of Bidl.*	

Register of Seamen, Series I (1835-1836), S - Z (BT 120/5)

This simple system was soon overwhelmed by the mass of crew lists and was replaced by a second series.

Register of Seamen, Series II, 1835-1844

Introduction

The *Register of Seamen, Series II (BT 112)* should incorporate all the entries for seamen included in the first series (BT 120). The reference number assigned to those seamen in the first series was used again in Part 1 of the second series and the voyage details should have been copied across - though one may find it easier to interpret the entries as recorded in the first series. Naturally BT 112 contains details of additional seamen not recorded in BT 120 and probably further voyages for those who were.

The arrangement of the second series, until recently, has not been well understood and anybody who has previously used it may find it worth repeating the searches based on the new finding aid mentioned below. The register in fact consists of two distinct parts, covering the period 1835 to February 1840 (Part 1) and December 1841 to 1844 (Part 2) - there is nothing corresponding to the missing dates. Originally Part 1 consisted of probably some 19 volumes in which the entries were arranged according to a numeric system with an associated set of name indexes (now in BT 119/1-27). Part 2 probably consisted of some 71 volumes in which the entries were arranged approximately alphabetically; a single index volume (BT 119/28) showed the page allocated to each surname (plus forename for common surnames). At some stage, probably during its actual use by the RGSS, these two sets of volumes were dismembered and reassembled in a vain attempt to rationalise them into a single coherent alphabetical series of some 79 volumes. All of the original material, except that for letter A of Part 1, has survived, but in a jumble that presents a nightmare to the present-day researcher. The author has examined the material extensively and produced a finding aid (of over 40 pages) that allows the researcher to identify the correct portions of the registers and indexes for any part of the alphabet. This finding aid is available at the PRO and anybody wishing to search these registers is strongly advised to make use of it.

Part 1, 1835 - February 1840

The entries in Part 1 are numerically arranged, and the index should be consulted to find reference numbers that may refer to the individual sought. The indexes are mostly to be found in Alphabetical Index to Seamen BT 119, pieces 1 - 27, but the finding aid referred to above will tell you if they have been misplaced or are missing. In our own researches, for a great-grandfather James Watts, we found the following entry (in BT 119/24):

Name	Age	Born	Reference	Ship(s) served in
WATTS, James	17	Haisbro	4621	Aerial

and, as luck would have it, we discovered that his two elder brothers had also been to sea:

WATTS, John	18	Haisbro	2432	Osprey, Harriet
WATTS, Robert	18	Haisbro	4562	Thainston

It should be noted the index might only give seamen's names and the reference number.

Return to the finding aid, mentioned above, which will tell you which volume, in BT 112, and which folios contain entries corresponding to the required reference numbers for seamen whose surnames begin with a particular group of letters. Note that reference numbers are only unique within initial letter pairs. This may sound complicated, but will become much clearer when you see the finding aid.

The corresponding entry in the Register for James Watts was (BT 112/74):

Name	Reference to Voyages
4621 WATTS, James 17 Haisbro	Co 75.8 June 39 Aerial

The last column, under the heading 'Reference to Voyages', gives a cross-reference to a sailing on the ship Aerial in the half year ending June 1839, and explained below:

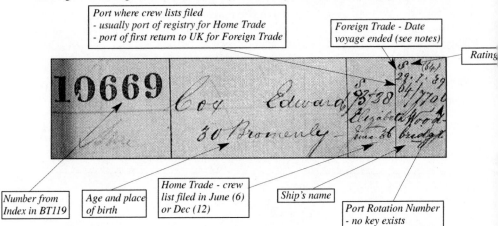

Notes:
- The dates given are those on which the various schedules were filed and not actual arrival dates. These can only be determined by consulting the crew lists or, in the case of foreign voyages, by consulting *Lloyd's List*.
- No key to Port Rotation Numbers has been located. Crew lists for this period are preserved at the PRO in series BT 98 and are arranged, for the whole period, by port of registry and then ship's name.
- A list of commonly-found abbreviations, including those used for 'Rating' are given in Appendix 1.

Part 2, December 1841 - 1844

Part 2 is rather easier to consult since the entries are arranged in an almost alphabetical sequence, although there is an index (mostly in BT 119/28) which tells you which page to look at for a particular surname (plus forename, for common surnames). Again use of the finding aid mentioned above will be necessary in order to locate quickly the relevant portion of the register itself in BT 112.

A typical example from Part 2 is as follows (BT 112/73):

	Name	Reference to Voyages
45.915	WATTS, James 25 Haisbro	Co 16.20 Minstrel 20/11/44*
(*An error in copying was made here the Crew List itself gives 20 Nov 1843)		

The entries under 'Reference to Voyages' may be interpreted in a manner similar to those found in Part 1, namely:

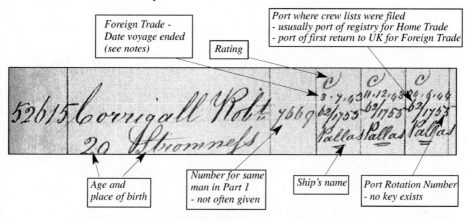

Foreign Trade -
Date voyage ended
(see notes)

Rating

Port where crew lists were filed
- ususally port of registry for Home Trade
- port of first return to UK for Foreign Trade

Age and
place of birth

Number for same
man in Part 1
- not often given

Ship's name

Port Rotation Number
- no key exists

Notes:
- The dates given are those on which the various schedules were filed and not actual arrival dates. These can only be determined by consulting the crew lists or, in the case of foreign voyages, by consulting *Lloyd's List*.
- No key to Port Rotation Numbers has been located. Crew lists for this period are preserved at the PRO in series BT 98 and are arranged, for the whole period, by port of registry and then ship's name.
- A list of commonly-found abbreviations, including those used for 'Rating' are given in Appendix 1.

An unexpected use of these registers was to help us to trace the birthplace of another ancestor who died before the 1841 census. He was James Watts's father-in-law Thomas Thorn, a mariner, who died in South Shields, County Durham, in 1839, aged 42. Family tradition held that one branch of our Tyneside family originated in Devon or Cornwall. We searched the index, to Part 1, and found 9 Thomas Thorns; some were clearly duplicate entries so that one born in 1793 came from Ilfourdcombe (the old name for Ilfracombe), while one born in 1802 came from Ilford Cove. 'Both' were on ships sailing from Tyneside, and when we searched the Ilfracombe Parish Registers there was only one Thomas Thorn, baptised in 1797; moreover the Devon family names (Robert, Mary, William and Thomas) agreed precisely with the names given to children in South Shields.

Register of Seamen's Tickets, 1845-1854

In 1844 new regulations were introduced in order to establish a Register Ticket system; each British seaman leaving the United Kingdom had to have a Register Ticket. There is an *Alphabetical Register of Seamen's Tickets (BT 114)*, which we consulted for James Watts and, along with about 100 others, we found (in BT 114/21):

	Birthplace	Ticket No.
WATTS, James	Harbro' (sic)	47874

Using the Register Ticket number we could consult the *Register of Seamen's Tickets (BT 113)* and were to find there (in BT 113/24):

Register of Seamen's Tickets, 1845-1854 (BT 113/24)

24

The Register Ticket gives some fascinating biographical information; besides furnishing a description of our great-grandfather, the Ticket was the only source giving his date of birth, omitted from the baptismal registers of Happisburgh (pronounced Haisboro) in Norfolk. Moreover the Register contains a list of 'Reported Voyages' by year, in numerical code, derived from the Crew Lists and, provided their meaning can be unravelled, one can trace the corresponding crew lists with their details of the voyages. The Register Ticket Number will be found against each man's name on the crew lists (except Schedule A).

The entries under 'Reported Voyages' can be interpreted as:

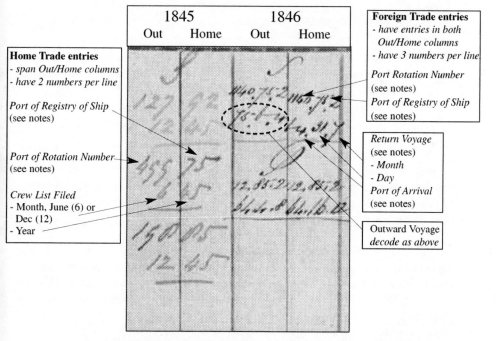

Notes:
- The dates given are those on which the various schedules were filed and not actual arrival dates. These can only be determined by consulting the crew lists or, in the case of foreign voyages, by consulting *Lloyd's List*.
- No key to Port Rotation Numbers has been located. Crew lists for this period are preserved at the PRO in series BT 98 and are arranged, for the whole period, by port of registry and then ship's name.
- A list of commonly-found abbreviations, including those used for 'Rating' and a list of the numbers used for abbreviations for Ports (arrival, departure, registry) is given in Appendix 1.

You need to be aware of several points about the index and the entries in the registers:

- The registers only go up to ticket number 546,000 although entries may be found in the index with higher numbers. In such cases no further information is available.
- Many entries will be found, towards the end of the life of the register ticket system, where no details have been entered for the seaman although his name appears in the alphabetical index in BT 114.
- If a ticket number found in the index includes a letter (e.g. S or A, B etc) the supplementary volumes at the end of BT 113 should be consulted to find the correct ticket.
- Under 'Reported Voyages' no entries seem to have been made for the years 1849, 1850 and 1854; it should not be assumed that no crew lists were filed for those years.
- It seems to have been normal practice, for at least part of this period, for sailors in the Royal Navy to be issued with a Register Ticket; this can be readily seen as the place of issue for the ticket will be given as 'HMS ...'
- Register Tickets were also often issued to those in the Coastguard Service; this will either be clearly stated in the register or can often be deduced from the 'capacity' given.

This set of registers is particularly important to the genealogist as it supplies the place of birth, usually prior to 1837, of seamen; this is vital since a seaman will not be found in the census returns unless he happened to be ashore at the time or unless his ship was in a UK port at the time of the census.

These registers are office copies; the original ticket (sized approx. 7 ½ ins x 4 ½ ins) was given to the seamen himself. He was supposed to carry this with him to sea and was provided with a small metal container, approximately ¼ in thick, that attached to his belt and into which he could just fit the ticket after folding it into eight. So, not surprisingly, few have survived and those that do are in very poor condition. If one has survived it will be in private hands.

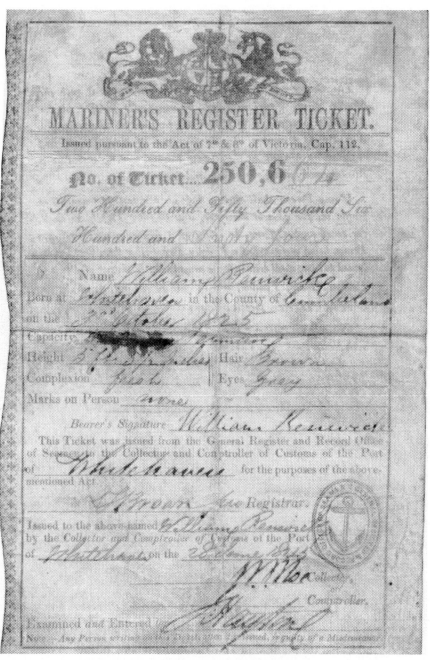

An original seaman's ticket

Register of Seamen, Series III, 1853-1857

The ticket system was unpopular with seamen and difficult and expensive to enforce and was abolished in October 1853. A new register, of 106 volumes, was started, listing seamen alphabetically - *Register of Seamen, Series III (BT 116)* - and giving their age, place of birth and details of voyages (ship's name, date and port of departure), together with their existing Ticket number (if any), e.g:

NAME AND DESCRIPTION			Age	VOYAGES					
				1853		1854		1855	
				Out	Home	Out	Home	Out	Home
No.	No. of Certificate	No. of Ticket	*15*						
James Watt									
Born at *Lanark*									

Register of Seamen, Series III, 1853-1857   (BT 116/98)

The gap - 1858-1912

Even the simplified system represented by the Register of Seamen, Series III was discontinued in 1857 as unworkable. It was also considered unnecessary since the information required by statute was available in other documents, such as Agreements and Crew Lists. But, in 1910, an Advisory Committee on Merchant Seamen proposed that a Central Index Register of Merchant Seamen be created. They argued that the statutory need was not being met simply by retaining Agreements and Crew Lists as these were not a Register as specifically required by statute.

So for the period between the end of the Register of Seamen, Series III (late 1857) and the start of the surviving records of the Central Index Register (1913) the only available records for the ordinary seamen are the Agreements and Crew Lists. As you will see, in a later section of this book, although all these have been preserved they are scattered around several archives world-wide - and there is no index to the names in them. So without the name, and port of registry, of a ship on which a man sailed it is a hopeless task trying to track down his seafaring career.

Where the name of a ship on which the individual sailed, during this period, is not known from other sources then two possibilities present themselves. The first is to check whether the individual served in the Royal Naval Reserve. The second is to make a check in the census returns to see if he was aboard ship at the time. There is a specific index to those on board ships in the 1861 census (of England and Wales) and the 1881 and 1901 censuses have comprehensive indexes that can be searched by computer. Both these possibilities are discussed elsewhere in this book.

Central Indexed Register, 1913-1941

Introduction

The Central Indexed Register, sometimes referred to as the Fourth Register of Seamen, was started in October 1913 and was maintained until 1941. It is believed that the main series (CR 1 and CR 2 cards) for the period 1913 to 1920 were destroyed in 1969, although there is also a special index surviving covering the period 1913-1921 (CR 10 cards).

These records include details of all categories of persons who went to sea, not just ordinary seamen; included are details of mates, engineers, trimmers, cooks, stewards, etc. The CR 10 cards do include information on masters, but the others (CR 1 and CR 2) rarely seem to do so. A small proportion of the Central Indexed Register cards refers to women reflecting the start of their acceptability as seafarers.

If an individual cannot be located here this may be because service was recorded on CR 1 and CR 2 cards for the period 1913-1920, which have been destroyed, or it continued after 1941 and the record has been transferred to the subsequent Central Register of Seamen (1941-1972).

The Register consists of four large card indexes (approximately 1.25 million cards have survived), available on microfiche at the PRO; the original cards are preserved at Southampton Archives Service. These are arranged as described below.

CR 10 Cards - PRO series BT 350
Registrar General of Shipping and Seamen: Register of Seamen, Special Index, Alphabetical Series (CR 10), 1918-1921. The CR 10 cards form a special index (made by a 1918 Order under the Defence of the Realm Act) and, as well as including similar information to the CR 1 cards described below, bear a photograph of the seaman. This series, which is alphabetically arranged, seems to have been primarily intended to record the issue of seamen's identity certificates.

CR 1 Cards - PRO series BT 349
Registrar General of Shipping and Seamen: Register of Seamen, Central Index, Alphabetical Series (CR 1), 1921-1941. The CR 1 cards are arranged alphabetically by surname and include:

- Place and date of birth;
- Discharge book (Dis.A) number - follow this up in the CR 2 cards and perhaps the Mixed series;
- Royal Naval Reserve (R.V.2) number - follow this up in BT 377 (for ratings) or, when it comes to the PRO, in ADM 240 (for officers);

- Rating or rank, with certificate numbers for officers - follow up in BT 352
- A short description of the individual.

A few of these cards, normally related to non-British subjects, also bear a photograph of the seafarer. These cards should be consulted to find a Dis.A number before proceeding to the CR 2 cards.

CR 2 Cards - PRO series BT 348
Registrar General of Shipping and Seamen: Register of Seamen, Central Index, Numerical Series (CR 2), 1921-1941. The CR 2 cards are arranged numerically by discharge book (Dis.A) number, ignoring any initial letter, although it is significant indicating the seaman's nationality or country of origin (see Appendix 1 for details) - individuals have been found with the same number but with differing initial letters. The card includes a brief record of the ships on which the seaman served (normally by ship's official number, but occasionally giving the ship's name) and the dates of signing on - these are mostly on the reverse of the card, but do not overlook the one on the front of the card!

Where the ship's name is not given this can be determined, at this date, from its Official Number by consulting PRO series *BT 336 (Registrar General of Shipping and Seamen, Registers of Changes of Masters)*, which happens to be arranged conveniently in ship's number order. But do confirm what you find by subsequently checking in the alphabetical lists given in the *Mercantile Navy List*. [Note: the official list, called Appropriation Books, arranged in numerical order is still in use by the Registry of Shipping and Seamen, who could be approached if this process fails.]

Mixed series - PRO series BT 364
Registrar General of Shipping and Seamen: Register of Seamen, Combined Numerical Index (CR 1, CR 2 and CR 10). This fourth index is believed to have been compiled, for reasons that are unclear, by extracting the cards from the other three indexes. It is arranged numerically, with the CR 1 card leading, and there are usually three cards (CR 1, CR 2 and CR 10) for each seaman. Because of its numerical arrangement, and the fact that the CR 2 and any CR 10 card should have been extracted from the alphabetical series described above, there is no convenient means of reference to these cards. But if a seamen's Dis.A. number is already known (these are given on crew lists at this date) then the series can be consulted. It is, though, always worth checking here even if a card has already been discovered in the other series giving a Dis.A. number - sometimes the supposed extraction process was imperfect!

An example of a CR 10 card for an early woman seafarer is:

C.R. 10.   No. of Identity Certificate........S.1.7.5.76

○   M.N.S. Region.......................Regional No.....................

Surname................*morgan*.....................................

Christian Name..............*Nellie Edith*..............

Rating....*Gail Stdess*.......R.N.R. No.....................

No. and Grade of B/T Certificate.............................

Date and Place of Birth..2.1.4.1880 *manden kent*

Nationality ...*Brit*....... Father..........*Brit*..............

Height.................Colour Hair..............Eyes...............

Tattoo Marks...

Dis. A No...................N.H. Insurance No...............

Name and Address of Next of Kin..............................

....

(32581) Wt. 20167—23. 100m. 8/18. Av. P. (503)
(11693) Wt. 5203—11. Rpt. 20m. 5/19. Av. P. (1272).

127659   14.3.19.
134093   21.4.17.
132093   16.5.19.
"   3.7.19.

817736

CR 10 card from the Central Indexed Register, 1918-1921

31

One possible way around the problem described above is available for seamen who sailed to the United States. From 1917 onwards the masters of all vessels, whatever their nationality, calling at a US port had to file a List or Manifest of Aliens Employed on the Vessel as Members of Crew and a list of any changes that had taken place prior to departure; these would, of course, have included any British or colonial seamen. Collections of these forms are to be found at the US National Archives (in Record Group 85, Records of the Immigration and Naturalisation Service) and some are available on microfilm - e.g. those for vessels arriving at Gulfport, Mississippi (1919-1945*); Mobile Alabama (1925-1931); Pensacola, Florida (1907-1939); Philadelphia, Pennsylvania (1918*). [* indicates that only changes in alien crew, not the full list]. It is likely that other lists do survive in manuscript form. Those related to the port of New York and Ellis Island have been transcribed and indexed (as part of a larger project related to passenger manifest) and are available on the internet at www.ellisislandrecords.org - having found an entry be sure to look at the image of the original document since it often contains information not found in the index or transcript. Typically the manifest will record details of each seaman's name, age, sex, race, nationality, height, weight, physical marks, whether able to read, where and when engaged and position in ship's company, length of service at sea. Provision is made on some, but not all lists, to record the number of the seamen's identification card - and you may be lucky to find the Dis.A. number recorded here. The Ellis Island database covers the period 1892-1924.

Dating also from 1917, seamen's identity cards were issued by the US authorities to alien seamen[30]. In addition, from August 1940, US law required the registration of alien seamen - a provision that cover the period 1940-1944. Collections of these are to be found in the US National Archives, either in Washington or at a regional branch.

Central Register of Seamen, 1942-1972

Introduction

In 1941 a Merchant Navy Reserve Pool was created to ensure that seamen would always be available to man vessels; the Government paid them to remain in the Reserve Pool when they were ashore. Thus continuous paid employment instead of casual employment was available to all seamen, and comprehensive and effective registration became possible.

All those who had served at sea during the previous five years were required to register and a new Central Register of Seamen (sometimes referred to as the Fifth Register of Seamen), was established. CR 1 and CR 2 cards of seamen who were still serving in 1941 were removed from the old Central Indexed Register and placed in the new Central Register of Seamen (CRS 10), index. The Central Register of Seamen was maintained until 1972; it consisted of two series of documents described below.

CRS 10 Docket books - PRO series BT 382
The CRS 10 Docket Books are the main component of the register containing a entry
for each seafarer; they are arranged alphabetically within a number of groupings:

- Series 1, seamen mainly of European origin (1941-1946)
  Note: Information later than indicated by these dates may often be found here.
- Series 2, seamen mainly of European origin (1946-1972)
- Asiatic Seamen, mainly of Indian origin (1941-1965)
- Asiatic Seamen, mainly of Indian origin (1966-1972)
- Seamen of Indian, Chinese and Foreign Nationalities - Unnumbered Series
  (1941-1972)
- Allied Prisoners of War and Internees (1941-1945)
- Service on Royal Navy Ships: Auxiliary War Vessels (T124, T124T, T124X etc)
  (1939-1945)
- Deaths of Merchant Seamen recorded for pension purposes (1944-1951)

Note: The series described as 'mainly of European origin' do include many
individuals from British colonies outside Europe.

The main series include the following information:
- Place and date of birth;
- Discharge book (Dis.A) number [any initial letter indicates the seaman's
  nationality or country of origin (see Appendix 1 for details) - individuals have been
  found with the same number but with differing initial letters];
- Rank or rating, with certificate numbers for officers;
- Details of any other qualifications;
- A list of ships, with date and place of engagement, rank or rating, F or H
  (for Foreign or Home trade voyage), with date and place of discharge and
  character. When ashore the sheet will bear the entry MNRP (Merchant Navy
  Reserve Pool) with date and place.

Note: Whilst this list of voyages should be complete, examples have been found
where the contents of an individual's pouch (in BT 372) have revealed additional
voyages.

On the front of a CRS 10 form (this one is from BT 382/400) are given details about the individual:

The reverse of the same form gives details of the individuals voyages:

Central Register of Seamen BT 382/400

Seamen's pouches - PRO series BT 372

In addition to the Docket Books (CRS 10) a series of seamen's pouches (referenced CRS 3) were created. Records relating to individual seamen were filed together in the pouches, which appear to have been used as a kind of 'safety deposit box'. Their contents, however, cover the period 1913 to 1972. When seamen were discharged some or all of their documents were placed in the pouches and these include discharges of seamen who were originally registered in the Central Indexed Register of 1913 to 1941. Most pouches contain the individual's British Seaman's Identity Card (BSIC), bearing a photograph and finger prints, for example (from BT 372/400):

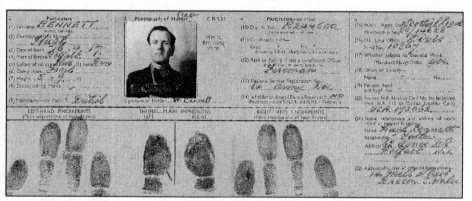

The pouches are preserved at the PRO in record series *Central Register of Seamen: Seamen's Records (Pouches) (BT 372)*; they are arranged in order of discharge number, irrespective of any initial letters, but the on-line catalogue includes seamen's names, date and place of birth. Pouches with discharge numbers up to about 95,000 were destroyed sometime before 1988. Additionally pouches were either not created, or do not survive, for every seaman. Information later that 1972 is sometimes found in a pouch.

After 1972

From 1973 onwards the current register is maintained by the Registry of Shipping and Seamen. In it are recorded details of the when the seafarer joined, the granting and renewal of certificates, and any disciplinary matters; voyage details are not given. Information is only released to the individual or, if deceased, the next of kin. It is called the 'UK series' as discharge book numbers bear the prefix UK. Both ordinary seafarers and officers are included in this register which has a supporting alphabetical index. As with the earlier Central Register of Seamen, Seamen's Pouches contain supporting miscellaneous documentation.

CERTIFICATES FOR SEA OFFICERS

Introduction

Prior to the introduction in the mid-19th century of examinations, and certification, for sea officers, there are no coherent sources for tracing their career. One must rely on the sources described elsewhere in this book such as Port Books, Shipping Returns, Letters of Marque, Mediterranean Passes, Receivers of Sixpences, and court records such as those of the High Court of Admiralty.

Even after the introduction of certificates there are still a number of incidental sources that will be also be described in this chapter.

Information on a master or mate in the service of the East India Company should be sought amongst the Oriental and India Office Collection at the British Library. Details of those in its employ 1760 may be found in Charles Hardy's book published in 1835[31].

Incidental sources

Alphabetical Register of Masters, 1845-1854
At the same time as compiling a Register of Seamen's Tickets, the Registrar General of Shipping and Seamen compiled an *Alphabetical Register of Masters (BT 115)*. This contains similar information to that given in the various earlier seamen's registers. But, as it was compiled solely from information contained in the filed crew lists, it does not contain the same useful genealogical information contained in the seamen's tickets. Voyage details found therein may be interpreted in the same manner as already described for the Register of Seamen's Tickets. BT 115 covers the period 1845-1854.

Changes of master.
The registration documents for a ship should contain details of the master, giving his certificate number – these are described in the section on Shipping Registers – Transcripts and Transactions.

From 1894 to 1948, a specific *Register of Changes of Master (BT 336)* was maintained. This is organised numerically by ships' official number giving the date and port at which the master joined the vessel, together with his name and certificate number.

Official and semi-official publications
Lloyd's Register, which is described more fully in the section on Lloyd's Marine Collection, includes against each vessel the name of the master. But as it is an annual publication, arranged by ships' names, it will be a tedious process to follow the career of any individual master here. For masters sailing between Britain and Australia the

Society of Australian Genealogists has compiled a Sea Captains' Index; this card index is taken from the 1834, 1836, 1848 and 1852 editions of *Lloyd's Register*. Lists of those passing the voluntary examinations (1846-1852) appeared at the time as appendixes to *Lloyd's Register*.

The *Mercantile Navy List*, an official government publication since 1850, contains lists of Certificated Masters and Mates etc. Initially these lists were complete, but later simply consisted of newly granted certificates. The *Mercantile Navy* List for 1863 contains an alphabetical list of masters and mates, 1845-1862; the same year it also included a list of those certificates that had been cancelled between 1857 and 1863.

The *London Gazette* also published lists of those granted masters' and mates' certificates; look in the index under 'Merchant Shipping: Masters and Mates Examinations'.

From time-to-time reports made to parliament about seafaring may yield the names of masters; these should be sought amongst the printed series of *Parliamentary Papers*, to which there is a good index on CD-ROM.

A wide range of books has been published covering many aspects of maritime activity; many of these name specific ships and their masters. A few of these books are listed in the bibliography.[32]

Certification for Masters, Mates and Engineers, 1845-1965

Voluntary examinations, 1845-1850
From 1845 onwards a system of examinations was introduced for masters and mates; at first it was voluntary and applied only to foreign-going vessels, but its scope was extended and gradually made compulsory from 1850. Masters and mates passing the voluntary examination, prior to 1850, should be included in the *Certificates of Competency and Service, Miscellaneous (BT 143)*, for example:

Certificates of Competency, Miscellaneous.	BT 143/1
Date:	*May 4, 1848*
Name:	*Henry Lambell*
Class of Certificate:	*Third*
Name of Board by whom Examiners appointed:	*Marine Board, South Shields*
Year born:	*1818*
Where born:	*Chatham, Kent*
No of Register Ticket:	-
Remarks:	*PS Northam of S. Shields 221 tons, as Mate.*

Lists of those passing these voluntary examinations appeared, between 1846 and 1852, in appendixes to *Lloyd's Register*: for example, in 1848:

An Alphabetical List of all the Masters and Mates in the Merchant Service, who have voluntarily passed an Examination, from time to time, and obtained Certificates of Qualification for the Class against each assigned under the regulation issued by the Board of Trade.

MASTER	Class	Age	Present or last service	No of Register Ticket	Where Examined	When
Watts, William	2nd	26	*Free Trade* 277 Tons (as Mate)	345865	London	10 Dec 1847

The *London Gazette* also published, monthly between 1845 and 1854, details of those passing these voluntary examinations. The names of those from Devon are included in *The London Gazette: Devon Extracts, 1665-1850* published by the Devon Family History Society (1987). Extract containing these details from the *London Gazette* should also be found in BT 6/218-219.

Certificate registers, 1850-1921
From 1850 examinations became compulsory for masters and mates of foreign-going vessels; from 1854 this requirement was extended to masters and mates of home trade vessels. Certificates obtained by examination are termed Certificates of Competency. Few examination registers seem to have survived but where these do they should be sought locally.

Masters and mates, examined by the Corporation of Trinity House, might be granted pilotage exemption certificates to allow them to pilot their own vessels in waters where they would otherwise need to take an independent pilot. Records of these survive at the Guildhall Library, amongst the records of Trinity House: *Registers of exemption certificates 1850-1957 (Ms 30182)*, giving age and physical description and the vessel's name and shipping company, and *Registers of masters' and mates' examinations 1864-1986 (Ms 30184)*.

Those who had sufficient experience as a master or mate, as well as those retiring from the Royal Navy, were eligible without formal examination for Certificates of Service. Those granted certificates of service who wished to progress to a higher grade had to pass the appropriate examination.

A similar system of certificates was instituted for Engineers in 1862 and for Skippers and Mates (Second Hands) of Fishing vessels in 1884.

Whilst at this period, masters and mates should have had certificates, it was certainly not unknown, especially in the coastal trade, for an owner to save money by employing a non-certificated officer. This was particularly true with mates, and the fact that a man was described on, for example, a civil marriage certificate as a mate does not always mean he will be found amongst these records. If he is not to be found there then the records of ordinary seamen, already described, should be searched.

Details of the certificates were entered into registers arranged in numerical order: name of officer, place and year of birth, register ticket (if any - referred to as 'Pilotage Certificate'), rank examined for, or served in, and date of issue of certificate; for example:

Certificates of Service, Masters and Mates, Foreign Service (BT 124/18)

In addition (but only up until 1888) each man's voyages after the certificate was granted are recorded, and may be followed up in the Crew Lists.

<u>Interpreting entries for Home Trade Voyages</u>

These entries do not simply record a single voyage, but rather a period of time during which the officer was engaged on a particular ship in the home trade.

The example below is taken from BT 126.

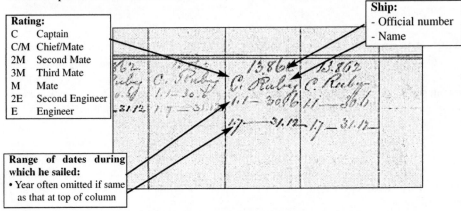

Rating:
C   Captain
C/M   Chief/Mate
2M   Second Mate
3M   Third Mate
M   Mate
2E   Second Engineer
E   Engineer

Ship:
- Official number
- Name

Range of dates during which he sailed:
• Year often omitted if same as that at top of column

Interpreting Entries for Foreign Trade Voyages

These entries record a single voyage, from the UK back to the UK, during which the officer was engaged on a particular ship. The example below is taken from BT 124.

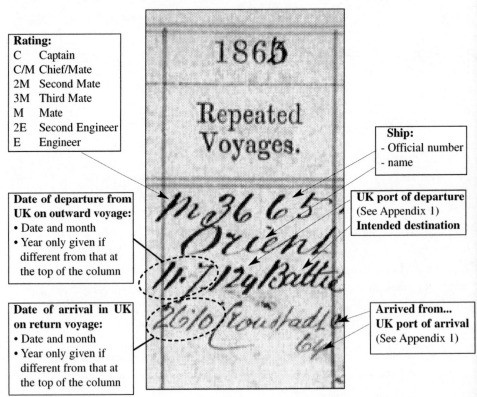

Rating:
C   Captain
C/M   Chief/Mate
2M   Second Mate
3M   Third Mate
M   Mate
2E   Second Engineer
E   Engineer

Ship:
- Official number
- name

Date of departure from UK on outward voyage:
• Date and month
• Year only given if different from that at the top of the column

UK port of departure (See Appendix 1)
Intended destination

Date of arrival in UK on return voyage:
• Date and month
• Year only given if different from that at the top of the column

Arrived from...
UK port of arrival (See Appendix 1)

If the entry is annotated with the letters BB followed by a number, this implies that disciplinary proceedings were taken against the Certificate holder.

These Certificates do contain rather less information than in the corresponding registers for ordinary seamen. However it should be remembered that virtually all masters and mates would have held a Register Ticket before applying for their Certificate. This should also be followed up for earlier information about him. The Pilotage Certificate referred to, in the example above, is in fact actually his Register Ticket.

Care should be taken in using these records as there may be several registers covering a particular certificate number, and date of issue; these will cover and record different periods of service for the certificate holder - all of these should be consulted until the man ceased to go to sea. In addition there may be a summary volume, which gives basic details about the certificate holder, including perhaps his date of death or giving up his certificate, but it will not provide voyage details.

Fuller details may often be found with the Applications for Certificates described later. These Certificates are contained in 12 series of registers according to the type of certificate and type of trade:

BT 122	Registers of Certificates of Competency, Masters and Mates, Foreign Trade	1845 - 1900
BT 123	Registers of Certificates of Competency, Masters and Mates of Steamships, Foreign Trade	1881 - 1921
BT 124	Registers of Certificates of Service, Masters and Mates, Foreign Trade	1850 - 1888
BT 125	Registers of Certificates of Competency, Masters and Mates, Home Trade	1854 - 1925
BT 126	Registers of Certificates of Service, Masters and Mates, Home Trade	1854 - 1888
BT 128	Registers of Certificates of Competency, Masters and Mates, Colonial	1870 - 1921
BT 129	Registers of Certificates of Competency, Skippers and Mates of Fishing Boats	1880 - 1921
BT 130	Registers of Certificates of Service, Skippers and Mates of Fishing Boats	1883 - 1917
BT 139	Registers of Certificates of Competency, Engineers	1861 - 1921
BT 140	Registers of Certificates of Competency, Engineers, Colonial	1870 - 1921
BT 142	Registers of Certificates of Service, Engineers	1862 - 1921
BT 143	Registers of Certificates of Competency and Service, Miscellaneous	1845 - 1849

There are three consolidated indexes to these volumes, namely:

BT 127	Index to Registers of Certificates of Competency and Service, Masters and Mates, Home and Foreign Trade	1845 - 1894
BT 138	Index to Registers of Certificates of Competency and Service, Skippers and Mates of Fishing Boats	1880 - 1917
BT 141	Index to Registers of Certificates of Competency and Service, Engineers	1861 - 1921

Note: BT 127 does not include details of those who obtained voluntary certificates (1845-1850) but many who obtained those probably went on to obtain compulsory ones and will thus be found there for that reason.

When searching these indexes, you will find that names beginning with Mc or Mac are usually to be found under the letter following that prefix, and not under the letter M; so, for example, MacDonald will appear under 'D'. The entries in the index provide details of a man's place and year of birth together with a certificate number. This certificate number given is that which was allocated when he was granted his first certificate; he would not necessarily have be given a new number when he progresses to a higher grade; though a new number will sometimes be allocated if a replacement certificate has to be issued. The certificate number indicates:

MASTERS AND MATES

Certificate Number	Certificate Type		Trade	Series commences	Series
1 - 34,999	Competency	Master or Mate	Foreign	1 Jan. 1851	BT 122
35,000 - 54,999	Service	Master	Foreign	Dec. 1850	BT 124
55,000 - 69,999	Service	Mate	Foreign	Dec. 1850	BT 124
70,000 - 78,999	Service	Master	Foreign	April 1851	BT 124
79,000 - 80,999	Service	Mate	Foreign	May 1852	BT 124
81,000 - 99,999	Competency	Master or Mate	Foreign	Oct. 1868	BT 122
100,000 - 119,000	Competency	Master or Mate	Home	March 1855	BT 125

MASTERS AND MATES

Certificate Number	Certificate Type		Trade	Series commences	Series
120,000 - 134,999	Service	Master	Home	April 1855	BT 126
135,000 - 150,000	Service	Mate	Home	April 1855	BT 126
01 - 0500	Yacht Master				-
0501 - 045,000	Competency	Master or Mate	Foreign	July 1875	BT 122
Note: BT 122 contains those with numbers up to 034,999; those from 035,000 to 039,989 are currently in BT 123/5; no records exist in either series for numbers from 039,990.					
001 - 0021,000		Master or Mate	Foreign, steam	April 1881	BT 123
Note: No records exist in these series for numbers from 0016,000.					
21,001 -		Master or Mate	Foreign, steam	May 1927	-

ENGINEERS

Certificate Number	Certificate Type		Series commences
1 - 400	Service	1st class Engineer	1862
401 - 3,000	Service	2nd class Engineer	1862
3,001 - 5,000	Service	1st class Engineer	
5,001 - 5,999	Service	2nd class Engineer	March 1930
6,000 upwards	Competency	Engineer	1862

SKIPPERS & MATES OF FISHING BOATS

Certificate Number	Certificate Type	Series commences
01 - 03000	Skippers, English	December 1883
03001 - 04888	Second Hands, English	December 1883
05001 - 05765	Skippers, English	January 1884
05800 - 05999	Skippers, Scottish	May 1907
06000 - 07561	Second Hands, English	July 1887
07600 - 07881	Second Hands, Scottish	May 1907
08000 - 08180	Skippers, Scottish	May 1907

Where a certificate number has one or more letters appended (e.g. NSW) this indicates that the certificate was issued in the colonies.

The *Mercantile Navy List*, an official government publication since 1850, contains lists of certificated masters and mates etc. Initially these lists were complete, but later simply consisted of newly granted certificates. The *Mercantile Navy List* for 1863 contains an alphabetical list of masters and mates, 1845-1862; the same year it also included a list of those certificates that had been cancelled between 1857 and 1863.

The *London Gazette* also published lists of those granted masters' and mates' certificates.

A 'Return of the Names of those Certificated Masters of the Mercantile Marine who, between the 1st day of January 1870 and the 1st day of July 1875, have passed the Board of Trade Examination in 'Steam' and 'Compass Deviation' appears under that title in the *House of Commons, Parliamentary Papers (1875) vol LXVIII p 303 (mf 81.538)*. This contains two lists, one for each examination giving simply each man's name; though it does not say so, it is presumed that this must be in date order.

Information regarding the granting of foreign-going masters certificates was passed regularly to Lloyd's, the insurance society. From this they compiled what is now known as *Lloyd's Captains Register*; this covers the period 1851-1947. Details of this are to be found in the section on Lloyd's Marine Collection.

Applications for Certificates 1845-1928
In addition to the registers preserved at the PRO, the National Maritime Museum holds the office copies of certificates issued; on file with these are the Applications for Certificates. The Certificate Number, found from the indexes at the PRO, or in *Lloyd's Captains Register*, is needed for the Application to be produced. As some of these documents are outhoused at Woolwich it is wise to enquire about their availability before making a visit.

The documents held at the NMM cover the whole period of operation of the certificate system in this form (i.e. up to 1928) and comprise:

MASTERS AND MATES

Type	Number	Comments
Masters and Mates, Competency, Foreign Trade	1 - 34999	
Masters, Service, Foreign Trade	35000 - 54999	
Mates, Service, Foreign Trade	55000 - 69999	
Masters, Service, Foreign Trade	70000 - 78999	
Mates, Service, Foreign Trade	79000 - 80999	
Masters and Mates, Competency, Foreign Trade	81000 - 99999	
Masters and Mates, Competency, Home Trade	100000 - 119000	
Yacht master	01 - 099	
Masters and Mates, Competency, Foreign Trade	0500 - 044217	044050 to 044217 seem to relate to duplicates issued 1926 to May 1940.
Masters and Mates, Competency, Foreign Trade, Steam	001 - 0021000	001700-003299 wanting.
Masters and Mates, Competency, Foreign Trade, Steam	1001 - 23800	

ENGINEERS

Type	Number	Comments
Engineers, Certificates of Service	1 - 4129	
Engineers	6000 - 22999	
Engineers - 1st	6404 - 22999	
Engineers - 1st and 2nd	23000 - 24999	
Engineers - 1st and 2nd	25000 - 34199	
Engineers - 1st and 2nd	34200 - 38999	
Engineers	39000 - 39299	
Engineers - 1st and 2nd	39300 - 63200	
Engineers	63201 - 64301	

FISHING

Type	Number	Comments
Skippers	1 - 5999	
Skippers Certificates	6000 - 15249	
Skippers and 2nd Hands	15250 - 17300	
Skippers, Certificates of Service	01 - 0349	
Skippers and 2nd Hands	05800 - 05999	
2nd Hands	07400 - 07899	07900 - 07999 noted as missing.
Skippers	08000 - 08199	
2nd Hands	1A - 139A	
Skippers	2960A - 3099A	

MISCELLANEOUS

Certificates of Pilotage, Ports A-W: 1859-1897	1 box of documents	

Where the certificate number is preceded by one or more letters (e.g. C for Canada; NSW for New South Wales) this indicates that it was issued in the colonies. In that case any surviving application should be sought in the appropriate archives of that state or country.

These documents are very interesting as the applicant for a Certificate of Service had to list in detail all the voyages that he had undertaken over at least the previous four years, in addition to giving essential information such as date and place of birth and current address. This information is contained on a form that the applicant himself filled in and signed. A signed office counterpart of the actual certificate is on file also. For example:

MATE'S CERTIFICATE OF SERVICE   No 57589

No of REGISTER TICKET   49 872

Number   *Fifty Seven Thousand Five Hundred & Eighty Nine*

Robert Thorne

Born at *South Shields County of Durham* on the *23rd Decr 1829*. Has been employed in the Capacity of *App Seaman & Mate 19 years in the British Merchant Service in the Coasting & Foreign Trades.*

Bearer's Signature   *Robert Thorne*

Issued at   *South Shields*   this *11* day of *July* 18 *63*

Thus in order to trace the career of a master or mate it will be necessary to consult the Seamen's Registers, the Applications for Certificates as well as the Registers of Certificates themselves. Additionally *Lloyd's Captains Register* may yield useful information.

Issuing of certificates, 1910-1965
From 1910, a combined index to masters, mates, engineers and skippers and mates of fishing boats was started to replace those formerly kept in registers. This is available on microfiche at the PRO as series *BT 352 (Index to Certificates of Competency, Masters, Mates, Engineers and Fishing Officers, Home and Foreign Trade, 1910-1930).*

The term 'index', as used by the RGSS, is a misnomer as it is not an index to any other records. In effect it replaced the earlier registers and indexes and became a self-indexing register. It was kept in card form covering the period 1910 to approximately 1965. It gives:

- Name
- Date and place of birth
- Certificate number
- Grade of certificate
- Date of passing
- Port of examination
- RNR number, if any

Also recorded are any reissues of certificates and any formal notations on a man's record. Voyage details are not given.

The cards are actually of different colours depending on the type of qualification; white cards are for Masters and Mates, pink cards are for Engineers and green for Skippers and Mates of fishing boats. Although the colour is not now discernible as the cards are only available on monochrome microfiche, the information it indicated is easily deduced from the written content.

Three series of documents record the actual issue of the certificates, namely:

BT 317	Registers of Masters and Mates Certificates Passings and Renewal	1917-1977
BT 318	Registers of Examinations for Certificates of Masters, Mates and Engineers, Returns of Passings and Failures	1928-1981
BT 320	Registers of Engineers Passings and Renewal	1913-1935

The registers in series BT 317 (pieces 1 - 7) give brief details of the issue of certificates. Each volume is subdivided according to the type of certificate.

Piece no:	Certificate type	Dates covered
1	Foreign Trade (incl. steam ships)	1 Jan 1917 - 28 Nov 1922
	Steam, compass deviation etc	13 Sept 1917 - 22 May 1922
	Home Trade	3 Jan 1917 - 28 Nov 1922
2	Foreign Trade (incl. steam ships)	1 Dec 1922 - 28 Aug 1929
	Home Trade	4 Dec 1922 - 30 July 1929
3	Foreign Trade	2 Sept 1929 - 30 June 1938
	Home Trade	6 Sept 1929 - 24 Dec 1937
	Voluntary endorsements	19 Dec 1935 - 17 March 1938
4	Foreign Trade	1 July 1938 - 26 June 1948
	Home Trade	1 July 1938 - 21 July 1948
	Voluntary endorsements	22 July 1938 - 10 April 1947
5	Foreign Trade	25 June 1948 - 22 Oct 1957
	Home Trade	27 July 1948 - 29 Dec 1958
	Master, Foreign Tug 2 Jan 1950 - 7 Aug 1977	
	Dublin: Foreign and Home Trade	14 July 1948 - 21 Oct 1953
	Endorsements	8 July 1948 - 27 Dec 1961
6	All	22 Nov 1957 - 3 Aug 1962
	All	3 Aug 1962 - 8 Apr 1968

The entries, within those categories, are arranged in date order and give:

- Date received
- No
- Surname
- Christian name
- Grade
- Port of examination
- When [examined]
- Port sent to
- Date

Some entries are in red ink, probably indicating the issue of replacement certificates; others are in black, which seem to indicate the issuing of a new certificate. Additionally some entries are made in large writing and some in small writing, which may be of significance but the reason is not known.

Series BT 318 and BT 320 are in the process of transfer to the PRO.

These series of documents are not the first place to look since the information recorded in them should be contained on an individual's card in BT 352, which is more readily consulted.

The *London Gazette* also published lists of those granted masters' and mates' certificates.

Information regarding the granting of foreign-going masters certificates was passed regularly to Lloyd's, the insurance society. From this they compiled what is now known as *Lloyd's Captains Register*; this covers the period 1851-1947. Details of this are to be found in the section on Lloyd's Marine Collection.

Modern - 1966 onwards
The RSS maintains an alphabetically organised card index, covering masters, mates, engineers and fishing officers, that is very similar to that described above for 1910-1965. Information about the issuing of certificates to sea officers, from 1966, should be directed to the Registry of Shipping and Seamen (RSS), P.O Box 165, Cardiff, CF14 5FU. Tel: 029 20 768227. E- mail RSS@mcga.gov.uk; a charge is made for this service.

Registration of Cooks
Registration of cooks began on 30 June 1908. Cooks could obtain their certificates as a result of examination (Certificates of Competency) or by exemption due to long service (Certificates of Service).

The *PRO Guide* lists a series *Registers of Cooks Certificates of Competence and Service (BT 319)*, but these records are, in fact, held at the National Maritime Museum. The NMM holds registers related to Cooks covering the period 1915 to 1958, bearing numbers 5001 - 41021. Two volumes of indexes though are held at the PRO in series BT 319 covering 1913-1956.

Disciplinary proceedings
Sometimes an entry in one of the registers of certificates will be annotated with the letters 'BB' followed by a number. This indicates that disciplinary proceedings were taken against the certificate holder. The number refers to the page in the Black Books to be found in the series *Precedent Books, Establishment Papers etc (BT 167)*, pieces 33 - 37. The Black Books, which cover the period 1851 to 1893, also have an index volume (BT 167/37).

The Black Books contain an account of the circumstances surrounding the events leading up to disciplinary proceedings being taken against the certificate holder. Where a 'BB' reference is found in the later series of cards (BT 352), it will usually be accompanied by a brief explanation.

The numerous references given in the left hand column of the Black Books, and on the cards in series BT 352, refer to the registered files of the Marine Department of the Board of Trade. Such files as do survive, which are few indeed, are now to be found in series *Ministry of Transport: Marine Correspondence and Papers, 1854-1969 (MT 9)*.

AGREEMENTS, CREW LISTS AND LOG BOOKS

Introduction and early lists

From as early as 1747, masters or owners of merchant ships were required to keep and file a Muster Roll giving details of the crew and of the ship's voyages. These lists, which were kept as a result of an Act for the Relief of Disabled Seamen[33], were filed with the Seamen's Fund Receivers at the ports of sailing and arrival. They form part of the PRO series *Agreements and Crew Lists, Series I (BT 98)* but survive for the period 1747-1834 for only a few ports, namely:

Port	Start Date
Shields and other Northern Ports	1747
Plymouth	1761
Dartmouth	1770
Liverpool	1772
Other ports	from 1800

A few muster rolls survive in other series, e.g. those for Plymouth (1776-1780) are in CUST 66/227 and those for Scarborough (1747-1765) are in CUST 91/111-112 and it is possible that others still await discovery. Additionally a few early muster books can be found in local record offices; for example Whitby Museum holds muster books for Whitby ships, 1708-1805 and 1835-1838.

Unfortunately there are no simple indexes to the names in these muster books and they are arranged by year and port of filing. Sometimes they include a full list of the crew's names, but more commonly name only the master and identify the number of crew members.

Following the 1835 Merchant Shipping Act, crew lists and other documents were filed with the Register Office of Merchant Seamen (the forerunner of the RGSS) and these, up to 1860, now form part of the PRO series BT 98 mentioned above. The Registrar extracted from them certain essential information about each seaman and entered it in either the Seamen's Registers or Officers' Certificate Registers already described. Clearly, in one's searches for details of a particular seaman, one must nowadays follow the reverse procedure working from the registers back to the crew lists.

The type and extent of information that can be gathered, with perseverance, about an individual seaman is typified by the 'Table of Voyages of James Watts between 1839 and 1851 compiled from Crew Lists' in Table 1.

1835 - 1844

During this period two main types of Crew List are to be found. *Schedule C, Crew List (Foreign)*, was completed by the master of each ship undertaking a foreign voyage, and filed within 48 hours of the ship's return to a UK port. (The term 'Foreign Going Ship' means 'every ship employed in trading or going between some place or places in the United Kingdom and some place or places situate beyond the following limits, that is to say, the Coasts of the United Kingdom, the Islands of Guernsey, Jersey, Sark, Alderney and Man and the Continent of Europe between the River Elbe and Brest inclusive'). *Schedule D, Account of Voyages and Crew for Home Trade Ship (Half Yearly Return)*, was completed by the master of a ship engaged in the coastal or fishing trade, giving the voyages and crew for the preceding half year, and filed within 21 days of the end of June or December.

These two types of list give similar genealogical information, and to see how this may be traced from the entries in the Seamen's Registers, let us follow one of the 'References to Voyages' quoted previously. The symbols:

16.20

Minstrel

20/11/44

were included opposite the entry for James Watts in BT 112/73. The major clue to the whereabouts of the Crew List is contained in the number 16; this is the Port Number which was used as a shorthand for the ship's Port of Registry. In this case 16 stands for Bridlington. The full list of Port Numbers for this period runs almost alphabetically from Aberdeen to Yarmouth and numerically from 1 to 108; it is available with the PRO series list for BT 98, and is included here in Appendix 1.

The crew lists for the whole period 1835-1844 are filed by ship's Port of Registry (by name, not number); for each port the lists are grouped by the initial letter of ships' names into boxes, but within each box the lists are randomly arranged. However, since the ship's name is known, from the Seamen's Register, only a short search is needed to locate the required lists. For example, for the Minstrel of Bridlington in 1843, we found the following details for two of the crew:

Christian and Surnames of Men	William YATES	James WATTS
Age	*21*	*23*
Place of Birth	*Stroud*	*Hasbro*
Quality	*Apprentice*	*Seaman*
Ship in which he last served	*Minstrel*	*Lord Wellington*
Date of joining ship	*3th Decr 1842*	*2th Oct 1843*
Place where	*Hull*	*Quebec*
Time of death or leaving ship	*Killed by a fall down the F.Hatch way 29th March*	*Discharged 19 Novr 1843*
Place where	*Patras*	*Hull*
How disposed of	*Interred in the Church Yard of St. Andrew*	*Discharged*

So far no mention has been made of the second number quoted in the Seamen's Register; i.e. the 20 of 16.20. This is the 'Port Rotation Number' and, whilst it uniquely identifies a ship, within its Port of Registry, no key to these numbers has been discovered. When one has found the required Crew List (in this period by making use of the ship's name), this Port Rotation Number will be found marked on it, and thus forms a check that the correct ship has been found.

1845 - 1854

From 1845 onwards further lists were introduced, and three key ones are found in addition to the Schedules C and D already mentioned. *Schedule A, Agreement for Foreign Trade,* (commonly called 'Articles') was an agreement between master and crew, and was filed within 24 hours of the ship's return to a UK port. *Schedule B, Agreement for Home Trade,* was the equivalent for the coastal and fishing trade and was filed within 30 days of the end of June or December. *Schedule G, Names and Register Tickets of Crew (Foreign Trade),* was a list of crew, with their Register Ticket numbers, filed for a foreign-going ship on sailing.

These lists give information which is very similar to the example quoted above but additionally include a man's Register Ticket Number (except on Schedule A). A typical list, the Home Trade Agreement (Schedule B) for the Hero of Scarborough for the half-year ending 31 December 1845 (BT 98/775) is reproduced on the cover of this book. References to voyages are given, under the heading of 'Reported Voyages', in the Seamen's Registers for this period (BT 113) and in the Alphabetical Register of Masters (BT 115). The major difference from the earlier period (1835-1844) is that the ship's name is that no longer given. Let us look, for example, at one of the Reported Voyages or James Watts for 1846; the entry in the Seamen's Register (BT 113/24) was:

1846

Out	Home
1140-75-2	1140-75-2
75-6-4	64-31-7

In brief, this means that James Watts was on a Newcastle registered vessel (75 in top line), which left Newcastle (75 in bottom line under 'Out') about 6 April 1846 and that he left the ship in London (64 in the bottom line under 'Home') when it arrived there about 31 July 1846. The dates actually refer to the date of filing of the various documents and so differ from the actual arrival and departure dates by a few days.

The Agreements and Crew Lists for this period are arranged by port of registry (name, not number) and by year; the lists for each port for each year may, for the larger ports, occupy 20 to 30 boxes, but they are grouped alphabetically. Unfortunately one normally does not know the name of the ship at this stage, only the Port Rotation Number, which in the example given above, is 1140. One must therefore be prepared to search all the boxes of lists for Newcastle for 1846 (27 boxes in all) until one finds the crew list marked 1140/75/2. This number identifies the ship, but no key has yet been found linking the ship's name and the Port Rotation Number.

In this way we located the Crew Lists for the voyage referred to in the example; they record that the *Pallas* of Newcastle sailed from there, on 4 April 1846, bound for Saguenay and Quebec and returned to London on 31 July. James Watts joined the ship as a seaman in South Shields on 4 April (his last ship having been the *Grantham*) and left it again in London on 31 July.

The search for a particular crew list, carrying a Port Rotation Number obtained from the Register of Seamen's Tickets, can sometimes be shortened by assuming that the Port Rotation Numbers were allocated initially from an alphabetical list of ships, with new ones being allocated as further ships were registered. Our experience shows, however, that this is not the full story. Naturally the laborious searching of boxes, for a port of interest over a range of dates of interest, can lead to the discovery of crew lists for a particular sailor, which have not been transferred to the seamen's registers (e.g. *Urania* for James Watts in Table 1). However the process is so time-consuming that it can hardly be recommended except in exceptional cases.

Lloyd's List can sometimes be used to determine the ship's name from its dates and ports of departure and arrival.

The crew lists do include the name of each seaman's previous ship and this ought to assist in tracing his earlier voyages. However, as Table 1 demonstrates, not all the crew lists that should have been filed were actually returned by ships' masters.

A strategy that we have found helpful in tracing voyages recorded in the Register of Seamen's Tickets is to concentrate initially on the later voyages so that advantage may be taken of the entries on the crew lists for previous voyages. Also searching for ships registered at small ports will shorten the search - try to avoid those registered at large ports such as London, Liverpool or Newcastle, where a dozen or more boxes of lists may need to be searched per year.

1853 - 1856

The arrangement of the crew lists remains unchanged from the previous period but the seamen's registers (BT 116), and certificate registers for masters and mates, from which voyage details may be found now give the ships' names. Thus locating a specific crew list, in BT 98, becomes relatively straightforward.

1857 - 1860

From 1857 onwards, each ship was allocated an Official Number on registration; these numbers were retained for the life of the ship, were not reused and may be found from the *Mercantile Navy List*. The Crew Lists are now arranged, in BT 98 still, by year and numerically by the ship's Official Number. All lists from 1857 to 1860 have been preserved in this way, and are to be found at the PRO. A few of the surviving log books, if not in BT 98, are to be found in *BT 165 (Ships' Official Logs 1857 -1972)*.

Locating voyage details for an individual during this period are not easy since no seamen's registers exist, but the certificate registers for masters, mates and engineers do give this information. Otherwise one needs to know, from other sources, the ships on which he sailed, as no index of any type exists to these crew lists.

1861 - 1912

From 1861 onwards, the location of these lists may be anywhere from Greenwich to Newfoundland, but finding them can be very complex. The vast majority of crew lists, agreements and log books (which are usually found together) are arranged by year and then by ships' official number. Where this is not known it can be found from the *Mercantile Navy List*.

For the period 1861 to 1912 crew agreements are located as follows:

- The PRO holds 10% of the total, in *BT 99 (Agreements and Crew Lists Series II)*, *BT 100 (Agreements and Crew Lists Series III (Celebrated Ships))*, *BT 144 (Agreements and Crew Lists Series IV (Fishing Agreements) 1884-1929))* and *BT 165 (Ships' Official Logs 1857 -1972)*. A set of lever-arch files, in the PRO reading rooms, give the ships (by official number) by year for which lists for this period are to be found in series BT 99.

- The National Maritime Museum, Greenwich, holds, for this period:

    - the remaining 90% for the years 1861, 1862, 1865, 1875, 1885, 1895, and 1905;

    - a number of yearly bundles of Fishing Agreements for the period 1884-1914 (with only one small bundle for 1914);

    - Crew lists, for the whole period 1861-1913, for ships without official numbers (arranged alphabetically by ships' names) and those for home trade vessels where the crew were employed on several vessels belonging to the same owner (e.g. Mersey Docks and Harbour Board, Great Western Railways, ICI);

- Some County Record Offices hold Crew Lists up to 1912 for ships with Ports of Registry within their area, namely:

Ship's name * (BT 98/n)	Port of Registry	Joined		Voyages	Left		Capacity
		Date	Place		Date	Place	
Aerial /407	Newcastle	13 June 1839	Shields	Shields to Schiedam and back	7 Jul 1839	Shields	Seaman
Minstrel /184	Bridlington	2 Oct 1843	Quebec	Canada to Patras to Hull	19 Nov 1843	Hull	Seaman
Urania /429	Newcastle	23 Apr 1844	South Shields	Newcastle to London – coal trade	1 May 1844	London	Seaman
Brothers /735	Newcastle	13 Jan 1845	Shields	2 voyages from Shields to London and back - coal trade	20 Mar 1845	Shields	Seaman
Hero /775	Scarborough	19 Sept 1845	Shields	2 voyages from So. Shields to Haver de Grace and back	11 Nov 1845	Shields	Seaman
Elizabeth /794	Sunderland	13 Nov 1845	Shields	Shields to London and back	20 Dec 1845	Shields	Seaman
Pallas /1045	Newcastle	4 Apr 1846	South Shields	Newcastle to Saguenay and back	31 July 1846	London	Seaman
Centurion /1074	Scarborough	3 Aug 1846	London	London to Quebec and back	9 Dec 1846	London	Seaman
Harvey /1706	Newcastle	13 Mar 1848	Jarrow	Newcastle to Carthagena and back to London	26 Sept 1848	London	Seaman
Brothers /2649	Newcastle	11 June 1851	Shields	Shield to London and back – coasting trade	30 June 1851	------	Seaman
Sirius /2720	Shields	10 July 1851	Shields	3 voyages from Shields to London and back	14 Sept1851	Shields	Seaman
Mary Clark /2715	Shields	22 Sept 1851	Shields	Shields to London and back	14 Oct 1851	Shields	Seaman
Brothers /2649	Newcastle	18 Oct, 17 Nov, 19 Dec 1851	Shields	3 voyages from Shields to London and back	Remained		Seaman Seaman Mate

Table 1: Voyages of James Watts, between 1839 and 1851 compiled from Crew Lists

Previous Ship * (incl. Port of Registry)	Seamen's Register Entry	Type	Tons	When built	Where built
Aeconomy (or *Occonomy*)	Co 75.8 June 39 Aerial	Snow	265	1839	Sunderland
Lord Wellington	16.20 Minstrel 20/11/44	Barque	357	1811	Hull
			Owner: T. Ward (Hull)		
Two Sisters	Not found in register (75/1191)	Snow	279	1799	Plymouth
			Owners: Whinney (So. Shields) Metcalf (No. Shields)		
Two Sisters	499-75 6-45		155		
			Not identified in Lloyd's Register		
Ivy	198-85 12-45	Snow	174	1808	Sunderland
			Owners: Wear & Co.		
Hero	127-92 12-45	Snow	266	1836	Sunderland
			Owners: Read & Co.		
Grantham	1140-75-2 75-6-4 64-31-7	Snow	253	1840	Sunderland
			Owner: T. Jackson		
Pallas	12-85-2 64-4-8 64-16-12	Barque	467		
			Not identified in Lloyd's Register		
Elizabeth	No G 701-75-2 64-25-9	Snow	303	1790	London
			Owners: J. Donkin (No. Shields)		
Quay Side, Shields	2550-75 6-51	Brig	209	1820	Leith
Brothers, So. Shields	189-124 12-51	Snow	224	1824	Shields
			Owner: Young & Son		
Sirius, So. Shields	189-124 12-51		224		
			Not identified in Lloyd's Register		
Mary Clark, So. Shields *Brothers*, Newcastle *Brothers*, Newcastle	2250-75 12-51	Brig	209	1820	Leith

* From the names of Previous Ships given, it can be seen that not all ships have been found in the Crew Lists.

Record Office or Library[34]		Ports of Registry/Dates held
Anglesey CRO	✓	Beaumaris (1863-1913)
Berwick-upon-Tweed RO	(✓)	Berwick (1863-1913) *
Bristol RO	✓	Bristol (1863-1913) *
Cambridgeshire CRO	✓	Wisbech (1863-1913)
Carmarthenshire RO		Carmarthen, Llanelly (1863-1913)
Centre for Kentish Studies, Maidstone	✓	Faversham (1863-1913)
Ceredigion Archives		Aberystwyth (1863-1913) (small sample) *
Cheshire RO	✓	Runcorn (1863-1913)
Cornwall RO	✓	Falmouth, Fowey, Padstow, Penzance, St. Ives, Truro (1863-1913)
Cumbria RO, Barrow in Furness	✓	Barrow (1863-1913)
Cumbria RO, Carlisle	✓	Carlisle, Maryport (1863-1913)
Cumbria RO, Whitehaven	✓	Whitehaven (1863-1914), Maryport (1863-1911)
Devon RO	✓	Barnstaple, Bideford, Dartmouth, Exeter, * Ilfracombe, Plymouth, Teignmouth (1863-1913)
Dorset RO	✓	Bridport (1863-1901), Lyme Regis * (1863-1912), Poole, Weymouth, (1863-1913)
East Kent Archive Centre	(✓)	Deal (1863-1874), Dover (1863-1913), * Folkestone (1880-1897), Ramsgate (1863-1913)
Essex RO	✓	Harwich, Colchester, Maldon (1863-1913)
Flintshire RO	(✓)	Chester (1863-1913) [records originally at * Chester County Archives] plus some misc.
Glamorgan RO	✓	Cardiff (1863-1913)
Glasgow City RO		ports in Scotland [Later transferred to Newfoundland]
Gloucester CRO	✓	Gloucester (1863-1913)
Gwent RO	✓	Chepstow, Newport (1869, 1879, * 1889, 1899, 1909)
Gwynedd, Caernarfon area RO		Caernarvon (1863-1913)
Gwynedd, Dolgellau area RO	✓	Aberdovey ships (registered Aberystwyth) (1863-1913)
Hull City Archives		Hull fishing vessels (1884-1913)

Record Office or Library[34]		Ports of Registry/Dates held	
Lancashire RO	✓	Fleetwood, Lancaster, Preston (1863-1913)	
Lincolnshire Archives		Boston (1863-1913), Gainsborough (1862-1881)	
Liverpool RO	✓	Liverpool (1863-1913)	*
Manchester Local Studies Unit Archives	✓	Manchester (1894-1913)	
Manx National Heritage Library		Castletown, Douglas, Peel, Ramsey (1863-1913)	*
Rochester upon Medway Studies Centre		Rochester	
Merseyside Maritime Museum		Misc. small sample (1863-1913)	*
National Archives of Ireland, Dublin	✓	Ports now in Eire (1863-1921)	μ
National Archives of Scotland		Scottish ships (1867-1913)	
National Library of Australia		Voyages to Australia and New Zealand (only 81 ships, 1861-1900)	
National Library of Wales	✓	Aberystwyth (1863-1913)	*
NE Lincolnshire Archives, Grimsby		Grimsby (1863-1914)	*
Norfolk RO		Great Yarmouth, 1863-1913 [Later transferred to Newfoundland]	
North Yorkshire CRO		Middlesbrough Whitby, Scarborough (1861-1867, 1872),	μ
Northumberland RO	✓	Blyth (1863-1913)	
Pembrokeshire RO	✓	Cardigan, Milford Haven (1863-1913)	*
Portsmouth City Museums and Records Service	✓	Portsmouth, Cowes (1863-1913)	*
Public Record Office of Northern Ireland	✓	Ports in Northern Ireland (1857-1938): Belfast, Coleraine, Londonderry, Newry, Strangford	μ
Somerset Archives and Record Service	✓	Bridgwater (1863-1913)	*
Southampton Archives Service	✓	Southampton (1863-1913)	*
Suffolk RO, Ipswich	✓	Ipswich, Woodbridge (1863-1913)	*
Suffolk RO, Lowestoft		Lowestoft (1863-1913)	*
Tyne & Wear Archives Service	✓	Shields (1863-1913) [formerly at Northumberland RO]	*
West Glamorgan Archives Service, Swansea	✓	Swansea (1863-1913)	*
West Sussex RO	✓	Arundel, Chichester, Littlehampton, Shoreham (1863-1913)	*

An ✓ indicates that the holdings of those record offices or libraries have been included in *A Guide to the Crew Agreements and Official Logbooks, 1863-1913, held at the County Record Offices of the British Isles* published by the Maritime History Archive, Memorial University of Newfoundland; but a significant number of transfers between record offices have taken place since that publication was complied.

A μ indicates that the collection has been filmed. Those for Ireland are available through LDS Libraries; copies of those at Northallerton are available at the Teeside Archives Service in Middlesbrough.

An * indicates that some indexing of names has taken place - enquire at the relevant archives in the first instance.

Some County Record Offices have published lists of their holdings[35] .

• Finally the Maritime History Archive, Memorial University, Newfoundland holds the remainder (70% for 1863-1913)[36]. The Maritime History Archive publishes a list of its holdings for this period[37]; they also offer a postal photocopying service at a modest charge.

Locating voyage details for an individual during this period is not easy since no seamen's registers exist. The certificate registers for masters, mates and engineers do give this information, but only up to 1888; after then some voyage details are obtainable from *Lloyd's Captains Register* for appropriate categories of seafarer. Otherwise one needs to know, from other sources, the ships on which he sailed, as no index of any type exists to these crew lists.

A few projects are underway to index crew lists held by county record offices and some indexes have appeared on the web; those about which we currently know are included in the bibliography[38]. A more ambitious project, the Crew List Indexing Project (CLIP), is compiling an index to crew lists held in county record offices; it is hoping to publish an index to its work so far on CD-ROM.

The CD-ROM, *Ships and Seafarers of Atlantic Canada*[39] includes a database compiled from the crew agreements for St. John, NB, Yarmouth, Windsor and Halifax for 1863-1914 and another with a 1% sample taken from non-Canadian vessels.

1913 - 1938

For the period 1913 to 1938, all crew agreements have been retained and are to be found located as follows:

• The PRO holds 10% of the total, *in BT 99 (Agreements and Crew Lists Series II), BT 100 (Agreements and Crew Lists Series III (Celebrated Ships)), BT 144 (Agreements and Crew Lists Series IV (Fishing Agreements) 1884-1929)) and BT 165 (Ships' Official Logs 1857 -1972).* A set of lever-arch files, in the PRO reading rooms, give the ships (by official number) by year for which lists, for the period 1913-1923, are to be found in series BT 99; this finding aid may not be comprehensive.

- The National Maritime Museum, Greenwich, holds the remaining 90% for the years 1915, 1925 and 1935; including those for home trade vessels where the crew were employed on several vessels belonging to the same owner (e.g. Mersey Docks and Harbour Board, Great Western Railways, ICI);

- The NMM also hold a number of yearly bundles of Fishing Agreements for the period 1884-1914 (with only one small bundle for 1914); from 1915 it is believed that agreements for fishing vessels are to be found in the regular series of crew lists arranged by ships' official numbers.

- No County Record Offices hold Crew Lists for this period, but the Public Record Office of Northern Ireland holds those for vessels registered at ports in Northern Ireland and the National Archives in Dublin those (up to 1921) for ports now in the Republic of Ireland. Crew lists held in the two Irish archives have been microfilmed and are available through the LDS library system.

- Finally the Maritime History Archive, Memorial University, Newfoundland holds the remainder (80% for 1913-1938). The Maritime History Archive publishes a list of its holdings for this period[40]; they also offer a postal photocopying service at a modest charge. The MHA also holds the agreements (T124) for vessels hired by the Admirality for the period of World War 1 (1914-1920).

Details of the ships on which an individual served may be found from the Central Index Register or possibly the records of the Royal Navy Reserve or from *Lloyd's Captains Register* for appropriate categories of seafarer. The first normally records the ships' official number; the others should give both the ship's name and official number. If these records give only the ship's name this can be converted into its official number using the *Mercantile Navy List*.

World War 2 (1939-1950)

All the surviving log books and crew agreements, of merchant and fishing vessels, for the period 1939 to 1950 are to be preserved at the PRO. Those for 1947 and 1948 are to be found in series BT 99. In addition, within BT 99, are to be found some lists related to miscellaneous vessels for a wider period:

- Home trade vessels where the crew were employed on several vessels belonging to the same owner - described erroneously in the catalogue as 'Railways' for 1939 (BT 99/7816) 1939-1945 (BT 99/6847-6906), 1947 (BT 99/7271-7273), 1948 (BT 99/7595-7597); other years may be found in BT 380.

- Personnel files of those serving on Cable Ships, arranged alphabetically by seaman's surname, for 1940-1948 (BT 99/7694-7751).

- Crew lists for British members of the crew of foreign-ships requisitioned or chartered by, or on behalf of, HM Government - described in the catalogue as Merchant, Dutch RT&C for 1941-1948 (BT 99/7752-7757)

- Auxiliary War Vessels for 1939-1946 (BT 99/7758-7801 and 7803-7815). These are the crew lists (T124 and variants) for British vessels requisitioned complete with their crews for war service.

The crew lists for 1949 and 1950 are in series *BT 380 (War of 1939-1945: Log Books, crew agreements and associated records)*. The remainder, and vast majority of the material covering the period 1939-1946, is in the process of transfer to the PRO; it should be sought, in due course, in series BT 380 and *BT 381 (World War II log books and crew lists, 1939-1946)*. The main run of documents is arranged by year and type of trade (e.g. deep sea, small coastal vessels, fishing, Hong Kong based/operated vessels) then by ship's official number. Some special categories (e.g. provisional registrations, crew employed on multiple home trade vessels by the same owner, merchant navy reserve pool) may be arranged differently.

Details of the ships on which an individual served may be found from the Central Indexed Register (up to 1941) or Central Register of Seamen (from 1942) or possibly the records of the Royal Navy Reserve or from *Lloyd's Captains Register* for appropriate categories of seafarer (up to 1947). The first normally records the ships' official number; the others should give both the ship's name and official number. If these records give only the ship's name this can be converted into its official number using the *Mercantile Navy List*.

Included within these various series should also be found miscellaneous catgories of crew lists related to allied vessels, all of which are arranged alphabetically by ship's name:

- British members of the crew of foreign-ships requisitioned or chartered by, or on behalf of, HM Government.
- Some official log books of allied vessels, with British crew, who were lost at sea
- British seamen who served on Dutch and Norwegian ships

1951 - 1976

For the period 1951 to 1976, all surviving crew agreements and log books have been preserved and are to be found as follows:

- The PRO holds 10% of the total, *in BT 99 (Agreements and Crew Lists Series II), BT 100 (Agreements and Crew Lists Series III (Celebrated Ships)* and *BT 165 (Ships' Official Logs 1857 - 1972);*

- The National Maritime Museum, Greenwich, holds the remaining 90% for the years 1955, 1965 and 1975 (those for 1975 are under arrangement and therefore unavailable); including those for home trade vessels where the crew were employed on several vessels belonging to the same owner (e.g. Mersey Docks and Harbour Board, Great Western Railways, ICI);

- No County Record Offices hold Crew Lists for this period;

- Finally the Maritime History Archive, Memorial University, Newfoundland holds the remainder; they also offer a postal photocopying service at a modest charge. Those up to 1953 have been arranged and listed so far; thereafter locating documents for a particular vessel can be somewhat difficult.

Voyage details for an individual during this period are found, from the Central Register of Seamen.

1977 - 1994

From 1977 the following crew agreements and log books have been preserved:

- The PRO holds 10% of the total, *in BT 99 (Agreements and Crew Lists Series II), BT 100 (Agreements and Crew Lists Series III (Celebrated Ships).*

- The National Maritime Museum, Greenwich, holds the remaining 90% for the year 1985 but these are currently under arrangement and therefore unavailable.

The remaining crew agreements and log books have been destroyed. No convenient way exists to access the details of service for an individual seaman as no register exist and the documents are unindexed.

1995 onwards

Records from 1995 onwards are held in their entirety at the Registry of Shipping and Seamen. A certificate of sea service for individual seaman who sailed on ships from this period may be obtained from these records; a fee is payable.

Log Books

The requirement for the master to keep an official log book goes back relatively early for specific categories of vessel. Usually this relates to some form of tax or subsidy for their trade. Arctic and Southern whalers had, from 1786 (26 Geo III, cap 41and cap 50), to compile a log book and surrender it to the Collector of Customs at the end of the voyage. From 1789 (29 Geo III, cap 66) slave-ships had to keep a general log book, a copy of which was to be handed over to the port authorities on return to the UK; even earlier than this the surgeon had to keep a medical journal. From 1803 (43 Geo III, cap 56) any ship carrying passengers had to keep a medical journal; if the ship had more than 50 people aboard, it had to carry a surgeon, and both he and the master kept official medical journals recording details of the health of both passengers and crew. Whilst surely some examples of these must survive, there seems to be no comprehensive collection of them.

The Mercantile Marine Act of 1850 required masters to keep a ship's Official Log recording illnesses, births and deaths on board, misconduct, desertion and punishment, and a description of each man's conduct. They were to be deposited after each foreign voyage, or half-yearly for home trade ships. They begin to appear amongst the records from 1852 onwards, though many have been destroyed; usually only those recording a birth, marriage or death have survived. There is a separate series at the PRO, *BT 165 (Ships' Official Logs)*, that nominally covers the period 1857-1972 although the majority of logs therein are from the period 1902 to 1919; others logs are mostly to be found with the Agreements and Crew Lists at the PRO or elsewhere.

Log books for 1902-1912 were preserved where they contained entries of birth, marriage or death; these together with all surviving logs for the period 1914-1919 are found in series *BT 165 (Ships' Official Logs)*. Selected logs for 1913 are in series BT 99.

Certificates of Discharge

Following the 1854 Merchant Shipping Act, both the master and seamen had to sign Certificates of Discharge and Character (E-1) on termination of a voyage. These had to be signed before the relevant port official or Shipping Master in a colonial port. For example:

NEW SOUTH WALES - PORT OF NEWCASTLE
(E.) CERTIFICATE OF DISCHARGE AND CHARACTER
GIVEN BEFORE THE SHIPPING MASTER

Name of Ship	Official Number	Port of Registry	Registered Tonnage	Description of Voyage or Employment
"Lord of the Isles"	51051	Lpool	656	Colonial

Name of Seaman	Place of Birth	Date of Birth
Frank Emms	Yarmouth	1843

Capacity	Date of Entry	Date of Discharge	Ability	Report of Character Conduct	Sobriety	Declines
Steward	24 Feby 1868	4 August 1868	G	G	G	X

I Certify that the above particulars are correct and that the above named Seaman was discharged accordingly at the date above mentioned.

(Countersigned) *F. Emms* Seaman   (Signed) *[illegible]* Master

Dated at Newcastle, and given to the above-named Seaman, in my presence, this 5th day of August 1868.

[signature illegible]   Shipping Master

These documents were given to the seamen and may survive, as the one quoted above does, amongst personal papers; sometimes a discharge certificate (List M or N) may be found with the crew lists. A Discharge Book, again carried by the seaman, later replaced individual documents; these books in effect recorded his complete seafaring career. Some Discharge Books may have survived in official records, by chance, in the Seamen's pouches (BT 372).

However some material related to the discharge or desertion of seamen in Australia does survive there in State and Commonwealth archives. Also to be found there are various crew lists, log books and the like. Reference to their whereabouts is included in Appendix 2.

Other sources

Casualty and Death Lists
When a vessel was lost at sea, its official logbook would have been lost with the vessel. In these circumstances the owners would submit the copy of the crew list that had been retained on shore (the 'Red Copy') to the RGSS; these lists were used for the registration of the deaths of the crew. These lists may sometimes be found filed with the crew lists. Casualty and deaths lists (C&D) for the years 1920-1938, along with casualties and deaths on fishing vessel's (List D) for the years 1920-1938, are at the National Maritime Museum. The records are organised by ship's official number.

Many lists C&D are included with the 1939-1950 logbooks and crew agreements held at the RSS some of which are currently in the process of being transferred to the PRO; they are to be found in the numerical sequence of logbooks and crew agreements.

Lists kept by owners
The records described so far are of the RGSS, with whom the crew lists had to be filed. But it should be remembered that the owner, or operator, of a ship might have also kept a copy of the crew list for his own reasons, though the vast majority of these will have been considered ephemeral and thus not have survived in any archive whether public or private.

Many railway companies operated ferries and so some of the RAIL series of documents may contain crew lists (e.g. RAIL 113/53, RAIL 227/488 to 489 and RAIL 1057/3556 to 3568), since their records have passed into the custody of the PRO. A useful starting point in locating these is the British Transport Historical Records card index located in the Research Enquiries Room at the PRO.

Aliens' returns
The record series *Aliens Act, 1836: Returns and Papers (HO 3)*, consists mostly of returns of alien passengers made by masters of ships made under that Act. They will identify the ships' master and bear his signature, but in some instances they will list the crew if they are aliens. The returns are in date order covering the period 1836-1869; there are no indexes to the names in them.

Other Home Office files may reveal details of foreign seamen who came to the attention of the authorities. For example nearly 300 West Indian and West African seamen, who were caught up in riots in Cardiff and Liverpool in 1919, are listed in HO 45/11017/377969 subfile 44. In the same year, the authorities became interested in Chinese seamen involved in opium smuggling activities and the names of some suspected of involvement are listed in HO 45/24683.

In PRO record series HO 45 and HO 144 is to be found correspondence related to special certificates of British origin, issued to coloured seamen, following the Special Restriction (Coloured Alien Seamen) Order 1925. These may be located under the heading of 'Nationality and Naturalization'.

Census returns
The annual censuses in England and Wales attempted, from 1851 onwards, to enumerate merchant seamen by the use of shipping schedules; the scope and accuracy of this is discussed in Edward Higgs' book[41]. With the exception of those for 1861, the schedules are to be found at the end of the returns for the port in which the ship was on census night, or to which it returned within the required time. For 1861, though, they all filed together at the end of the complete run of returns. There is a specific index to those on board ships in the 1861 census and the 1881 and 1901 censuses have comprehensive indexes that can be searched by computer.

Where a schedule is found for a vessel, it should be remembered that the master was normally the enumerator and so his signature, which should appear on the schedule, ought actually to be his.

In Scotland similar enumeration of merchant vessels took place from 1861 onwards; these are kept separate from the parochial returns but are still available at the General Register Office for Scotland. No specific indexes to those on vessels have been compiled but there are excellent indexes available to the complete censuses of Scotland for 1881, 1891 and 1901. The 1881 index is available on CD-ROM, microfiche or on-line; that for 1891 as microfiche or on-line; the 1901 index on-line only.

Seamen's Working conditions

Some idea of the seaman's lot can be gained from the wages and provisions he received on his voyages. For instance, on the ship *Harvey*, which James Watts joined at Jarrow on 13 March 1848, for a voyage to Quebec and back, the rates of pay were 'per calendar month, share or voyage' (BT 98/1706):

		£	s	d
Alexander Hood	Master	10	0	0
Wm. Lowrie	Mate	4	15	0
Wm. Currie	Carpenter	4	15	0
Edwd Johnson	Cook	3	5	0
James Watts	Seaman	3	5	0
3 other seamen	each	3	0	0

The rates of wages for a voyage to America or the Baltic were generally quoted per month, while those in the coal trade were per voyage[42]. Of course rates fluctuated and even gradually increased over the years; by 1851, James Watts was paid £4-10-0 per voyage while working on the *Brothers* on the rather more arduous coal trade.

The provisions to be supplied to the crew during a voyage were supposed to be recorded on a daily chart with headings such as Biscuit, Spirits, Salt Beef, Salt Pork, Flour, Peas, Tea, Coffee, Sugar and Water. These tables were rarely completed, although some conscientious masters might make an entry, as did the master of the *Marmora* involved in the home trade for the first half of 1865 (List at NMM):

Bread	1 lb every day
Beef	1lb on Sun, Mon, Wed, Thurs, Sat
Pork	1lb on Tue, Fri
Flour	½ lb on Sun, Mon, Wed, Thurs
Peas	¼ pt on Tue, Fri
Tea	½ lb per man per month
Coffee	1½ lb per man per month
Sugar	4 lb per man per month
Rice	½ lb on Sat
Butter	1 lb per man per week
Equivalent substitutes as comforts or necessity may require.	
No Spirits	

Sometimes the Agreements would record conditions of employment, for example (*King Coal*, half-year ending 30 June 1875; document at NMM):

And it is also agreed that any member of the crew be found smuggling he shall forfeit all his wages, it is also agreed that any member of the crew wishing to leave the ship he shall give 24 hours notice or forfeit all his wages. It is also agreed that any member of the crew wishing to leave the ship and the ship is going to sea the same day he shall forfeit half one days pay to the man who shall succeed him. Wages to rise and fall as customary.

Often all the Official Log will record about a man will be VG (Very Good) under the two headings of 'General Conduct' and 'Ability in Seamanship'. Sometimes though other details may be entered as for example in the log books for the ships Robert Thorne sailed in following his receipt of a Mate's Certificate of Service. An entry in the Log Book (preserved at the Maritime History Archive, Memorial University of Newfoundland) for the *Rosario* of North Shields, 266 tons, Barque, Official Number 56461, provided a surprising reminder that relatives often sailed together. In it Robert Thorne recorded the following information about his nephew (and our grandfather) Thomas Watts:

April 1st 1871, No. Shields.

This is to Certify that thomas Watts Ordanary Seaman Derseated from the Barque Rosario Leaving his Effects on Board.

Robert Thorne (Mate)

This incident did not seem to count too strongly against our grandfather who repeated his behaviour on the *Stornoway* of Newcastle, 482 tons, Official Number 10520 (Document preserved at the Maritime History Archive, Memorial University of Newfoundland):

31st January 1872, Shields

William Drew A.B. and Thomas Watts O.S. came on board on Wednesday 31st January and at 5 p.m. went on shore without leave and did not return again untill Saturday the 3rd Febuary but went on Shore again without leave and did not return untill Monday the 5th Febuary when they resumed duty. Tow [i.e. two] substitutes being employed at the cost of 18 Shillings each.

Robert Thorne (Mate)   George Greener (Master)

Further general information on the life and conditions of the merchant seaman in Victorian times can be gained from many sources. There are several excellent examples of these: firstly Dr. Press' Ph.D. Thesis[43]; Walter Runciman's evocative stories of life on board sailing ships employed in the coal trade leave the smell of salt (and coal dust) in one's nostrils[44]; a well-illustrated and informative recent publication in the inexpensive Shire Album series, by David Marcombe, merely whets the appetite for more[45]; finally there is an excellent book by Basil Greenhill[46].

These references will lead you into the world of the apprentice sailor, who could rise to ordinary seaman and after a few years' experience become an able seaman, who had the pick of berths and food and expected the lower grades to sweep decks and tar rigging; the 'idlers' were the cook, steward and carpenter, who worked daylight hours except in small ships. The seaman on watch always had to be occupied, except at night or on Sundays; setting or furling sails, at the wheel, manning pumps, washing and holystoning decks, replacing or repairing sails and rigging - there was plenty to do.

A major reason for desertion was the requirement to assist with cargo in port, as shore leave was disallowed; an added incentive in the USA and Canada was the high wage obtainable for the trip home to the UK - which is why we found, in the crew lists, several sailors who deserted at Quebec. Discipline was harsh, with 'hazing' of crews common on British ships (a continuous pressure to work, performing pointless tasks); this was often complemented by the notorious behaviour of seamen when let ashore. Their accumulated earnings could be spent quickly on drink and women in the tough neighbourhoods that exploited seamen, although there were good conditions at homes (e.g. London Sailor's Home - 6d a night for berth, 10 - 14s. per week for full board and lodging).

The general conclusion (Press[47]) was that seamen fared quite well economically, when in employment, compared with the agricultural labourer, but were probably worse off overall as they rarely worked more than nine months in the year. Nevertheless, shortage of employment on the land, and possibly the lure of far-away places, attracted two to three hundred thousand of our ancestors to the sea in the 1840s and 1850s.

WAR SERVICE AND MEDALS

War Service

World War 1
During World War 1 government took on a wide range of responsibilities related not just to the moving of troops and supplies but to include control of mercantile shipbuilding. At the end of the war this responsibility was primarily related to the return of troops and prisoners of war and material back to the UK. The PRO holds a wide range of records related to these activities and these are described in *Records of Merchant Shipping and Seamen*[48].

Much of the available material relates to policy and statistics and this need not concern us here. The following should be noted when trying to trace information about somebody who served as a merchant seaman during World War 1:

- An alphabetical series of merchant seafarers exists; it was probably primarily intended to record the issue of seamen's identity certificates (1918-1920). This series of CR 10 cards, PRO series BT 350 is described in the chapter on Registration of Merchant Seamen

- Information about officers may be found, in addition, in BT 352 and, for appropriate classes of officer, in *Lloyd's Captains Register*. These are described in the chapters on Certificates for Sea Officers and Lloyd's Marine Collection respectively.

- Merchant seamen may have served in the Royal Naval Reserve; these records are described below.

- Fishermen may have served on a vessel that was requisitioned, complete with its crew, for minesweeping and similar duties. This service would have been recorded on a T124 form for the ship; these are now preserved at the Maritime History Archive, in Newfoundland, as *Agreement and Account of Crew of Commissioned Chartered Ships, T124, 1914-1920*. The records of the Royal Naval Reserve (Trawler Section) described below should also be consulted.

- Records of ships are to be found amongst the main series described in a later chapter on Registration of Shipping

- Lists of ships lost during World War 1 can be found in PRO record series *MT 25 (Ministry of Shipping, 1917-1921: Correspondence and Papers)*.

- Investigations into ship losses, where the papers have been preserved, may be found in PRO series *BT 369 (Shipping Casualty Investigation Papers, 1910-1968)*.

- Lists of British merchant vessels attacked by enemy submarines, with reports of actions and sinkings (1916-1918), are to be found in PRO record series *ADM 131 (Admiralty: Station records: Plymouth Correspondence)* - pieces 113 to 118.

- Many records relating to merchant ship and trawler losses are to be found in PRO record series *ADM 137 (War of 1914-1918: Admiralty Historic Section: Packs and Miscellaneous Records)*

- Lloyd's Marine Collection, preserved at the Guildhall Library, contains useful material related to the loss of merchant vessels during World War 1:

Ms 14,934A	Casualties to Shipping through Enemy Causes (Lloyd's Official List)	1914-1918
Ms 14,932	Lloyd's Loss and Casualty Books	1837-1972
Ms 14,933	Index to Lloyd's Loss and Casualty Books	Incl. 1878-1934
Ms 14,934/1-4	War Casualty Books	August 1914 - June 1922
Ms 14,935/1-2	Index to War Casualty Books	April 1917 - June 1922

These, together with other useful material, are described in the Guildhall Library's guide[49].

The Merchant Navy Association is also believed to have a significant archival holding on seamen and ships lost in both World Wars.

Records related to medals and prisoners of war are discussed below.

World War 2
Following the earlier precedent government again took close control over the merchant navy during World War 2. An outline of the material available is contained in *Records of Merchant Shipping and Seamen*[50]; a more detailed breakdown of the various records available is to be found in *The Second World War: A Guide to Documents in the Public Record Office*[51].

Much of the available material relates to policy and statistics and this need not concern us here. The following should be noted when trying to trace information about somebody who served as a merchant seaman during World War 2:

- Service of merchant seamen during World War 2 should be contained either in the Central Indexed Register (BT 349, BT 348 and BT 364) or in the Central Register of Seamen (BT 382 and BT 372) described in the chapter on Registration of Merchant Seamen.

- Information about officers may be found, in addition, in BT 352 and, for appropriate classes of officer, in *Lloyd's Captains Register*. These are described in the chapters on Certificates for Sea Officers and Lloyd's Marine Collection respectively.

- Merchant seamen may have served in the Royal Naval Reserve; these records are described below.

- Fishermen may have served on a vessel that was requisitioned, complete with its crew, for minesweeping and similar duties. This service would have been recorded on a T124 form for the ship; for 1939-1946 these forms are to be found in BT 99/7758-7801 and BT 99/7803-7815. A portion of the CRS 10 docket books, in the Central Register of Seamen (BT 382/3252-3284), covers merchant seamen working on HM Auxiliary War Vessels (T 124).

- Records of ships are to be found amongst the main series described in a later chapter on Registration of Shipping.

- Ship losses are recorded in the PRO series BT 347 *(Daily Casualty Registers and Index of Ships, War of 1939-1945)*. These consist of registers of casualty lists, within which each loss is briefly described, together with a card index. The card index (BT 347/8), available on microfiche, lists each ship alphabetically giving brief details together with references to the loss both in the Casualty Lists and in the printed *Lloyd's List*. The Admiralty publication *British Merchant Vessels Lost or Damaged by enemy action during Second World War* (HMSO, 1947) might prove useful. Other series that contain information on losses of particular merchant vessels are ADM 1, ADM 199 and ADM 267.

- Investigations into ship losses, where the papers have been preserved, may be found in PRO series *BT 369 (Shipping Casualty Investigation Papers, 1910-1968)*.

- Lloyd's Marine Collection, preserved at the Guildhall Library, contains useful material related to the loss of merchant vessels during World War 2:

Printed book	Lloyd's War Losses: the Second World War	
--	Lloyd's Marine Loss Cards	1939- 1972
Ms 14,932	Lloyd's Loss and Casualty Books	1837-1972
Ms 14,933	Index to Lloyd's Loss and Casualty Books	Incl. 1878-1934, 1936-1972

These, together with other useful material, are described in the Guildhall Library's guide[52].

- Convoy records are in PRO record series ADM 237 but only about half of the records have been preserved. A card index to convoys is available in the PRO reading rooms. Reports of interviews with masters and survivors of merchant ships lost by enemy action are to be found in ADM 199/2130-2148.

- The Registry of Shipping and Seamen holds ship movement cards (called Voyage Record Cards) recording the movement of merchant vessels between 1939 and 1946; these cards are in the process of transfer to the PRO as record series BT 385.

The Merchant Navy Association is also believed to have a significant archival holding on seamen and ships lost in both World Wars.

Records related to medals and prisoners of war are discussed below.

Royal Naval Reserve

Introduction

In 1860 the Royal Naval Reserve (RNR) was established to provide the Royal Navy with a body of experienced merchant seamen and fishermen should a crisis arise. Commissioned ranks were created from 1861, when the Admiralty was permitted to recruit masters and mates of the merchant service. In 1872, midshipmen, under the age of 18, were added to the list of officers - most of these came from those educated in the training ships *Conway* or *Worcester*.

The RNR consisted of experienced seamen and should not be confused with the Royal Naval Volunteer Reserve (RNVR), established in 1903, The RNVR consisted of both officers and ratings who undertook naval training in their spare time but were not professionally employed at sea as were men in the RNR. During both world wars, the RNVR was the main means by which officers entered the Royal Navy for the period of the war. Perhaps confusingly for the new researcher, the RNR and the RNVR were merged in 1958. The RNVR will not be discussed further here; those interested in men who served in the RNVR should consult Nicholas Rodger's book[53].

The RNR generally consisted of officers and men of deep-sea merchantmen. From 1911 the need was found to employ trawlers in war-time as minesweepers and patrol vessels; the Royal Naval Reserve Trawler Section was set up to enrol the necessary personnel. Although abolished as a separate section of the RNR in 1921, the RNR(T) always remained quite distinct from the RNR proper, and employed fishermen.

In both world wars a large number of trawlers were taken up by the Royal Navy complete with their crews, who were entered on a form T124 by which they engaged to serve in a named vessel for the duration of the war only*.

Also in 1911 the Royal Fleet Auxiliaries was formed, because of difficulties over the legal position of the crew of the hospital ship *Maine*, commissioned in 1902 with a civilian crew, although it was one of HM ships and part of the Mediterranean Fleet. Until 1921 the officers of the Royal Fleet Auxiliaries were nearly all RNR officers and ranked accordingly. Since then they have been ranked as other merchant navy officers.

In 1914 a separate element of the RNR was formed on the Shetland Islands. Known as the Shetland Royal Naval Reserve it was unlike the regular RNR in that it was a coast-watching and local defence organisation. It was disbanded in 1921†.

---

* The service records of ratings who served in the RNR (Trawler) section are probably an integral part of series BT 377 under letter codes such as WSA, SA, DA, ES and TS.

† The authors have been unable to locate the service records of those who served in the Shetland RNR. It is hoped that their records may be deposited locally in due course.

Some RNR Officers and Ratings saw service, on land, in the Royal Naval Division during World War 1; their records should be sought in PRO record series *ADM 339 (Royal Naval Division: Records of Service)*.

Some records relating to the RNR have found their way into local record offices:

Ceredigion Archives	RNR, Aberystwyth: Enrolment books etc	1908-1960
Gwynedd Archives, Caernarfon	RNR: Caernarfon Battery	1891-1904
Shetland Archives	RNR Relief Fund, Lerwick	1910-1931

A few records survive for the earlier Sea Fencibles in record series *ADM 28, Sea Fencibles: Pay Lists (1798-1810)*.

Officers

From 1862 onwards, RNR officers were included in the published *Navy List*, copies of which may be found in many libraries and archives. During both world wars key information potentially of use to the enemy was omitted from the published edition and confined to confidential editions reserved for service use. The *Navy Lists Confidential Editions* are available at the PRO in series ADM 177. For RNR officers the *Navy List* gives name, rank, date of commission, and seniority. Lists of RNR Officers also appeared in 1863 and 1864 editions of the *Mercantile Navy List*.

Promotions of officers will also be found in the *London Gazette*, indexed under Naval Promotions, Royal Naval Reserve, for example:

London Gazette, October 25, 1898 page 6235
Royal Naval Reserve
Assistant Engineer John Wallace to be Engineer, 12 October 1898

Records of officers serving from 1862 to 1909 and honorary officers from 1862 to 1960 are to be found at the PRO in series *Royal Naval Reserve: Records of Service of Officers (ADM 240)*. These show details of merchant as well as naval service and are arranged in numerical order of commission. There are no separate indexes as such, although some of the volumes do provide a partial index. Additionally RNR officers are indexed in ADM 196/26 although, as with many RN records of service, it is unclear as to which set of registers these indexes refer.

An example from these registers is:

Royal Naval Reserve: Records of Officers Service: Engineers	ADM 240/32
Surname	*Wallace*
Number of Commission	*0210*
Christian name	*John*
Date of birth	*1872, 30 December*
Date of Commission	*1898, 22 October*
Date of seniority	*1898, 12 October*
No. and description of Certificate of Competency	*1st class 31047*
	N 11698 *M 18388/98*
Date and cause of removal from the	*22.2.1906* *M 3865/06*
List of Engineers	*Promoted Senior Eng.*

Particulars are given of his service, conduct, character etc.
It records that he was promoted from Assistant Engineer and that he was selected to undergo the Instructional Course for Engineer Officers in the RNR commencing at Portsmouth on 6th June 1899 (N.6041 M 9691/99)

Service records for officers serving between 1910 and 1920 are currently with the Ministry of Defence but are due to for transfer to the PRO during 2002. Enquiries about those who served at a later date should be directed to the Ministry of Defence who will normally only consider releasing information to the individual concerned, or his proven next-of-kin; a fee is usually charged.

Ratings

Only a selection of the service records for ratings who served between 1860 and 1913 have been preserved; these are in series *Royal Naval Reserve: Representative Records of Service (BT 164)*. These consist of volumes and cards, each page or card covering five years' service in the RNR; any individual may therefore be entered in several volumes or cards. Letters (A, B, etc) were given to successive five-year terms; the entries are in numerical order of enrolment.

A typical example is:

Royal Naval Reserve: Representative service records: 1860, 1-400	BT 164/1
Surname of volunteer	*Anderson*
Christian names	*James*
Where born	*Eastbourne, Sussex*
Year when born	*1822* {Note: sometimes full date is given}
Usual abode	*22 Bilbury Street, Plymouth*
Height	*5 ft 6 ins*
Complexion	*Sallow*
Colour of eyes	*Grey*
Personal marks or peculiarities (if any)	*Mole on left cheek*
Name of father and mother	*James* *(M)*
	Ann
Finally disposed of	*Re-inrolled, 20.007 Cert. recd*

Listed are:
- Appearances at drill
- Payment of retainers etc.
- Particulars of voyages in Merchant service subsequent to Inrollment, namely: port, date, rating on engagement, name of ship, official number, voyage, date of expected return, discharge details.

Service records for RNR ratings, serving during and after World War 1, have been preserved in their totality. These are microfiche in series BT 377, arranged in service number order. Although the series does contain records up until the merger between the RNR and RNVR in 1958, there seem to very few records of those serving during World War 2.

Name indexes are available to all RNR ratings records[‡] even where, during the period 1860-1913, not all the records have been preserved. An individual's RNR number (variously referred to RV 2 or RS 2) may also be found in a variety of other record series mentioned elsewhere (e.g. the Central Indexed Register and the Medal Rolls in ADM 171 and BT 351).

[‡] The earlier of these indexes is not yet available for consultation.

Prisoners of War

World War 1
Lists of names of enemy prisoners and internees were routinely forwarded to the Prisoners of War Information Bureau in London that in turn informed the International Red Cross Headquarters in Geneva. The International Red Cross does not permit personal access to this material but searches will be made for a fee though this is quite expensive. Bombing in 1940 largely destroyed the lists compiled by the Bureau.

No comprehensive lists of prisoners of war on either side have survived at the PRO but some lists have been found amongst the correspondence of the Foreign Office and Colonial Office and others may await discovery:

Reference	Dated	Title or topic
FO 383/65 File 67310, Paper 146257	21 September 1915	List of Merchant Seamen and Fishermen detained as Prisoners of war in Germany, Austria-Hungary and Turkey
FO 383/352 File 4651, Paper 92439	31 March 1917	
CO 693/5 File 45094, folios 509-567	31 July 1917	
CO 693/9 MO file 3957, folios 454-503	31 Dec 1917	
CO 693/9 MO file 3957 folios 576-624	1 May 1918	
FO 383/183 File 31991, Paper 83624	25 April 1916	List of Royal and Merchant Navy Officers and Ratings taken to Germany by the surface raider ss *Moewe,*
FO 383/353 File 32672, Paper 122095	1917	List of Lascar seamen Prisoners of War who served on the ss *Author.*

Information varies but may include the name of the seaman and his address, age and place of birth, date of capture, the name and owner of the ship and the camp in which the seaman in interned.

Correspondence about both British and enemy merchant seamen taken prisoner is to be found in PRO record series *Marine Correspondence and Papers (MT 9, code 106).*

Other material may be found in the series *Foreign Office: General Correspondence: Political (FO 371)* for which there is a large card index for the period 1906 to 1919 in the PRO reading rooms. This can be searched by either the name of the ship or of the individual, though do not expect to find every seaman's name include in lists of prisoners to appear in the index.

World War 2

German forces during the World War 2 captured over 5,000 allied merchant seamen. Most were held at some time at the Merchant Navy Internment Camp at Westertimke, near Bremen, Germany, known as MILAG (from the German 'Marine Internierten Lager'). The key series of records is *Merchant Seamen Prisoner of War Records; 1939-1945 (BT 373)*. These records are arranged in various categories, typically by ship or by seaman's name; they list:

- Name of camp
- Prisoner of war number
- Name of Seaman
- Date and place of birth
- Discharge book number
- Rank or rating
- Name and official number of ship
- Date of loss of ship
- Next of kin, with relationship and address

Correspondence about British merchant seamen taken prisoner is to be found in PRO record series *Marine Correspondence and Papers (MT 9, code 106)*. Mention of merchant navy prisoners of war may also be found in other series, such as *War Office Registered Files (WO 32, code 91)* and *Directorate of Military Operations Collation Files (WO 193/343-359)*.

The *Index to General Correspondence of the Foreign Office 1920-1951*, available in the PRO reading rooms, contains numerous entries relating to prisoners of war. Not all files listed there have been preserved; those that have are to be found mainly in series *General Correspondence: Political (FO 371)*.

Papers of MI9, the division of Military Intelligence which dealt with escaped prisoners of all services and those who evaded capture, are in WO 208/3242-3566; reports related to merchant seamen are to be found amongst these records. This material mostly relate to the European/Mediterranean theatres of war and only represent a small percentage of the estimated 192,000 British and Commonwealth prisoners of war. It includes both escape and liberation reports and camp histories. Escape and liberation reports are to be found in pieces 3298-3327, 3336-3340 and 3348-3352 to which there is a nominal card index available in the PRO reading rooms. A camp history, and additional papers, relating to MILAG are in WO 208/3270 and 3501.

A section of the Central Register of Seamen applies specifically to Prisoners of War and Internees, namely BT 382/3232-3249.

Papers on RNR officers who were casualties, missing or prisoners of war, during World War 2, are in BT 164/23.

Medals
Gallantry
In the nineteenth and early twentieth centuries the main gallantry awards which merchant seamen, perhaps amongst others, were eligible to receive were:

- Albert Medal - instituted in 1886
  Register of awards and photographs of holders (1866-1913) in BT 97.
  Announcement in the *London Gazette*; any additional information should be sought in MT 9 code 6 and BT 261. Annotated copies of the *London Gazette* entries are in BT 339/5.

- Sea Gallantry Medal (for merchant seamen) - 1856-1981
  Registers, covering 1876-1880 and 1887-1981 in BT 261.
  Medal rolls for 1899-1902 are also found in ADM 171/51.
  Announcement in the *London Gazette*; any additional information should be sought in MT 9 code 6.

- Empire Gallantry Medal (1922-1940) - replaced by George Cross.
  Announcement in the *London Gazette*; any additional information should be sought in MT 9 code 6.

- British Empire Medal (from 1922 for meritorious service)
  Announcement in the *London Gazette*; any additional information should be sought in MT 9 code 6 and AIR 2.

- George Cross (from 1940 replacing the Empire Gallantry Medal, and from 1971, the Albert Medal)
  Announcement in the *London Gazette*; any additional information should be sought in MT 9 code 6 and AIR 2. Annotated copies of the *London Gazette* entries are in BT 339/5

- George Medal (from 1940)
  Announcement in the *London Gazette*; any additional information should be sought in MT 9 code 6, AIR 2, ADM 1, ADM 116 and ADM 199.

- Lloyd's awarded a number of medals, namely:

  - Lloyd's Medal for Services to Lloyd's (from 1913)
    Cumulative lists in *Lloyd's Calendar*, 1918-1975
  - Lloyd's Medal for Saving Life at Sea (from 1836)
    Cumulative lists in *Lloyd's Calendar*, up to 1940
  - Lloyd's Medal for Meritorious Service (from 1893)
    Cumulative lists in *Lloyd's Calendar*, up to 1940
  - Lloyd's Medal for Bravery at Sea (from 1940)
    Cumulative lists in *Lloyd's Calendar*, 1953-1955.

  Lloyd's Calendar, 1893-1975, is available at Guildhall Library. Citations for medals need to be sought from the Manager's Secretarial Department, Lloyd's, Lime Street, London EC3M 7HL A published list and history is available[54].

- Queen's Gallantry Medal (from 1974 for meritorious service).
  Announcement in the *London Gazette*.

Records of merchant navy officers and men receiving naval gallantry awards during both world wars can be found in record series ADM 1, code 85 and *ADM 116, code 85 (Admiralty Secretariat Cases)*; indexes to these are in ADM 12.

Recommendations for World War 1 awards may also be found in ADM 137. Nominal lists and copies of *London Gazette* entries for officers (1916-1920) are found in BT 339/6. Some recommendations for World War 2 awards may be found in ADM 1 Code 85, AIR 2 B Code 30, BT 164/23, BT 238, BT 261, MT 9 Code 6, PREM 2, and ZJ 1. *(London Gazette)*

Campaign
The key campaign medals to which a merchant seaman could be entitled include:

- Egypt Medal (1882)
  ADM 171/41

- Egypt Medal (1884) - for campaigns in Sudan
  ADM 171/42 - 43

- Sea Transport Medal (1899-1902)
  ADM 171/52

- World War 1 campaign medals, namely:

  - 1914-15 Star, British War Medal and Victory Medal
    RNR officers in ADM 171/92 - 93 and ratings in ADM 171/120 - 124; other merchant seamen in ADM 171/130 - 133
    The issue of the British War Medal and the Mercantile Marine Medal is recorded in BT 351.
  - Silver War Badge
    Lists of those receiving the Silver War Badge are contained in MT 9 code 6.
  - Medal rolls for those in the RNR attached to the Indian Navy are held in the Oriental and India Office Collections of British Library.

- World War 2 campaign medals
  Unlike those for World War 1 these campaign medals were not issued automatically; it is necessary for the individual or next of kin to apply for them. The records do not give entitlement but simply note whether the British authorities have issued a medal, or ribbon, to an individual; they do not provide any other information about the person. The records are not yet available to the public and enquiries should be directed to the Registry of Shipping and Seamen who will only release information to the person concerned or, if deceased, the next of kin.
  Medals to which a merchant seaman may have been entitled were:

  - 1939-45 Star
  - Atlantic Star
  - Africa Star
  - Pacific Star
  - Burma Star
  - Italy Star
  - France and Germany Star

Lists of men from the colonies who received campaign stars and award medals, together with correspondence, are to be found in the records of the *Colonial Office: Military Department (CO 820/62).*

Royal Naval Reserve
Records relating to the award of the RNR Long Service and Good Conduct medal are in ADM 171/70 - 72. Honours and Awards for the RNR during World War 1 are in ADM 171/77.

Issue of the RNR and Long Service and Good Conduct medals to ratings should be noted on their service record in BT 377.

Papers on awards to RNR officers during the World War 2 are in BT 164/23 and ADM 1.

The Roll of the Naval War Medals also contains entries for the RNR - officers in ADM 171/92 - 93 and ratings in ADM 171/120 - 124.

Awards and Testimonials
Between 1857 and 1864 the *Mercantile Navy List* includes lists of officers receiving awards and testimonials for exceptional service at sea, usually in connection with shipwrecks.

Later medals
Merchant navy personnel may be entitled to the following medals:

* Naval General Service Medal with Clasp Palestine (1945-1948)
* British Korea Medal (1950-1953)
* Naval General Service Medal with Clasp Near East (Suez) (1956)
* Naval General Service Medal Cyprus (1955-1959)
* Naval General Service Medal with Clasp Borneo (1962-1966)
* South Atlantic Medal (Falklands) 1982
* Gulf Medal 1990-91

Enquiries about them should be made to the Registry of Shipping and Seamen who will only release information to the person concerned or, if deceased, the next of kin.

APPRENTICESHIP, CHARITIES AND PENSIONS

Apprentices' Indentures

From 1823, masters of ships greater than 80 tons were required to carry a quota of indentured apprentices. To help ensure that this regulation was complied with, Apprenticeship Indentures had to be filed. From 1835, these could be filed either with local Customs or with the Registrar General of Shipping and Seamen (RGSS) in London. From 1844 on, those indentures filed with the Customs had to be forwarded quarterly to the RGSS.

The RGSS compiled an *Index of Apprentices* in these indentures, some of which go back to the 1820s; this is now PRO record series *BT 150*. The Indexes are subdivided into London and Outports, then by span of dates; the entries within each volume are sorted by first letter of apprentice's surname. A typical entry reads:

Index of Apprentices, Outports (K - Z), Oct. 1840-1844	BT 150/22
Month of registry	*June 1841*
No.	-
Port of Registry	*Yarmouth*
Date of Indenture	*1 June 1841*
Name of Apprentice	*Watts, J.S.H.*
Age of Apprentice	*15*
Term for which bound	*5 years*
Name and residence of Master	*A. Steward*
Name and Burthen of Vessels	*Harlequin 190*

Whilst indexes survive from 1824, not all the Apprentices' Indentures have been preserved. The PRO retained only those for every fifth year, in record series BT 151 and BT 152, a few went to the National Maritime Museum and the remainder were destroyed.

Those indentures that were originally filed with the local Customs should perhaps have survived amongst the Customs records. We have found no evidence of their survival, though some later ones do survive in various CUST series at the PRO and County Record Offices do hold some Apprenticeship Registers from Custom Houses but these usually date from the late 1800s. For instance North East Lincolnshire Archives holds registers of those apprenticed to the fishing industry in Grimsby (1879-1937) and the Cumbria Record Office, Whitehaven, holds those for Workington (1859-1892).

The Society of Genealogists holds 17 bound volumes of original indentures acquired, mainly from parish chests, by a Victorian antiquarian. This collection called *Crisp's Indentures* contains many indentures of seamen from the north-east of England dated between 1845 and *c*.1861.

A more general source, which does include details of many seafaring apprentices, is the PRO record series *Apprenticeship Books (IR 1)*, which records the payment of tax on indentures; it covers the period 1710 to 1811. These registers give names, addresses and trades of the masters together with the names of the apprentices and the dates of their indentures. Until 1752 the name of the apprentices' parent (usually father) is given but after that year rarely. Indexes to apprentices' names and to masters' names from 1710 to 1774 have been compiled and are available on microfiche at both the PRO and the Society of Genealogists amongst other places. These records specifically exclude those apprenticed on the common charge (e.g. parish apprentices) and rarely include those apprenticed within a family.

Care needs to be taken when using these indexes to be aware of the shorthand used by the compilers:

- In the index to apprentices, following the surname, the apprentice's forename appears first followed by that of his parent, with the words 'son of' omitted. The references given are the piece number and folio within series IR 1, followed by the year in which the indenture was registered (which could be up to one year after the date of expiry of the indentures).
- The index to masters does not directly index the Apprenticeship Books; they are actually an index to the names of masters within the volumes of indexes to apprentices, from which reference to the original register may then be obtained.

Public Record Office

BT 150	Index of Apprentices	1824-1953
BT 151	Apprentices' Indentures [Only every 5th year preserved]	1845-1950
BT 152	Apprentices Indentured for Fishing [Only every 5th year preserved]	1895-1935
BT 167/103	Colchester: Register of Apprentice seamen's indentures	1704-1757 1804-1844
CUST 52/112	Register of Apprentices - Ramsgate	1893-1908
CUST 57/28	Register of Apprentices Indentures - Littlehampton	1856-1897
CUST 56/89	Register of Apprentices Indentures - Newhaven	1893-1908
CUST 64/205	Indentures of Apprentices - Teignmouth	1853-1893
CUST 67/81	Register of Apprentices Indentures - Fowey	1825-1925
CUST 68/185	Register of Apprentices Indentures - Scilly Isles	1857-1878
CUST 69/224	Register of Apprentices Indentures - Bideford	1857-1880
IR 1	Apprenticeship Books	1710-1811

National Maritime Museum

Registered at	Dates of registry	Coverage
London	June 1845	
London	July - August 1847	
London	January - April 1850	
London	September - December 1850	
London	May - August 1851	
Outports	January 1845	K-Z
Outports	August 1845	K-Z
Outports	September 1845	A-J
Outports	December 1845	K-Z
Outports	August 1846	A-J
Outports	April 1848 K-Z	
Outports	October 1853	
Outports	November 1856	

Other repositories

County Record Offices	Apprenticeship Registers from some local Custom Houses.	Mostly late 1800s
Society of Genealogists	Crisp's Indentures	NE England, 1845-*c*.1861

Training ships and schools

A few schools specialised in training boys for a seafaring career, usually as officers. Details are given below of those where material has been traced in public archives, namely *HMS Conway, HMS Worcester* and Christ's Hospital Mathematical School. A most useful background description of the social situation out of which these institutions grew, together with details of another training ship, *Arethusa*, is to be found in an 'Early History of Shaftesbury Homes and Arethusa' published on the website of the Arethusa Old Boys Association at www.users.zetnet.co.uk/arethusa/history.htm. The records of that training ship are still with the Shaftesbury Homes and Arethusa who also publish a brochure outlining their history.

Conway

The records of *HMS Conway* are preserved in the archives of the Merseyside Maritime Museum, Liverpool. The major holdings relevant for details of an individual are:

D/CON 12/1-2	Indexes to Registers of Cadets	1859-1972
D/CON 13/1-40	Registers of boys	1859-1971
D/CON 14/1-57	*The Cadet* - magazine of *HMS Conway*	1889-1974

The registers are likely to record the cadet's name, when and where he was born, the name, address and occupation of his parent or guardian, the last school that he attended, when he was admitted and left. Regular reports on both his naval and school activities should be found.

Worcester
The National Maritime Museum holds minutes, financial records and news cuttings (1861-1968) for *HMS Worcester* (Thames Nautical Training College), Greenhithe, Kent and material from the training ship *HMS Worcester* at London (1863-1972). The Thames Nautical Training College published a magazine, *The Dog Watch*, three times per year; it first appeared in 1924.

Christ's Hospital Mathematical School
Boys from Christ's Hospital Mathematical School were examined by Corporation of Trinity House elder brethren and bound as apprentices for seven years to ships' captains. One register of 'ships' apprentices', covering 1816-1857, survives at the Guildhall Library (Ms 30338).

Charities

Introduction
Many charities have from time to time existed for the support of destitute seamen, and this presents an avenue, that we believe has hitherto been poorly explored, to obtain information about individual seamen. J.P. Press, in Chapter VI of his Ph.D Thesis[55], lists the following:

Marine Society (London)	1757	See below
British & Foreign Bethel Seamen's Union	1819	London
Seamen's Hospital Society	1821	Still exists
Seamen's Loyal Standard Association	1824	Tyneside
British & Foreign Sailor's Society	1833	
Shipwrecked Fishermen & Mariner's Royal Benevolent Society	1839	
Missions to Seamen	1856	Mainly local

But this list is by no means complete. For instance the records of the Sailors' Children's Society, founded in 1821, still exists providing welfare facilities for seamen in the Humber area including homes for aged seafarers in Hull and South Shields. The Hull Seamen's and General Orphanage, and the Clyde Marine Society (which evolved from the Glasgow's 'Sailor's Poor Box') date back some years, as no doubt do many others.

Occasionally one comes across papers, surviving in private hands, relating to individuals seeking or receiving benefit from one of these charities. Whether any comprehensive records do survive, either with the charity itself if it is still extant, or in a public archive is most uncertain. Perhaps the best way to pursue such an enquiry is first to search the computerised catalogue of the Historical Manuscripts Commission (available on-line at http://www2.hmc.gov.uk) or ask at the relevant local record office for the area in which the charity operated. Records of interest may possibly also be found at the Public Record Office in the various series of records from the Charity Commissioners (CHAR) but little work seems to have been carried out along this avenue.

Here we will limit ourselves to describe, albeit briefly, some key collections available publicly, namely: Trinity House, Marine Society, Dreadnought Seamen's Hospital, Trafalgar Square Aged Seamen's Homes (Sunderland), Great Yarmouth Shipwrecked Sailors Home and Jersey Merchant Seamen's Benefit Society. Some others are known to exist at the Merseyside Maritime Museum, namely the minutes of Liverpool Sailor's Home. 1838-1963 (D/LH); Royal Liverpool Seamen's Orphan Institution archives, 1869-c.1970, (D/SO).

Trinity House
The Corporation of Trinity House was incorporated by royal charter in 1514; it has had three main functions for most of its history, namely as:

- General Lighthouse Authority for England, Wales, the Channel Islands and Gibraltar.
- Pilotage Authority for London and forty other districts (termed outports); these included Southampton but not Liverpool, Bristol and several ports in the north-east of England.
- Charitable organisation for the relief of mariners and their dependants in distress.

The first two of these need not concern us here; those interested in these aspects should consult the brief guide (leaflet) available from the Guildhall Library where most of the records are held. The archive is subject to a fifty-year closure period and researchers must seek permission to see any record less than fifty years old.

Prior to the Merchant Shipping Act of 1854, the Corporation of Trinity House had at its disposal certain charitable funds for the benefit of seafarers and their dependants throughout the UK, independent of any previous connection with Trinity House. In order to benefit from these a seafarer (mostly mercantile mariners) or his dependants had to make application to Trinity House. This application took the form of a Petition, which gave details of his circumstances. An example, described by E.P. Stapleton as representative[56] reads:

> The humble Petition of James Wilson aged 44 Years residing at North Shields and where he has lived for sixteen years and followed the Occupation of Mariner. Sheweth
>
> THAT your petitioner went to sea at the age of Twelve years in a vessel out of the Port of Newcastle and served there as Aprentis seven years in the Coal and Baltic trade and latterly in the station of Master on board the Ship Louisa of London in the coal trade of which ship John Chambers was owner and in that capacity served for six voyages.
>
> THAT Your Petitioner has a wife Isabella Wilson aged 46 Years and one child under eleven years old, or through Infirmity incapable of earning their living whose names and ages are viz. Mary Wilson aged nine years and three more under 13.

Further details are then given of the petitioner's financial resources. Typically a master mariner might receive £3 per annum, decreasing to £1-19-0 per annum for seamen.

These records suffered badly by fire in 1666 and 1714; those that now survive cover the period 1787-1854. The original petitions, bound up in two alphabetical series, previously at the Society of Genealogists are now at Guildhall Library:

Ms 30218A	Main series of petitions	1787-1854
Ms 30218B	Second series of petitions	1787-1853

The records are available at both locations on microfilm; both series are indexed in the published Trinity House Petitions[57].

There are also some Apprenticeship Indentures (1780, 1818-45), presumably filed in support of an application, which are described and indexed in the *Genealogists' Magazine*[58].

E.P. Stapelton gives some further details in the article in the *Genealogists' Magazine*. There he mentions Pension Pay Books, dating from 1775, although these give little more information than is contained in the Petitions except probably recording the date of a pensioner's death. It is thought that the Pension Pay Books were destroyed in a wartime fire.

In addition to the petitions described above, the Guildhall Library also holds *Registers of almspeople and pensioners 1729-1946 (Ms 30218)*. These give the age of the applicant and the reason for assistance; but they are indexed for 1907-1939 only. The indexed *Registers of almspeople 1845-1971 (Ms 30219)*, which only cover almspeople, give age and reason for assistance. Southampton University Library also holds *Applications for pensions to the 1st Duke of Wellington, Master of Trinity House, 1829-1852* (reference MS 61).

The 'other' Trinity Houses

One needs to be clear that, despite its national coverage in very many matters, there were in fact other regional Trinity Houses - and their records may assist. The following are listed by the Historical Manuscripts Commission, in their National Register of Archive, as containing records about admissions, apprentices or pensioners:

Trinity House	Repository (reference)	Covering dates of collection *(see note)*	Includes material on
Trinity House, **Dundee**	Dundee City Archives (GD/Hu/SF)	1652-1974	Fraternity of seamen
Trinity House, **Hull**	Hull University, Brynmor Jones Library (DTR)	17th-20th century	
Trinity House, **Ipswich**	Suffolk Record Office, Ipswich Branch (HC426)	1955-1980	
Trinity House, **Leith**	National Archives of Scotland (GD.226)	16th-20th century	
Master, Pilots and Seamen of Trinity House, **Newcastle-upon-Tyne** (whose jurisdiction extended to **Sunderland, Stockport** and **Hartlepool**)	Tyne & Wear Archives Service (GU/TH)	1604-1982	Admissions, apprentices papers
Trinity House, **Newhaven and district**	East Sussex Record Office (A5387)	1857-1988	
Trinity House, **River Thames** Pilots Association	Medway Archives Office (U2919)	1936-1988	
Trinity House and Merchant Seamen's Hospital, **Scarborough**	North Yorkshire County Record Office (ZOX)	1747-1910	Muster rolls, pensioners records
Trinity House, **South Shields**	Tyne and Wear Archives Service (Acc 1477)	1804-1861	Pilot books

Note: The dates given are the covering dates of the whole collection and do not necessarily mean that the items of interest are available for the whole of that period.

For example information about seamen using Leith may be found amongst the records of Trinity House, Leith, preserved at the National Archives of Scotland in GD.226. It was a mutual benefit society supporting poor, aged and infirm merchant seamen and their dependants. The records include minutes and cash books dating from the mid-17th century that record payments by seaman as well as pensions to their dependants. Records related to individual harbour pilots are also in this collection.

Marine Society

Notable amongst collections giving personal histories of seamen is that of the Marine Society. The society was founded in 1756, and indentured some 16,000 boys into the Merchant Navy between 1815 and 1854; in fact it supplied, by about 1835, up to 10% of the total apprentices. It kept detailed records of the parents and guardians of the boys, who came mainly from the London area. The key items of interest, all of which are held at the National Maritime Museum, are more fully described in an excellent article by Roland Pietsch[59]; they include:

MSY/H/1-2	Registers of boys recruited for the Royal Navy	7 Years War
MSY/H/3-4	Boys returned to MS at end of 7 years war	
MSY/J	Marine Society: miscellaneous volumes and papers	
MSY/K	Registers of boys received and discharged from the Marine Society's ship	1786-1874
MSY/L	Register of admissions	1854-1958
MSY/O	Registers of boys entered as servants in the King's ships	1770-1873
MSY/Q	Registers of apprentices sent to merchant ships	1772-1950
MSY/S/1	Registers of men recruited for the Royal Navy	7 Years War
MSY/T	Register of girl apprentices under Hickes Trust	1772-1978

The Guildhall Library also holds some records of the Marine Society between 1762 and 1869.

Dreadnought Seamen's Hospital, Greenwich.

Dreadnought Seamen's Hospital was established in 1821, being based initially on a sequence of river-based ships, namely: *Grampus, Dreadnought,* (supported in times of need by the *Dover, Iphegenia, Devonshire* and *Belle Isle*) and another *Dreadnought* (previously called the *Caledonia*); in 1870 the hospital moved ashore. The secretary of the society has published an interesting history[60].

Records related to the hospital are now held at the National Maritime Museum but, as they are currently outhoused, an advance enquiry is advisable. Additionally there are some restrictions on the use of material more recent than 100 years old. Included in the collection are:

DSH/1	Admissions	1826-1977
DSH/101	Index to Admissions	
DSH/201	Outpatients	1857-1964
DSH/401	Nurses and records of training	1895-1968

Aged Seamen's Homes, Sunderland
This extant charity (Aged Seamen's Homes, Sunderland: Assembly Garth and Trafalgar Square), of which some of the original buildings still stand in the east end of Sunderland, supported mariners and their families from the mid-19th century. An article illustrating just what may be discovered amongst their records has been published[61]. The available material consist of a register, covering the period 1839-1854, into which details were copied from the nearly 2800 applications for assistance. Photocopies of the register are available at Sunderland Library but have also been published[62], in microfiche form, by the Northumberland and Durham Family History Society. That publication includes an index to the almost 4700 individuals named (seamen, wives, children) plus a copy of an article[63] published in 1903 giving a history of the homes. Anybody interested in a seafarer, or his family, with connections in Sunderland at this time is well advised to look at this material as it may reveal extensive details about individuals and their seafaring activities.

Great Yarmouth Shipwrecked Sailors Home.
Great Yarmouth Maritime Museum holds records related to the Great Yarmouth Shipwrecked Sailors Home, namely:

SO 4/1-3	Minutes	1805-1905
SO 4/4	Committee Minutes	1858-1862
SO 4/5-6	Daily Log Books	1858-1865
SO 4/7-8	Letter Books	1859-1930
SO 4/9-10	Annual Reports	1908-1964
SO 4/11-12	Ledgers	1908-1949
SO 4/13	Cash Journal	1908-1917
SO 4/14	Pass Book	1924-1938
SO 4/15-16	Log of Shipwrecks	1913-1964
SO 4/17	Letters of thanks from shipwrecked men	1902-1912
SO 4/18	Correspondence, mostly financial	1950s-60s

Jersey Merchant Seamen's Benefit Society
The Jersey Merchant Seamen's Benefit Society was created in 1835 by the States of Jersey when the English compulsory levy of 6d per month on merchant seamen's wages was abolished. The records are now held in the library of the Société Jersiaise[64] and consist of three series:

- Ledgers of Seamen (1835-1897) giving the names of their ships, the length of service in each, parish of origin and age; there are separate nominal indexes to these ledgers.
- Pensions and Allowances Books (1835-1964) recording contributions received and monies paid out in pensions to seafarers giving their names, sometimes ages, and places of origin; details of their deaths and subsequent payments to widows or families are often recorded.
- Books listing ships and their crews; these cover 1835-1900 but with gaps 1843-1845 and 1856-1860.

The records are more fully described on the website of the Société Jersiaise at www.societe-jersiaise.org.

Pensions

Whilst some provision was certainly made for the payment of pensions to both seamen and their dependants, out of the Merchant Seamen's Fund, we have not come across any comprehensive records relating to such payments. A report on the potential impact of winding up this fund is to be found in the *House of Commons, Parliamentary Papers (1844) vol VIII p 279ff (mf 48.61 to .64)* but the fund was not actually wound up until some eight years later. The report does give an interesting insight into conditions at the time.

The Seamen's Fund Winding-up Act of 1851 made provision for the payment of pensions, under certain circumstances, to seamen and masters and their widows and children. The Marine Department of the Board of Trade handled applications for these. Amongst the *Marine Out-Letters (MT 4)* are to be found office copies of the letters confirming granting of a pension. For example, in MT 4/22 (fo. 2997):

Office of Committee of Privy Council for Trade,
Marine Department,
Whitehall, 10 June 1856

5996
Sir,
  I am directed by the Lords of the Committee of Privy Council for Trade to acknowledge the receipt of your letter of the 6th Instant; and to inform you that Pensions have been granted to Widow Clarke and her four Children. The Pension Tickets have been forwarded to the War Office, and will in due Course be delivered to her by the Staff Officer for the District in which she resides.

I am
Sir
Your obedient Servant,
James Booth

John Key Esq're
Shipowner,
Harrington, Cumberland

These letter books are indexed, either within the series or in MT 5, however the required entries are often to be found there under the heading of War Office. This is because the responsibility for payment of such pensions rested with the War Office, which had the necessary facilities in place for payment to its own pensioners.

Whilst the Pension Ticket referred to is only likely to have survived amongst personal papers, additional details are to be found in *Royal Hospital Chelsea Pension Returns, WO 22 (1842-1883)*. WO 22/208, 1852 Miscellaneous Mercantile Marine, covers seamen and dependants admitted when the scheme started, and often gives a date of birth; pieces 256 and 257 also relate to merchant seamen. Later volumes, related to individual districts, include seamen in the same way as for soldiers[65]. For example:

Pension returns - Carlisle Pension District (1852- 1862)						WO 22/16
Monthly Return of Changes which have taken place among Out-Pensioners of Chelsea and Greenwich Hospitals and those belonging to the East India Company in Carlisle District from the 1st to the 30th June 1856 inclusive.						
III Pensioners newly admitted to Out-Pension						
Mercantile Marine						
Regt Number	**Rate**	**Date of Admission to Out-Pension**	**Rank**	**Name of Pensioner**	**Date on which pension commenced in the District**	**Remarks stating whether Perm. or Temp**
1346	*4-8*	*31 May*	*M W*	*CLARKE Mary Ann*	*1 April 1856*	*Life*
1148	*2-4*	*31May*	*M Child*	*CLARKE James Charters*	*1 April 1856*	*Temp.*
1149	*2-4*	*31 May*	*M Child*	*CLARKE Henry Milward*	*1 April 1856*	*Temp.*
1150	*2-4*	*31 May*	*M Child*	*CLARKE Ralph Tate*	*1 April 1856*	*Temp.*
1151	*2-4*	*31 May*	*M Child*	*CLARKE Ann Eliza*	*1 April 1856*	*Temp.*

As you might expect the children appeared again (under the section V Pensions expired or reduced) on reaching the age of 14.

Correspondence related to pensions to merchant seamen and their dependants will also be found in the series *Out Letters Secretary at War (WO 4)* with three volumes, 1851-1856 relating specifically to merchant seamen (WO 4/752-754). These contain name indexes, but the entries are not usually particularly informative; some entries do record that the individual chose to commute the pension to a lump sum payment.

Records of pension commutation, following the Pensions Commutation Act of 1869, are to be found in the record series *Pensions Commutation Board Minutes (NDO 14)* covering the period 1869-1970 (subject to a 75 year closure). *NDO 7 (National Debt Office, Correspondence)* contains two pieces (Correspondence, 1871-1897 NDO 7/49 and Advances 1871-1942 NDO 7/50) which are correspondence between the Pensions Commutation Board and the Treasury may contain extra detail. In particular NDO 7/49 contains a printed list of persons who commuted pensions between 1869 and 31 March 1883, with addenda up to mid-1884, though a quick search did fail to reveal any for merchant seamen. Permission had to be granted by the Treasury for commutation to take place, thus *Treasury Board Papers T 1* contains letters sent by the Pensions Commutation Board to the Treasury. The route to these is from the *Register of Papers T 2* under 'Public Offices, Pensions Commutation Board' or via *Subject Registers T 108*. It is doubtful if many files have been kept unless a particular matter of policy arose.

Information on Admiralty pensions granted to RNR ratings from 1922 to 1925 may be found in ADM 23/170.

Other record series, at the PRO, that may include information about pensions for merchant seamen include:

J 96 /112-142,	Supreme Court of Judicature,	1947-1979,
191-192	High Court, Queen's Bench Division,	1943-1968.
	Orders in Appeals and other papers	
	[against Pensions Appeal Tribunals]	
PIN 15	War Pensions	1901-1983
PIN 22	Ministry of Pensions and National Insurance:	1912-1974
	Registered Files, MA and MA(X) series	
PMG 56	Naval Establishment, Warlike Operations:	1914-1928
	Pensions etc.	

Records of the Liverpool Seamen's Pension Fund, 1909-1917, survive at the Merseyside Maritime Museum.

BIRTHS, MARRIAGES & DEATHS AT SEA

Introduction

There are several popular beliefs about the registering of births and deaths occurring at sea, and about the performing of marriage ceremonies at sea. Most of these do not hold up to detailed scrutiny. For instance, although some baptisms at sea from 1893 onwards are recorded in the registers of that church[66] , it is not true that all baptisms at sea were recorded at St. Dunstan, Stepney.

Masters of merchant vessels, it is popularly believed, may perform marriage ceremonies. Whilst this may perhaps be true of captains of RN vessels, we have yet to see any convincing evidence for such authority being vested in the masters of merchant vessels. Indeed the General Register Office, for England and Wales, put forward the view[67] in 1991 that marriages on board merchant vessels could not be legal under English law as no ships were buildings authorised for that purpose under the appropriate Marriage Act; a more in depth discussion on this point may be found in PRO record series RG 48. This does not, of course, preclude possibilities such the solemnisation of a marriage by a clergyman deriving his authority from a law other than that of England. Masters were required to record such marriages in the log book.

The Board of Trade was much clearer on this point. The guidance notes, printed as part of the Official Log Book (e.g. Form O9 during the 1910s) reminds masters of the requirement to enter in the log book details of each marriage that took place on board. But it goes on to state that 'Masters are reminded that they have no power to perform the marriage ceremony aboard their vessels, and that if such a ceremony is performed by them the marriage will not be a legal one.' This advice is based upon Section 240 (6) of the Merchant Shipping Act 1894.

In this chapter we will concentrate not so much on such myths, and legal niceties, but rather upon the more practical aspects of just what records of such events have survived, what they might reveal and where to find them. The prime source must be the log books of the ships, but these have not always survived or may not necessarily be readily accessible. So the first place to turn, even if it must strictly-speaking be termed a secondary source, are the registers kept by the Registrar General of Shipping and Seamen; next are the registers maintained by the various General Register Offices. Both of these are described more fully below. Discussion of the various supporting sources, which include log books, is delayed to this point as accessing them is best left until these two sources have been explored. Finally a range of miscellaneous material is examined.

Registers created by the RGSS

Introduction

The Seamen's Fund Winding-up Act 1851 required masters of British ships to hand on to a Shipping Master at the end of all voyages the wages and effects, or their proceeds, of any seaman who died during the voyage. Registers of these wages and effects were maintained by RGSS.

The Merchant Shipping Act 1854 made compulsory the deposit of official logs with RGSS. Registers were compiled from the entries in these logs of births, deaths and marriages of passengers at sea. Ships' masters were also required by the Registration of Births and Deaths Act 1874 to report all births and deaths on board ship to RGSS who then reported them periodically to the Registrar-General of Births, Deaths and Marriages of England and Wales, Scotland or Ireland as appropriate. Registers of reported births and deaths were kept by RGSS. Up to 1889 separate series of registers were kept for seamen and passengers but in 1890 a combined series was introduced.

It should be remembered that the legislation, and hence the records, applied to British vessels (including Britain's colonies at the time). So events relating to any foreign nationals aboard those vessels will be recorded along with British nationals. But events relating to British seamen, or passengers, aboard foreign-registered vessels will not be recorded here - details should be sought amongst the archives of the nation with whom the vessel was registered.

Wages and Effects of Deceased of Seamen, 1852-1889
The *Register of Wages and Effects of Deceased Seamen (BT 153)* records details of the deaths of seamen, 1852-1881 and 1888-1889; those for the period April 1881 to May 1888 have not survived. In them is recorded:

- name and register ticket number of the deceased seaman
- date of engagement
- place, date and cause of the man's death
- name and port of registry of his ship
- master's name
- date and place of payment of the wages
- amount of wages and date of receipt by the Board of Trade
- from 1866 they also record the seaman's age, his rating, and the ship's official number with a note of its voyages.

There are two indexes to these registers in BT 154 (by seaman's name) and BT 155 (by ship's name) that provide page numbers within the registers in BT 153.

Associated with these registers are *Monthly Lists of Deceased Seamen (BT 156)* that record:

- name, age and rating of deceased seaman
- nationality, or birthplace, and last address
- cause and place of death
- ship's name, official number and port of registry

Finally there is a series of *Registers of Seamen's Deaths Classified by Cause (BT 157)* that are arranged by cause of death. They record:

- vessel: name; official number; port of registry; UK, Colonial or Fishing; tonnage
- owner
- deceased: date of death; name; age; rating; cause of death; place of death
- voyage from and to
- remarks

This last series should not be ignored as it may reveal some surprises. Whilst looking for an individual who had purportedly been murdered at sea, we came across the entry for the *Young Dick*, a sailing vessel registered in Wellington, New Zealand, captained by J.H. Rodgers with 14 crew and 118 passengers (BT 157/8 fo. 274). It had sailed from Maryborough, Queensland to the South Sea Islands, in the labour trade in July 1886 - but had not made it, as can be seen from the remarks below:

Vessel missing - supposed to
have struck on Harrier Reef, Queensland

By paragraph in Shipping Gazette of 9.2.87
A letter dated Apia,
Navigators Island 13.12.86.
A number of Melanesian labourers
on their way to Malaita, Solomon Group
have eaten up the entire crew of the
ship & plundered the vessel -
The Cap't & mate were residents of Apia
the crew consisted of Patagonians &
other Polynesians.

Supposed to refer to the previous
voyage -

BT 153	Registers of Wages and Effects of Deceased Seamen	1852-1889
BT 154	Index to Seamen's Names (in BT 153)	1853-1889
BT 155	Index to Ship's Names (in BT 153)	1855-1889
BT 156	Monthly Lists of Deaths of Seamen	1886-1890
BT 157	Register of Seamen's Deaths, classified by Cause	1882-1888

Births, Deaths and Marriages 1854-1890
Registers of Births, Deaths and Marriages of Passengers at Sea (BT 158) contain details
of births, deaths and marriages of passengers taken from ships' official log books for the
following periods:

Births	1854-1887
Marriages	1854-1883
Deaths	1854-1890

There is an index to births and deaths from 1872 to 1890.

The death registers record:

- name, sex, age, rank, profession or occupation, and nationality or birthplace of the deceased
- last place of abode
- date, place and cause of death
- ship's name, official number and port of registry and trade

From 1874, the RGSS was required to report births and deaths at sea, aboard ships registered in Britain or its colonies, to the Registrars General of England and Wales, Scotland and Ireland (the General Register Offices). These are to be found in the series:

BT 159	Registers of Deaths at Sea of British Nationals	1875-1888
BT 160	Registers of Birth at Sea of British Nationals	1875-1891

There are separate volumes for England and Wales, Scotland and Ireland.

The death registers record:

- details of the ship
- date and cause of death
- name, sex, age, occupation, nationality and last address of deceased
- whether deceased was passenger or crew

The birth registers record:

- name and number of the ship
- date of ship's arrival in port
- date of birth
- name and sex of child
- name and occupation of father
- maiden name of mother
- parents' nationalities and last place of residence

Births, Deaths and Marriages, 1891-1972
From 1891 a new series of registers was introduced which combined records of the births, deaths and marriages of passengers at sea and the records of deaths and marriages of seamen at sea. The registers are in the PRO series *Registers and Indexes of Births, Marriages and Deaths of Passengers and Seamen at Sea (BT 334)*. The covering dates and information given in these registers is as follows:

- Births (1891-1960): name of ship, official number, port of registry, date of birth, name, sex, name of father, rank or profession or occupation of father, name of mother, maiden surname of mother, father's nationality/birthplace and last place of abode, mother's nationality/birthplace and last place of abode.

- Deaths (1891-1964): name of ship, official number, port of registry, date of death, place of death, name of deceased, sex, age, rating [for seamen], rank or profession or occupation [for non-seamen], nationality and birthplace, last place of abode, cause of death, remarks. *Note:* deaths of crew members taking place ashore, for instance in hospital, were required to be recorded wherever possible in addition to those that occurred actually at sea.

- Marriages (1854-1972): name of ship, official number, names of both parties, ages, whether single, widow or widower, profession or occupation, fathers' names, professions or occupations of fathers.

Marriages from 1854 to 1972 are in a single volume (BT 334/117), which has an integral index. The series also contains indexes to births and deaths. These are arranged both by ships' names and individuals' names. Later registers of births and deaths at sea are held by the RSS; a request for information from them may attract a fee.

One registers of deaths and births at sea, first reported at Falmouth (1892-1918), is to be found amongst the Customs records in CUST 67/74.

It should be noted that, although the RGSS was required to report deaths to the appropriate General Register Office, over half of the entries are blank in the column headed 'Which RG has been informed'. It appears that, where the vessel was missing or lost, the names of the individuals who were presumed to have died were entered in the RGSS's registers but details were not forwarded to any Registrar General. Also in some cases when the death actually took place ashore then details may again not have been forwarded - but the precise rules are not clear. Care also needs to be taken in interpreting the 'Which RG has been informed' column since either the abbreviations E (for England), S (for Scotland), I for (Ireland) and NI (for Northern Ireland after 1922) or alternatively L (for London), E (for Edinburgh) and D (for Dublin) may have been used. But the context will soon tell you whether E means England or Edinburgh.

In Australia, the Navigation Act 1912-1920 required the masters of all vessels, whether Australian, British or Foreign-registered, carrying passengers to Australia to report any births, marriages or deaths on board to the marine superintendent upon arrival at any port in Australia. These reports are likely to be found in, or with, the log books preserved in state or commonwealth archives.

General Register Office

Introduction

From 1874 onwards, the RGSS was required to report births and deaths at sea, on British-registered (including colonial) vessels to the appropriate Registrars General of Births, Marriages and Deaths (General Register Offices) for England and Wales, Scotland and Ireland. Similar onward-reporting arrangements only came into force in 1980 for the Isle of Man; none exist for any of the Channel Islands. These reports were limited to those with the appropriate nationality or who were normally resident in those countries. Each of these countries maintains a separate set of register related to events at sea - and some of these registers pre-date this reporting requirement.

As will be seen from the above description, the registers at the various General Register Offices are actually two steps removed from the original record. Incomplete reporting from the RGSS is evident from his records and a filtering process, based on nationality or residence, is known to have been applied. Thus the records held by the GROs are incomplete. But the start of the GRO's registers pre-dates the RGSS's reporting requirement and hence the former may actually contain, at that date, entries not in the RGSS's registers. Therefore the only prudent course is to consult both sources when searching for an individual event; though having found it, it is unlikely that the GRO's version will contain extra information about the event. It is also wise to consult the regular civil registration indexes in case the event sought happen not to be classified as 'at sea'.

England and Wales

Births and deaths occurring at sea are not usually found amongst the normal records at the General Register Office. Such events are recorded in the *Marine Register Books*, and there are special indexes to these at Family Records Centre. These relate to births and deaths, aboard British-registered (and colonial) ships, of British nationals normally resident in England and Wales. Records of British nationals normally resident in Scotland or Ireland will be with the General Register Office appropriate to those countries. In keeping with the GRO's view, explained earlier, they hold no registers of marriages at sea.

The Marine Register Books for England and Wales start on 1 July 1837, and thus could contain entries not recorded by the RGSS's registers. These earlier entries seem to have been compiled from log books sent directly to the GRO by ships' masters; they cover both the Royal Navy and the Merchant Navy. The GRO does not hold any actual log books:

the information has been transcribed into registers.

Marine Register Book - Births	1837 -1965 §
Marine Register Book - Deaths	1837 -1965 §

A typical entry in the Index to Deaths at Sea reads:

Year	Name	Age	Vessel	Page
1894	Cater, A.B.	23	J.M. Lennard	457

The corresponding certificate reads:

Return of Death of Seaman reported to the Registrar-General of Shipping and Seamen under the provisions of the 'Merchant Shipping Act 1854,' and 'Births and Deaths Registration Act, 1874,' and otherwise, during the month of October, 1894.					
Registrar-General to whom Death is required by the Act of 1874 to be reported	Name and Surname of Deceased	Sex	Age		Rank, Profession or Occupation
E	CATER, A.B.	Male	23		Asst. Engineer
Nationality or Birthplace	Last Place or Abode		Death		
			Cause	Date	Place
London	(London)		Drowned; vessel grounded capsized and sank	20.8.1894	Goole Reach, R. Ouse
Name of ship	Official Number	Port of Registry	Trade	Source of Information	Reference to Register
(S.S.) J.M. Lennard	70,435	Middlesbro'	Foreign	C & 3	1B.Z./b

Scotland

The General Register Office for Scotland holds registers, containing certified returns made by the RGSS, of births and deaths at sea, occurring on ships registered in Britain or its colonies, for Scottish subjects or those normally resident in Scotland. These *Marine Register of Births* and the *Marine Register of Deaths* both run from 1855, when civil registration in Scotland began; entries in these registers are included in the normal series of indexes.

---

§ Up to 1965 the indexes have been microfiched; enquiries about later events should be made at the Family Records Centre (Office for National Statistics).

Ireland
The RGSS supplied, until 1921, details of births or deaths, occurring aboard ships registered in Britain or its colonies, for all Irish subjects or those normally resident anywhere in Ireland to the General Register Office in Dublin; from 1922 these returns apply solely to the Republic of Ireland. These marine births and deaths, which cover the years from 1864 onwards, are included in the general run of indexes at the end of each volume.

From 1922 similar material was supplied to the General Register Office for Northern Ireland in respect of those from that part of Ireland.

Supporting material

Once the name of the ship on which the event occurred has been determined, either using one of the sources described above or from other previous knowledge, there are a number of sources that may be explored for further details.

Where an entry has been found in the *Registers and Indexes of Births, Marriages and Deaths of Passengers and Seamen at Sea (BT 334)*, the column headed 'Source of Information' should be looked at carefully as it may give a clue as to where to search next. Although we do not have a complete understanding of the abbreviations used, the following may assist:

Abbreviation	Refers to:	Search next in:
LB	Log book	Log books
C&D	Casualty & Death list	Casualty & Death list
I or 1	-	
W&E1	-	} B&D lists
CC 15	-	
RG	Registrar General's file reference	File of correspondence attached to B&D lists

These sources are described below.

Log books (LB)
The log book of the vessel is the most likely place to find additional information. Those for merchant vessels, after 1854, containing a report of a birth or death have usually been retained and guidance of how to find them is in the earlier chapter on Agreements, Crew Lists and Log Books. Log books for Royal Naval vessels are mostly to be found at the Public Record Office; details of these can be found in PRO's Readers' Guide by Dr. Nicholas Rodger[68].

Casualty and Death (C&D) Lists
Where the vessel has been lost at sea then any crew agreements and log book would not have survived. In such circumstances the owners of the vessel were required to send a copy of the crew list (the 'Red Copy') to the RGSS. *Casualties and Deaths Lists (C&D)*, would be used for the registration of the deaths of the crew members; some of these documents may be found in the various series of crew lists. The National Maritime Museum holds these for 1920-1933 in a single series covering the whole period arranged by ships' official numbers; these include casualties and deaths on fishing vessel's (List D) for the same period.

Many C&D lists are included with the 1939-1950 log books and crew agreements currently in the process of transfer from the RSS to the PRO.

Birth and Death (B&D) Lists
The National Maritime Museum holds these (sometimes described at 'Returns of Death'), in three series:

• January 1914 to 1919
  These are arranged by date (year and month) then alphabetically by vessel's name. There is also a single box of Births to Passengers, January - June 1915.
• 1939-1945
  These are arranged by date (year and month) then alphabetically by vessel's name; there are separate series for crew and passengers
• 1946-1964
  These are arranged date (year and month) then alphabetically by vessel's name; there are separate series for crew and passengers

No returns exist between 1920-1938; those from 1965 to the present day are held at the RSS. There are some gaps in these records.

A B&D List includes the name, official number and port of registry of ship together with, for a death, the date and place of death, name, age, rank/occupation, address and cause of death of deceased. On the reverse of the form there should be an extract of the ship's logbook giving an account of the events that led to any death at sea; log book extracts are not always included. Sometimes, especially in the 1914-1919 series, supporting papers giving the circumstances surrounding a death (e.g. papers from the Embassy or Consulate) may be attached.

The series for 1939-1945 contains details of many deaths aboard hospital ships, often at ports in the Indian subcontinent. Many researchers may overlook these not believing that such deaths would be classified as 'at sea'.

106

B&D lists also make provision for reporting births at sea, but such events are much rarer than deaths at sea and almost exclusively limited to passenger vessels.

Inquiries into Deaths at Sea
Inquiry reports concerning deaths at sea, conducted under the provisions of the Merchant Shipping Acts, are at the PRO in record series *Inquiries into Deaths at Sea, Papers and Reports (BT 341)*. These documents contain statements, log book entries, medical reports and other relevant information regarding the particular death at sea. Inquiries may relate to crew or passengers; the period covered is 1939-1946 and the year 1964. The Returns of Death that originally accompanied these papers are now held at the NMM - see above. These records are organised in year order and then in alphabetical order of ship's name.

Deaths of Merchant Seamen, World War 2
The NMM also holds a card index of deaths of merchant seamen during World War 2 (up to 1948). The Discharge Book (Dis.A) number of the seaman is usually given. This source classifies deaths by cause according to a numerical code, the meaning of which is not now clear.

The PRO holds, amongst the series *Registrar General of Shipping and Seamen: Rolls of Honour, Wars of 1914-1918 and 1939-1945 (BT 339)* five volumes related to the deaths of merchant seamen during World War 2. Two volumes (BT 339/1-2) are arranged alphabetically by ships' names recording: the ship's name plus the name, rank or rating, and date of death of the seaman. Two more volumes (BT 339/3-4) are arranged by seamen's name recording rank or rating, age at death, address (town), date of death and name of ship. The final volume (BT 339/8) is a Roll of Honour for T124 (i.e. Fishing Trawler crews employed on minesweeping and patrolling duties on a named vessel for the duration of the war 1939-1945); this is arranged according to seamen's names. Despite its title, the series does not contain similar rolls for World War 1.

Miscellaneous Sources

Births, marriages and deaths
Certain miscellaneous registers may also contain references to births, marriages and deaths of British and Commonwealth subjects aboard British or foreign ships. The General Register Office (England and Wales) formerly held these, but they are now preserved at the PRO:

RG 32	Miscellaneous Foreign Returns	1831-1951
RG 33	Foreign Registers and Returns	1627-1958
RG 34	Foreign Marriages	1826-1921

RG 35	Foreign Deaths		1830 - 1921
RG 36	Registers and Returns of Birth, Marriage and Death in the Protectorates etc of Africa and Asia		1895 - 1950
RG 43	Miscellaneous Foreign Returns of Birth, Marriage and Death: Indexes		1627 - 1947

The following are specifically known to contain a record of some events at sea:

Reference	Indexed in	
RG 32/1-16	RG 43/2	Some births and baptisms at sea, 1831-1931
RG 33/156	RG 43/7	Marriages aboard naval ships, 1842-1889 - possibly those in places where obtaining a valid British marriage was difficult.
RG 35/16 (in French)	RG 43/3	Deaths of British citizens aboard French ships, 1836-1871
RG 35/17 (in Dutch)	RG 43/3	Deaths of British citizens aboard Dutch ships, 1839-1871
CO 386/169-172		Registers of deaths of emigrants at sea, 1847-1869

Some notifications of deaths of prisoners of war for the World War 2 period are included in the series *General Register Office: Miscellaneous Foreign Returns (RG 32)*.

Baptisms, marriages and burials
Despite the disparaging comments made in the introduction to this chapter, it is still worth considering searching appropriate parish and similar registers. It should be remembered, for instance, that although a birth may have taken place aboard a ship, the baptism of the child may have not have been performed until the ship reached an appropriate port. The entry of baptism might be the only record relating to the birth of the child. Registers at port cities must surely contain more than the average for such events. Again although the legality of marriages at sea may be debatable, it is certainly true that registers of both marriages and baptism conducted by clergymen on board vessels at sea do survive. The collections held by the Guildhall Library are strong in such material[69]; e.g:

Ms 10,926 Indexed in Ms 10926C	Bishop of London's Registry: International Memoranda (baptisms, marriages and burials)	1816-1924 (but with some entries back to 1788)	Include some registrations made by clergymen on board ship.
Ms 23,607 Indexed in Ms 23607A	Bishop of Gibraltar: memorandum book of miscellaneous baptisms	1921-1969	
In Ms 11,531	List of certificates of marriage on board HM ships	1843-1879	Refers to Ms 10,926.

| Ms 11,817 | Certificates of baptism on British vessels | 1955-1961 | Indexed in Ms 15,061/1-2 under 'Sea'. |
| Ms 11,827 | Certificates of miscellaneous baptism and burial at sea | 1894-1952 | |

In addition to the above sources, it is worth looking in the International Genealogical Index (IGI) which has a separate section for events that occurred 'At Sea'.

Burial registers of coastal parishes do sometimes contain information on shipwrecks recording the names of the ships and their crew, where known, even if the bodies were never found.

For lost marriages of seamen, it is worth checking for a marriage licence, as seamen were often unable to meet the residence requirements for marriage by banns.

Graves and memorials
Those from the merchant navy and fishing fleets, who gave their lives during the two world wars, and were either lost buried at sea and have no known grave are commemorated on the Tower Hill Memorial, London; they are also included in the Tower Hill Memorial Registers.

Information kept by the Commonwealth War Graves Commission (CWGC) includes merchant seamen who were buried in various graves and war cemeteries around the world as well as those who have no known grave and are commemorated on the Tower Hill Memorial and the Halifax Memorial. The best way to access this information is from the CWGC website at http://www.cwgc.org, which includes an on-line searchable register.

Officers, men and women of the Merchant Navy and Merchant Fleet Auxiliary, who died during World War 1, are listed in the recently published Volume 5 of the Cross of Sacrifice[70]. The information it contains is based on the Commonwealth War Register.

Churchyards in coastal parishes do sometimes contain monuments to ships lost, recording the names of their crew, where known. The National Maritime Museum has, for a long time, been compiling a record of monuments to people connected with the sea[71].

Wills
The Wills, or Letters of Administration, of those dying at sea after 12 January 1858 with property in England and Wales should be included in the normal series of probate

records. Prior to 1858, jurisdiction over those dying at sea rested with the Prerogative Court of Canterbury, thus a search amongst their records may prove fruitful[72]. The indexes are quite helpful in that they usually name the ship or say 'Parts' (i.e. died in foreign parts). Also the Commissary Court of London (London Division), whose records are at the Guildhall Library, include many wills of merchant seamen from the late 17th century to 1857.

In Scotland testaments of seafarers should be sought amongst the records of the various Commissary (or later the Sheriff's) courts; these are to be found in the main at the National Archives of Scotland. Two useful lists of seventeenth and eighteenth century Scottish seafarers, compiled from Scottish, English and colonial sources, have been published[73].

Royal Navy

Although strictly-speaking beyond the scope of this book, researchers should be aware that there is some specific material that relates to the deaths of Royal Naval personnel:

- Army/Service returns of birth, marriage and death (1881-1955)
  Despite their title, these records include Royal Naval personnel and their families. The General Register Office, for England and Wales holds the registers, and an index is available at the Family Records Centre and on microfiche. Extracts related to persons normally resident in Scotland are available at the General Register Office for Scotland. Separate registers, and indexes, applying to the two world wars are listed below.

- Naval War Deaths (1914-1921)
- Naval Officers' War Deaths (1939-1948)
- Naval Ratings' War Deaths (1939-1948)
  The General Register Office, for England and Wales holds the registers, and an index is available at the Family Records Centre and on microfiche. Extracts related to persons normally resident in Scotland are available at the General Register Office for Scotland. Copies of these registers are available at the Public Record Office in series ADM 242 and ADM 104/122-149.

A wide range of other records, particularly at the PRO, may give details of events related to RN personnel[74].

LLOYD'S MARINE COLLECTION

Introduction

The underwriters at Lloyd's have been undertaking marine insurance for nearly 300 years. The publications and records arising from this business are potentially of great interest to the family historian. Some, such as *Lloyd's Captains Register* are directly so. Some such as *Lloyd's Register* and *Lloyd's List* can assist rather more indirectly, by helping to pinpoint ships on which an ancestor sailed. Others, such as *Ships' Surveys* and *Missing Vessel Books* fill out background about seafaring ancestors.

Lloyd's Marine Collection has been deposited at the Guildhall Library in London. It contains some unique manuscript material, which is in the Manuscript Section there. Additionally there are copies of most of its printed publications, together with an index to *Lloyd's List* in the Printed Books Section, though much of this material (apart from the index) may also be seen at many other libraries. *Lloyd's Ships' Surveys* are deposited at the National Maritime Museum, Greenwich.

Only an outline description of the key material is given here; a fuller description of the collection can be found in the Guildhall Library's guide[75].

Lloyd's Register

Lloyd's have been publishing an annual register of shipping since at least 1764, the date of the first surviving issue. *Lloyd's Register* is concerned with factors affecting a ship's seaworthiness and thus records briefly essential details about each ship, whether British or Foreign, of interest to Lloyd's brokers and underwriters, together with its owner's and master's names, port of registry and destined voyage. For example the 1844 volume (covering 1st July 1844 to 30th June 1845) includes the following entry:

Ship	Master	Tons	Build Where	When	Owners	Port belonging to	Destined Voyage	Classif-ication
Harvey Sw	A. Hood	303	London	1790	J. Donkin	N Shilds	Shl. Amer.	Æl
ptd 47 pt 48 ptF&S 48			ND&TSds 31 Sprs 44 & 47					3

The abbreviation Sw tells us that the Harvey was a Snow. The entries on the bottom line indicate the nature and date of significant repairs carried out to her. Her overall condition, at the time of her inspection in March, was classified as Æl. All these terms are described in tables at the beginning of the register.

If more details are required about any ship, then these can be obtained from the *Ships' Surveys* described later.

Until 1890 *Lloyd's Register* was almost entirely restricted to British-registered vessels although some foreign vessels that traded regularly with the UK are included. Apart from the period 1834-1837 only after 1875 were vessels that had not been surveyed by Lloyd's included. From 1775 to 1954/5 the set of *Lloyd's Register* held at the Guildhall Library were marked up with details of casualties to the vessels.

Lloyd's Register can be useful in determining a ship's master and intended voyage so that one may differentiate between various possibilities for vessels of the same name on which an ancestor may have sailed. Also they may be used to find out brief details of the type of ship on which somebody sailed. Caution is necessary in their use because, since 1834, they have been published mid-year with the contents covering the following period of 1 July to 30 June. But, until 1868, the volumes have been labelled simply with the single year of publication.

Numerous appendixes have been published with *Lloyd's Register,* one of which has already been described - that of masters and mates passing the voluntary examinations. Some of the more useful ones, for our purposes are:

Appendix content	Dates
Changes of vessel name	1876/7 onwards
Shipowners and their fleets	1876/7 onwards
Shipbuilders and their existing vessels	1890/1 onwards
Royal Navy ships	1779-1783
East India Company ships	1778-1833

The Society of Australian Genealogists has compiled a card index (the *Sea Captains' Index*) which includes masters sailing between Britain and Australia, taken from the 1834, 1836, 1848 and 1852 editions of *Lloyd's Register.*

Copies of *Lloyd's Register*, the first surviving issue of which is dated 1764, are available at many large libraries including Guildhall Library, National Maritime Museum, British Library, Tower Hamlets Library and many others besides; the PRO hold only a selection of years. Gregg Press produced a facsimile reprint edition, for the years 1764 to 1833, and these may be more widely available.

Mercantile Navy List

The *Mercantile Navy List,* published by the Registrar General of Shipping and Seamen, was the official list of British-registered ships. It first appeared in 1850, although most collections start in 1857; it ceased publication in 1976. It lists each vessel by name giving its official number, port of registry and, from 1871, date and place of building and name and address of the owner. Vessels registered at overseas ports in the colonies were included but, only between 1858 and 1864, were some foreign vessels included and then in appendixes.

Until 1864 the list of vessels was in order of ship's official number; after that date the arrangement is alphabetical but split (from 1871) into steamers and sailing vessels and (from 1922) into sailing vessels, steamers and motor vessels.

The *Mercantile Navy List* also published a number of short-lived appendixes, some of which may be useful e.g.

Appendix content	Dates
Royal Navy ships	1857-64, 1869, 1871
East India Company Navy/HM Indian Navy	1857-64, 1869, 1871
American naval and merchant vessels	1860-64
Vessels removed from register while current issue going through the press	1875-1904

Between 1857 and 1864 the *Mercantile Navy List* includes lists of those holding:

* Masters and mates certificates
* Pilots
* Receivers of wrecks
* British consuls abroad
* Royal Naval Reserve officers (1863 and 1864 only)

Also for those dates are included annual obituary lists and cumulative lists of officers receiving awards and testimonials for exceptional service at sea, usually in connection with shipwrecks.

113

Lloyd's List

Lloyd's List was originally a weekly newspaper, but was published twice a week during the hundred years until 1 July 1837 since when it has been published daily, Monday to Saturday. It published general commercial information, together with information on shipping movements and casualties. The last two categories are likely to be of most interest to us. *Lloyd's List* did not restrict itself to British-registered ships nor to those surveyed by Lloyd's.

Reports of shipping movements were arranged geographically by port, beginning with Gravesend (under which all London arrivals were initially reported) and working clockwise round the British Isles; a similar arrangement was adopted for other regions of the world. Under each port there are headings for arrivals and departures, reports being ordered chronologically thereunder. Essentially this system lasted until the end of the nineteenth century when an alphabetical arrangement by ship's name was adopted. *Lloyd's List* also includes lists of 'speakings' (communications between ships at sea) and reports of ships lost or damaged.

The first issue is believed to have appeared in April 1734, but no copies survive before 2 January 1740/1. A typical entry, from the issue dated Thursday September 14, 1843 reads:

QUEBEC		arrived from
12 August	Lord Wellington, Hill	London

The name 'Hill' is the master's name - this is the usual way to differentiate between ships of the same name.

Copies of *Lloyd's List* are available at the Guildhall Library, the National Maritime Museum and the British Library Newspaper Library. The Guildhall Library also has indexes originally compiled by Lloyd's - copies are also available at the NMM and the Maritime History Archives. Casualties are indexed between 1741 and 1799 (with gaps); casualties and movements are indexed from 1838 to 1926 on microfilm; from 1927 to *c*.1970 *Lloyd's Voyage Record Cards* can be used as an index. Ships are indexed by name, giving master's name, issue dates and column numbers. There is no index to movements prior to 1838. The series of Voyage Record Cards, maintained by the RGSS, will be assist those wishing to trace the movements of a particular vessel - these records are described later.

Lloyd's List can be used to help solve the problem posed by the seamen's registers for the period 1845-54, when two ports together with dates of arrival/departure are known, but the ship's name is not given. Consulting *Lloyd's List* can sometimes isolate the ship down to one of a small number.

Other newspapers, published locally at most major ports, may also assist with similar information about arrivals and departures at that port, and also details of movements of local ships sometimes world-wide. Examples of such papers are the *Shields Gazette* and the *Port of Tyne Pilot*. Copies of these should be sought at the British Library Newspaper Library or locally[76].

Lloyd's Captains Register

Lloyd's Captains Registers were compiled from information supplied, at regular intervals, by the RGSS about masters holding Certificates of Competency or Service. The information was arranged, by Lloyd's, into an alphabetical sequence of masters' names, known as Captains' Registers. These were compiled from 1869 in manuscript, but the earliest sequence (Ms 18567 Vols. 1 to 15) also contain pasted-in summaries of the qualifications and service from 1851 of masters who were still active in 1869. These were cut from an original printed register of 1869.

Lloyd's Captains Registers lists, for each person:

- the name, place and year of birth;
- the date, number and place of issue of the master's certificate obtained;
- any other special qualification, including the 'steam' certificate from 1874;
- the name and official number of each ship; the date of engagement and discharge as master or mate; the destination of each voyage; casualties to vessels;
- any special awards (e.g. war service)

Some of the commonly-used abbreviations are included in Appendix 1

Lloyd's Captains Register consists of five distinct sections, namely:

- *Lloyd's Captains Register, 1851 - 1911 (Ms 18567)*
  These comprise alphabetical lists of persons holding masters' certificates with records of service, as described above. Indexes to this section of the register, for surnames beginning with the letters 'A', 'B' and 'K', are available both at the Guildhall Library and at the PRO.

- *Lloyd's Captains Register, 1901-1948 (Ms 18568)*
  These comprise alphabetical lists of persons holding masters' certificates with records of service, as described above. In dates, this series overlaps with Mss. 18567 and 18569.

- *Lloyd's Captains Register, 1885-1948 (Ms 18569)*
  These comprise alphabetical lists of persons holding masters' certificates with records of service, as described above. This series complements Ms 18568 apparently comprising non-current sheets extracted from it. For overlapping dates see Ms. 18567.

- *Lloyd's Captains Register, 1912 - 1914 (Ms 18570)*
  These comprise a card register of individuals holding master's certificates who received appointments only as mates; they contain a record of services etc. as described above. Upon appointment as a master, a captain's register entry was begun (in Mss. 18568-9); details of service as a mate were then transferred and the card was destroyed.

- *Lloyd's Captains Register, 1933 - 1947 (Ms 18571)*
  These comprise a card register of individuals holding master's certificates who had not taken up an appointment. They give details as described above.

These records clearly are a vital source for anybody interested in a master mariner, and complement the records of the RGSS already described sine they give voyage details for some periods where this information is not to be found in the records of the RGSS. They are preserved in the Guildhall Library, Manuscript Section and microfilm copies are available at some locations. For 1869 only, this material was printed as *Lloyd's Captains Register*[77] and has been reprinted on microfiche by the Society of Genealogists. A specimen entry (fictitious) reads:

> **SMITH, William.** London, 1826. (C. 23,405, Bristol, 1850.)   *Violet*, 1856, B.   *Herald*, 17,610, 1858-9, Ct., B.   *Stafford*, 2,929, 1860, A. Robert Taylor, 3,504, 1861-2, A. Percival, 23,406, U.S., 1863. Miriam, U.S., lost May 3, 1864, *Stromboli*, 23,484, U.S., 1865-8.

This means:
William Smith, born in London in 1826, was examined at Bristol and received a certificate of Competency as Master (No. 23,405) in 1850. He was Mate of the 'Violet' in 1856, when she was in the Baltic trade; of the 'Herald' (Official No. 17,610) in 1858 and 1859 in the coasting and Baltic trades; and of the 'Stafford', 2,929 in 1860 in the African trade. He was then made Master of the 'Robert Taylor' (3,504), and remained in the African trade with her during the years 1861 and 1862. In 1863 he was appointed to the 'Percival' in the American trade; and in 1864 to the 'Miriam' in the same trade. On May 3, 1864, the 'Miriam' was lost, and he remained unemployed either as a Master or a Mate until 1865, when he was appointed Mate of the 'Stromboli', in which ship he served to the end of 1868.

Loss Books

One of the main concerns of Lloyd's was to know promptly about missing vessels. There are, preserved at the Guildhall Library, two sets of records relating to mishaps to ships. The first, the *Missing Vessels Books* list those vessels posted missing, but whose fate was not known; this was done to allow insurance claims to be settled. *Lloyd's Missing Vessels Books*, which contain integral indexes by ships' names, cover the period 1873-1954 and are preserved in the Printed Books Section.

In the Manuscript Section are to be found the *Lloyd's Loss and Casualty Books (Ms. 14932)* covering the period 1837-1972. These manuscript volumes contain reports of casualties and losses for which specific information was available. The early volumes contain integral indexes, but from 1852 there is a separate index in Ms. 14933. A typical entry reads:

Lloyd's Loss Book, 1894.	Ms. 14932/53 fo. 244
Tuesday 21st Aug	WSW
J.M. Lennard (s) of Middlesbro'	
coal for Jersey	
caught the ground last night's tide about ½ mile below Goole drove athwart & capsized - now lying on beam end, head to bank almost submerged at high tide - 2 men drowned .	Agt Goole

There will normally be reports in *Lloyd's List* for all vessels reported missing or lost, and these will often be fuller than those in the two sets of records described above. The Guildhall Library has other records from Lloyd's relating to the loss of vessels, which are described in their published guide[78]. Some of this material relates specifically to the two world wars.

Those with an interest in World War 1 might also refer to *Admiralty, Merchant Shipping (Losses); House of Commons Paper 199 (1919)*[79]. Those interested in merchant shipping losses during World War 2 should consult also the PRO record series *Daily Casualty Registers and Index to Ships: War of 1939-1945 (BT 347)*; the index to this contains many references to Lloyd's List as well as to the casualty reports themselves.

The PRO holds a series of *Shipping Casualty Investigation Papers (BT 369)*, arranged by the name of the vessel, covering the period 1910-1988; this may also be a useful source.

The National Maritime Museum holds a series of *Wreck Reports* originating from Lloyd's. These contain details of accidents and shipwrecks and often contain a 'Report of Survey for Repair'. There is a numerical arrangement of bundles within which the reports are arranged by ships' names. There is a card index to the bundles, by ships' names, at Greenwich but the reports themselves are out-housed. The series covers approximately 1900 to 1968.

The NMM has another set of records of use to those interested in finding information about missing ships, namely the *Wreck Registers* which covers the period 1855-1898. These are arranged alphabetically within spans of years. The entry relating to the ss *J.M. Lennard* reads:

Wreck Register, 1881 - 1898 (E - L)	
Official Number	*70435*
Port of Registry, Number and Date	*Middlesbro 10/75*
Tonnage	*285*
Name of Ship with Report of Wreck	*J.M. Lennard: s. stranded near Goole.*
or Casualty	*L.G. 24.8.94*
Date of Wreck or Casualty	*20.8.94*
Date of GR62 or Closing of Register	*19.10.94 J20 1.11.94*
Date of Receipt of Schedules	*C 10.9.94*
No of lives lost	2
Name and Address of Managing Owner	*J.M. Lennard, Middlesbro*

The Board of Trade *Wreck Registers*, 1855-1858, have been indexed on cards by the Maritime History Archive for those vessels registered at the ports of St. John, NB, St. John's, Nfld., Halifax, NS, Charlottetown, PEI, and Yarmouth, NS.

A privately run project, the 'UK Shipwreck Computer Index' is aiming to list all known shipwrecks around the coast of the British Isles mainly concentrating on the 12th to 19th centuries. Records of World War 1 and World War 2 wrecks are already well covered by the records of the Hydrographic Department at Taunton.

Ships' Surveys

Lloyd's were naturally most concerned with the seaworthiness of the vessels that they insured. The system of rating is well known; it was based upon regular inspections and surveys. The details, given in *Lloyd's Register*, are just a summary of the information available. The actual *Ships' Surveys*, on which that rating was based, survive at the NMM, from 1834-1914 and, from 1870, include plans. The series is arranged by port of survey and then numerically by then ships' official numbers; some of the ports of survey are overseas, e.g. Hamburg, Auckland, Sydney, PEI. There are manuscript indexes to them:

LLY/IND/1	Lloyd's Ships' Surveys, Index A - J	1839-1868
LLY/IND/2	Lloyd's Ships' Surveys, Index K - Z	1839-1868
LLY/IND/3	Lloyd's Ships' Surveys, Index A - J	1868-1892
LLY/IND/4	Lloyd's Ships' Surveys, Index K - Z	1868-1892
LLY/IND/5-8	Lloyd's Ships' Surveys, Indexes	1893-1914

The index includes, under each ship's name, the master's name, tonnage and where and when built; for example (from LLY/IND/1):

Harvey	Simpson 303	London	1790
	Nwc 29-418-Sld 867-Brs ...		

The corresponding survey reads:

No 5	Port of *Newcastle*	Date *8 April 1834*
Survey of the	*Barque Harvey*	
Master	*J. Jordinson*	
Tonnage	*303*	
Owners	*John Richardson*	
Belongs to	*Newcastle*	
By whom built	*Unknown*	
Where built	*River Thames*	
When built	*1790*	
Destined voyage	*Quebec*	

There then follows a full description of the ship. We learn that it was copper and iron fastened, was four-masted (a 21½" Bowsprit, a 18½" yellow pine Fore Mast, a 19" pine Main Mast and a 12" red pine Mizen Mast). Its sails comprised Fore Topmast Stay Sails, a Fore Sail, Fore Top Sails, Main Sails and Main Top Sails. It had three boats, a Long boat, a Skiff and a Jolly boat. From this amount of detail it ought to be possible to reconstruct how the ship looked!

The major surveys have been preserved for each ship, and from 1870 include plans, though the annual inspections have not usually been kept.

REGISTERS OF SHIPPING

Introduction

Documents relating to the registration of shipping may assist the family historian in several ways. The first, and obvious way, is by providing background information about vessels on which an ancestor sailed. But the registers also list the name of each ship's master, and document changes as they occurred. They also include details of ownership of each vessel - traditionally in sixty-fourths. The list of owners often contains some surprises. One should expect to find well-off men there, as well as masters owning a part share. But it is not uncommon to find ordinary seamen, carpenters and shipbuilders as well. This often arose when the owner could not immediately meet debts arising from the building or repair of his vessel and would get his ship to sea by offering part share in it as payment to craftsmen for their services. So the sorts of record that we are about to describe can profitably be searched for information about the lower classes of seafarers. Indeed it is a practical proposition, at least for the smaller ports, to search these Registers of Shipping speculatively over a number of years.

1786 - 1854

Ships have been registered in England since the mid-17th century, but no central government records pre-date the introduction of general registration in 1786. For background on Ship Registry - 1707-86, see the article of that title by Rupert Jarvis[80]. From that date all owners of British ships with a deck and a burden of greater than 15 tons were required to register them with the Customs at their home port. The information to be provided included port registry number, name and home port of the ship, date and place of registration, owners' names and addresses, master's name, place and date of the ship's building (or capture as a prize) together with technical details about the ship. Changes in ownership were to be endorsed on the Certificate of Registry granted to the ship. The Customs officers copied the information into a book (now usually held locally). A copy, known as a *Transcript* was sent to the Custom House in London or Edinburgh. Edinburgh then sent a further copy of the transcripts to London.

The provisions were strengthened by another Act in 1825. Ownership of vessels then had to be held in sixty-fourth shares. Any changes in ownership of shares (known as *Transactions*), as well as changes in master had to be marked up on the Transcripts.

The copies sent to London are now preserved, at the PRO, as *Transcripts and Transactions, Series I (BT 107)*. None of these survived the fire at the Custom House in 1814, so the series starts then. To the series have been added the registration books for the Port of London. This class is arranged in nine geographical regions, each starting at different dates:

London, Coastal Vessels	1786-1820
London, Foreign Trade Vessels	1787-1854
Northern Ports	1814-1825
Western Ports	1814-1825
England and Wales (amalgamating Northern and Western Ports)	1826-1854
Irish Ports, Channel Isles and Isle of Man	1824-1854
North British (i.e. Scottish) Ports	1817-1854
East Indies and Australia	1824-1854
Plantations (covering all other colonial ports)	1812-1854

Although no documents survive at the PRO, prior to 1814, for ports other than London, the local copy kept by the Customs officer at the port of registry often still survives. These, which in many cases go back to 1786, are normally now to be found at the relevant County Record Office for English and Welsh ports. Those for the Isle of Man, which were at the PRO, are on permanent loan to the Manx Museum.

At least one set of original registration books have been printed (those for Liverpool 1786-1788[81]), and guides to others published[82]. The National Maritime Museum has a project underway to make proforma transcripts of these local Ship Registers. A dictionary of Tyne sailing ships[83], compiled mainly from Custom House registers but augmented from other sources, has been privately published. This contains, in addition to details about the ships and, lists of shipbuilders, owners, shareholders, masters and some seamen.

In Scotland, the National Archives of Scotland holds registers for Leith, Bo'ness, Kirkcaldy, Banff, Peterhead, Fraserburgh, Grangemouth, Arbroath, Methil, Burntisland, Anstruther and Granton. Other registers for Aberdeen, Dumfries, Kirkcudbright, Wigtown, Stranraer, Montrose, Dundee, Arbroath, Campbeltown, Inverness, Isle Martin, Fort William, Kirkwall, Perth, Lerwick, Bo'ness, Alloa, Grangemouth are held at local authority archives. Further registers that were, until recently, in the custody of the Greenock Customhouse Museum, have been or are in the process of being transferred to the National Archives of Scotland or local archives.

Other associated registers may sometimes be found locally. For example the owners' declarations required under the 1739 Wool Act, which was concerned to prevent the export of wool from Ireland in non-British vessels, are to be found at the Merseyside Maritime Museum; they cover the years 1739-1792. Also held there are a similar series of registers aimed at controlling abuse in the Plantation Trade; these Plantation Registers record, especially, early Liverpool vessels in the slave trade and privateers (1743-1784). Both sets of registers give details of the vessel together with the names of the master and owners.

For those interested in vessels registered in Atlantic Canada, the Maritime History Archive, Memorial University of Newfoundland, has transcribed and published, on microfiche and on CD-ROM[84], the *Shipping Registries of Atlantic Canada up to 1914*; these list owners and all shareholders. The following ports have been covered:

Halifax, Nova Scotia	1820-1914
Miramichi, New Brunswick	1828-1914
Pictou, Nova Scotia	1840-1914
Richibucto, New Brunswick	1880-1914
Saint John, New Brunswick	1820-1914
Windsor, Nova Scotia	1849-1914
Yarmouth, Nova Scotia	1840-1914
Prince Edward Island	1787-1914
Charlottetown, Newfoundland	1820-1936
Sydney, Nova Scotia	1820-1914

The National Archives of Canada has a card index of Canadian-registered ships that includes transaction data.

A typical example of an entry from this period (BT 107/325) reads:

No. *247/1849*

Official No. *24,737*

Certificate of British Registry

THIS is to certify, that in pursuance of an Act passed in the Eighth and Ninth Years of the Reign of Queen VICTORIA, intituled, "An Act for the Registering of British Vessels",

John Curry of South Shields in the County of Durham Ship Owner

having made and subscribed the Declaration required by the said Act, and having declared that [*??*]

[*???*] *S. Shields*

sole Owner (in the proportions specified on the Back hereof) of the Ship or Vessel called the *John & Isabella* of *Shields* which is of the Burthen of *Two Hundred & Twenty-four 324/350* Tons and whereof *John Fletcher* is Master, and that the said Ship or Vessel was *Built at Monkwearmouth in the County of Durham in the year One Thousand Eight Hundred and Forty Eight as appears by a Certificate of Registry granted at this Port 21st August 1848 No 113 now delivered up and cancelled the property being altered in description ----------- and William Penny TideSurveyor at this Port* having certified to us that the said Ship or Vessel has *One* Deck and *Two* Masts and *a Topsail Mast,* that her length from the inner part of the Main Stem to the fore part of the Stern Post aloft is *Eighty four* feet *five* tenths, her breadth in Midships is *Twenty two* feet *seven* tenths, her depth in hold at Midships is *Fourteen* feet *six* tenths, that she is *Square* rigged, with a *Standing* Bowsprit; is *Square* sterned *Carvel* built; has *No* Galleries, and *No Figure* Head; and the said subscribing Owners having consented and agreed to the above Descriptions, and having caused sufficient Security to be given, as is required by the said Act, the said Ship or Vessel called the *John & Isabella* has been duly registered at the Port of *Shields.*

Certified under our Hands, at the Custom-House, in the said Port of *Shields* this *Fourteenth* Day of *December* in the Year One Thousand Eight Hundred and *Forty Nine* –

The reverse of the form has details of owners, and changes in Master:

Names of several Owners within mentioned	Number of Sixty-fourth Shares held by each Owner	Form of Endorsement for Changes of Master
John Curry	Sixty four 64	Shields 24 Oct 54 Robt Mole (vice Jno Fletcher)
		Newcastle - 22 Sep. 1855 Geo Annison (30,165) Master
		N'castle 14/6/56 Thos May 44262 No
		Newcastle 18/6/57 Ralph Younger
		Newcastle 14 July 1857 William Anderson - 50029 vice Younger
		N'castle 3 Novr 57 Ralph Younger
		Do 22-4-58 Robt Mole 9120 No
		Do 17-8-58 Ralph Younger No
		N.Castle 22-4-61 Robt Rowell 52672
		Newcastle 11-11-61 Ralph Younger

This shows the information available about masters. Another example, the registration of the *Eliza* of Ilfracombe in 1826 (BT 107/185) illustrates better the point made earlier about ship ownership; this lists the owners as:

Richard Thorne	Esquire of Pilton	4 shares
William Lamb	mariner of Ilfracombe, executor of the late William Walters	12 shares
Thomas Pugsley	of Barnstaple, attorney-at-law, legatee under will of late Charles Pugsley	8 shares
James Bowen		16 shares
Eliza Bowen		16 shares
Catherine Parry Squire		4 shares
William Christo		4 shares

If one is interested in a specific port, then these documents can conveniently be accessed by reference to the series list at the PRO, or via the on-line catalogue. If a ship's name is known, then there is an index, in *BT 111 Transcripts and Transactions, Index to Ships' Registries,* covering 1786-1907. BT 6/191-193 also contain information on ships registered between 1786 and 1793.

1855 - 1889

In 1854, the system of filing documents changed. The Transcripts and Transactions are separately filed. Reference to Transactions is made by endorsement of the Transaction number and Year on the reverse of the Transcript. Thus a later Transcript for the *John & Isabella* besides repeating a description of the ship has, on the reverse, the List of Masters and 'References to Transactions', for example (BT 108/72):

> 1 & 2 - 6692   6/73

Looking up Transaction number 6692, in 1873, (BT 109/265) we find:

> ..that by a Bill of Sale dated 26 June 1873, and registered 28 June 1873 at 10.30 am, John Curry sold 64/64th of the *John & Isabella* to George Wardell of Sunderland, innkeeper, who on the next day sold 21 shares to James Street of Sunderland, master mariner.

The Transcript already referred to (BT 108/72) additionally tells us:

> Vessel lost at Stonehaven 21 October 1875. Certificate lost with the ship. Registry closed 25th January 1876 per Form as received 26th January 1876.

The records for this period are preserved in the following classes:

BT 108	Transcripts and Transactions, Series II, Transcripts	1855-1889
BT 109	Transcripts and Transactions, Series III, Transactions	1855-1892

The Transcripts (BT 108) are grouped into seven sections, namely London, England & Wales, Ireland, Channel Isles & Isle of Man, Scotland, Plantations (1855-1868), East Indies (1855-1868) and Colonial (1869-1889); the last amalgamates Plantations and East Indies. These are indexed by ships' names in BT 111 as earlier. Reference to Transactions is made from the endorsements on the back of the relevant Transcript.

The Merchant Shipping Act of 1854 brought with it the entitlement for owners of foreign-going and home trade passenger ships to vote in elections for members of the

Local Marine Board. The minute books for the ports of Cardiff, Glasgow, Greenock, Hull, London, Newcastle on Tyne, South Shields, Stockton on Tees and Sunderland (1850-1947) survive in PRO record series *Local Marine Boards (MT 26)*. Those for South Shields, 1866-1875, (MT 26/6) contains an alphabetical list of such persons - others may also be found here or locally.

1891 - 1994

From 1890 the system changes yet again, and all the papers related to a ship's registration are kept together until the registry is closed. They are then all filed together under the date of the ship's de-registration. These are now to be found in class *BT 110 Transcripts and Transactions, Series IV, Closed Registries.* They are filed therein by decade of de-registration, then alphabetically by ships' names or official number; UK and Colonial registered ships are filed separately. To access the correct file, it is necessary to find first the date of de-registration, which must be found by a process of elimination using the *Mercantile Navy List* or *Lloyd's Register.* In some cases where a ship has been bought back from foreign owners and thus the registry was re-opened, the papers have been carried forward and are filed under the second date of de-registration.

The records in *BT 110* cover the period from 1891 to the end of the manual registration system. In 1994 the registration system was computerised; registries still open at the date of change form the record series *Transcripts and Transactions, Registries open as at 21 March 1994 (BT 340)*; this series is arranged by ship's names.

Two other series contain information on ships' registration:

BT 374	Registers of Changes of Names of Ships	1959-1993
BT 368	Shanghai Registry: Papers related to Registry of Ships	(in process of transfer)

Related Topics

Voyage Record Cards

The usefulness of *Lloyd's List* and *Lloyd's Voyage Record Cards* in tracing the movements of a vessel has already been described in the section on Lloyd's Marine Collection. The RGSS also maintained records of the movements of merchant vessels and these survive for the period 1928-1980. Those for the period of World War 2 (1939-1946) are in the process of transfer to the PRO as *Index to World War 2 Ships Logbooks and Crew Agreements (BT 385)*; the remainder are at the National Maritime Museum although, being under arrangement, they may not be available for research at present. The cards are divided into two categories (large ships and fishing vessels) each of which is alphabetically arranged according to ships' names; recorded on them are basic details about the vessel:

- Port of registry
- Build (iron, steel, wood)
- Tonnage
- HP of engines
- Rig
- Managing owner
- together with a record of each voyage:
  - port of departure, intermediate ports, destination
  - if sunk the details of sinking, including location
- closing of the ship's registry or selling foreign are normally noted.

Photographs and pictures
Having discovered something about your ancestor's seafaring career, it is only natural to wish to find a picture of the vessels on which he sailed. In many cases, especially if the ship on which he sailed was of modest size, this may be an over-optimistic objective. But even if you cannot find a picture of the specific ship you may be able to find one of a sister ship or a similar vessel. But where should you search for this?

The National Maritime Museum has a very large collection in its Historic Photography Library and its catalogue is probably the first place to think of searching. The Merseyside Maritime Museum also has a good collection, and the many smaller maritime museums around the country may also have something of relevance.

The larger shipping companies will have almost all maintained a collection of pictures or photographs of their fleets. A few have published histories of the company and these usually contain illustrative material. The P&O Company, for instance, has a historical art collection containing some 2000 original works, produces a selective catalogue[85], and sells copies of items in the collection. Many of the large shipping companies have a website, often illustrated with pictures of their vessels, that may steer your enquiries. Indeed the web is a useful place to seek out such material and the Palmer List described below may be good starting point.

Finally a search of, or enquiry in, a magazine such as *Sea Breezes* may turn up something relevant.

Palmer List of Merchant Vessels
Michael Palmer, an experienced nautical historian, has created an on-line database of merchant vessels, both sail and steam, from a variety of sources. Each entry described the ship giving, where possible, details of its masters and voyages; some also include a picture of the vessel. Full source information is given to support the entries. The database is to be found at http://www.geocities.com/mppraetorius

Shipbuilding
We will not attempt to cover the topic of shipbuilding in any depth here - it could be, and indeed has been, the subject of many books. Ones that have come to our attention that might typify what may be available about the area in which you are interested are:

- A monograph, published by the National Maritime Museum, related to North Devon[86] that lists ships built there from 1786.

- A two-volume work on shipbuilding in the North East of England[87].

- A Directory of shipowners, builders and marine engineers[88].

Primary source information is to be found in a number of different archives; the survey by L.A. Ritchie[89] should assist in locating it. The databases of the National Register of Archives and its sister organisation in Scotland, the National Register of Archives (Scotland), should also provide useful information on locating material.

MISCELLANEOUS

Introduction

In surveying any set of records, it is inevitable that there will be a number that do not fit the chosen categorisation. Additionally there will always be some records which are peripheral to the subject, but which cannot be totally ignored. Lastly there are those sources which are so obvious that they are often overlooked completely by the researcher! In this chapter we cover a number of such sources. Their inclusion here does not imply that they are any less important to a particular problem, but rather they reflect the individuality of every research problem. The Society of Genealogists' library guide to maritime sources[90], provides a useful bibliography to printed material that may assist.

One special group, namely fishermen and fishing vessels, has actually already been well covered though perhaps not explicitly. The records already described will cover these categories of individual and vessel. After 1883, though, specific provision was made in legislation to cover fishing vessels under 80 tons; records relating to them have already been described within the main chapters of this book.

Those interested in somebody in the employ of the Hudson's Bay Company (1751-1870) may find useful material amongst their archives in Winnipeg; copies of these are available on microfilm in the National Archives of Canada, and at the Public Record Office, Kew.

Deserters from merchant vessels in the colonies may possibly be found amongst the various series of *Government Gazettes* preserved at the PRO in the files of the Dominion Office (DO) and the Colonial Office (CO). One published index is noted in Appendix 2 under State Records, New South Wales.

The records of the various Harbour Masters may give details of shipping arrivals and of ships' masters. These should be sought in the appropriate state or provincial archives of the relevant former colony; some are known to survive in Canada (for St. John's, Liverpool and Halifax) and in Australia (see Appendix 2).

East India Company

Until this point no real consideration has been given to a special group of seamen, namely those employed on the ships of the Honourable East India Company (EIC). We do not intend to give anything more than give an outline here as other works cover this particular subject more fully already[91].

From its incorporation, in 1600, the East India Company had a monopoly of trade with India until that was abolished in 1833. The EIC itself was abolished, and India came under the direct government of the Crown, in 1858 following the Indian Mutiny. In order to carry out this trade, and to maintain its monopoly, the EIC needed two categories of naval force. The military was a fighting force employed by the EIC that, in association with the Royal Navy as and when appropriate, protected the interests of the Company including convoys of its mercantile ships. The mercantile marine was the trading arm, although its ships were usually well armed for self-protection. The ships, and seamen, of the mercantile marine did not always belong to the EIC but could be employed, as and when needed, though many of its officers were directly in the employ of the EIC. So, as with the more general seafaring communities already discussed, we must be prepared to distinguish between the various categories of seafarer, namely military or mercantile, officer or seaman. Unfortunately name changes have made this differentiation less clear than it might have been:

- Bombay Marine/Indian Navy (1613-1863)
  The Bombay Marine was the fighting navy of the EIC in Asian waters; it was renamed the Indian Navy in 1830. The Indian Navy was abolished in 1863, being replaced by a revived, but non-combatant, Bombay Marine.

- Bengal Marine (-1877)
  The Bengal Marine was an independent armed force under the administration of the Bengal government. Its main duties were patrolling the Hoogly and its approaches. In later years its steamers sometimes acted as dispatch and supply vessels for the Bengal Pilot Service.

- Royal Indian Marine/Navy
  This revived Bombay Marine was combined with the Bengal Marine, in 1877 to form HM Indian Marine. In 1892 this became the Royal Indian Marine and then, in 1935, the Royal Indian Navy.

- Pilot Services
  The Bombay and Bengal Pilot Services provided appropriate pilotage services.

- EIC's Mercantile Marine (1600-1833)

In addition, during the period of the EIC's monopoly, 'free mariners' traded in private English merchant vessels registered in Calcutta or Bombay. These vessels termed 'country ships' operated, under licence from the EIC in eastern waters, ranging from as far afield as the east coast of Africa to Botany Bay, but never to the west of the Cape of Good Hope. The various publications[92] by Anne Bulley provide an excellent guide to their activities and records.

The main collection that will assist in tracing both officers and seamen sailing on the mercantile ships in the employ of the EIC, and free mariners, is the Oriental and India Office Collections (OIOC)* of the British Library. The series most likely to assist with such a search are:

L/MAR/A	Ships Logs of East Indiamen	1605-1701
L/MAR/B	Ships Logs of East Indiamen (often contain muster lists of officers, crew, passengers and deaths that occurred on the voyage)	1702-1834
L/MAR/C/644	EIC merchant marine appointments	1736-1810
L/MAR/C/650-651	EIC merchant marine officers' services	1737-1832
L/MAR/C/652-666	EIC merchant marine services	1771-1833
L/MAR/C/667	EIC merchant marine pensions	1828-1834
L/MAR/C/668	EIC merchant marine register of masters/mates of extra ships	1790-1825
L/MAR/C/669-670	EIC marine officer's certificates of baptism etc.	c.1780-1820
L/MAR/C/671; 687	EIC midshipmen's certificates of baptism and competence	1820-1840
L/MAR/C/680-681	EIC officers and men aboard ships (arranged by ship)	1766-1837
L/MAR/C/774-777	EIC masters and mates for extra ships,	1796-1833
L/MAR/C/779-780	EIC marine petitions for relief	1795-1798 & 1801-1873

The handlist to the Marine Department records (OIOC reference L/MAR), available on the shelves in the Reading Room expands on the above list.

There are two excellent works, by Anthony Farrington that will assist in tracing both individuals and ships[93].

---

* Often still referred to by its previous names of the India Office Library, or the India Office Library and Records.

In addition some useful material, specifically related to EIC mariners may be found elsewhere. The Guildhall holds the surviving records of the Jerusalem Coffee House, in Cornhill; this London coffee house was a meeting place for managing owners of EIC ships, East India merchants and brokers:

Ms 31372	Register of shipping - listing of EIC vessels arrived at English ports with names of passengers carried.	1799-1809
Ms 31373	Jerusalem Coffee House lists of the commanders, managing owners, principal officers, surgeons and pursers of EIC ships.	1785-1833
	Annual lists of ships in the service of the EIC, includes managing owner, commander, when sailed and destination.	1757; 1759-1762; 1801-1873
Ms 31374	Register of sailings from England giving name of ship, captain and destination.	1813-1828
Ms 31376	Society of EIC Commanders - memorandum book. This group functioned as a friendly society and also represented the interests of the commanders of the East India Company ships to the EIC.	1774-1828

Further material that may assist is to be found amongst the collections at the National Maritime Museum *(including the Percy-Smith Collection (MS 88/006))*, Tower Hamlet's Library, John Rylands Library and the Society of Genealogists; this is described in Geraldine Charles's book[94]. And finally, all the material already described in this book may be of assistance depending on the career path of the individual being traced.

Allied occupations

Introduction
In searching for a merchant seaman ancestor, it is quite likely that one will come across somebody who was in an allied occupation. Perhaps the most obvious are those in the Royal Navy or in the employ of the East India Company; mention of these has been made already. Less obvious perhaps is an occupation such as carpenter. In sailing ships, carpenters were sometimes carried, especially if the ship had only recently been undergoing repairs that had not been totally completed when she had to sail. Records do exist of shipwrights: for example those of the Shipwright's Company of London are deposited at the Guildhall Library[95], whilst those for the Shipwrights of Newcastle have been published[96].

There is no doubt that there are many other such occupations besides, and other sets of records exist that will assist particular searches. Remember that a man may have had a number of jobs, progressing from one to another during his lifetime. The records of any, or all, of them could yield valuable information.

Similarly much helpful material about seafaring must exist locally. For example the Norfolk Record Office has the records of Yarmouth Port and Haven Commissioners. Material at the Devon Record Office includes, amongst the Quarter Session records, for example, a 'Register of Barges and numbers of men raised by the county for service in Navy' (1795) and "Enrolment of men for Navy, North Division" (*c.*1800).

A few categories, about which we have been asked questions in the past, are briefly discussed below.

Coastguards
The Coastguards are an occupation that often attracted ex-seafarers, though more often ex-Royal Navy personnel.

The Coastguard was formed in 1822, by amalgamation of three of the services for the prevention of smuggling. Most records of them are to be found at the Public Record Office in particular in series ADM 175, ADM 119, ADM 23, PMG 23 and PMG 70. These, together with many other useful sources, are described in their leaflet; this is available on their website.

PRO record series ADM 175 contains, for the period 1816 to 1918, records of appointments etc. of coastguards serving at a shore establishment; on a guard ship, but based on shore (ADM 175/27-73 for 1861-1879); on a sea-going Revenue Cruiser (ADM 175/1 and /24-26 for 1816-1868). Those on a sea-going Revenue Cruise for 1824-1854 are to be found in series ADM 119.

Those serving on Coastguard Revenue Cruisers were usually given a merchant seaman's ticket and so may be found in series BT 113 (indexed in BT 114) covering 1845-1854; this has been described elsewhere in this book.

The printed *Navy List* contains a section listing RN Officers serving in the Coastguard Service. *Parliamentary Papers* include some lists of Coastguards; those relevant are listed in the PRO leaflet or may be located using the CD-ROM index.

A Coastguards' Index is being compiled by Mrs Eileen Stage (150 Fulwell Park Avenue, Twickenham, Middlesex TW2 5HB). She will undertake searches therein for a modest fee.

Customs and Excise

Until recent times, the Customs and Excise services were entirely separate. The Customs service was responsible for collecting duty on imports and exports and for prevention of smuggling; the Excise service was responsible for the collection of taxes on home goods.

The main series for tracing the career of either a customs official or an exciseman are the Establishment Books - effectively staff and pay lists. These are arranged, usually annually for each service, by place. In addition some records of pensions granted to these officials may be found. All of these records are at the Public Record Office; their leaflet, available on their website, gives further details.

Lifeboatmen

All lifeboatmen were experienced seamen. Because of the nature of their work one can expect to find mention of them, from time-to-time, in the local, and perhaps even national, newspapers. Records of the Royal National Lifeboat Institution are held at RNLI Headquarters, West Quay Road, Poole, Dorset BH15 1HZ. Perhaps if you have cause to enquire of them you may wish to think of making an appropriate donation towards their work.

Lighthouse Keepers

Lighthouse Keepers are another occupation often followed by ex-seafaring folk. Information about them may be sought amongst the records of Trinity House. Surviving records, which relate almost exclusively to staff serving after 1940, are at the Guildhall Library but access to them is currently restricted.

Pilots

Most Pilotage Authorities have records relating to those licensed to operate as pilots. Since the trade often ran in families, these records can be particularly useful. Many, such as those of the Port of London Authority, will still be with the authority itself; others such as those of both the Sunderland and Tyne Pilotage Authorities have been deposited at a County Record Office (the Tyne & Wear Record Office in that case). For example, on enquiring of the Tyne Pilotage Authority (before the records were deposited) about a family called Young, who were Tyne pilots at the end of last century, we were given the names, dates of birth, dates of licensing and dates of death of four possible candidates, together with the same details about the two sons of one of them and the address of the widow of one of these as well. The records of the Liverpool Pilotage Service, back to the 18th century, are at the Merseyside Maritime Museum; those of the Newport Pilotage Authority are at Gwent Record Office.

One of the Admiralty miscellaneous series, preserved at the PRO, contains letters related to pilotage, namely: *ADM 6/134 Trinity House - Letters (1704-1797)*. These may reveal information about individuals.

Watermen

Thames Watermen were another allied profession that was controlled. Information about them can be found in the records of the Company of Watermen and Lightermen, many of which have been deposited at the Guildhall Library[97]. A leaflet describing these is available from the Guildhall Library's website.

Name indexes to apprentice bindings (1692-1949), apprentices affidavits (1759-1949), and contract licences (1865-1926) have been compiled by R.J. Cottrell (19 Bellevue Road, Bexleyheath, Kent DA6 8ND). He will make searches in these indexes for a modest fee. Microfiche copies of the indexes are available for purchase and may also be consulted at both the Guildhall Library and at the Society of Genealogists.

The Corporation of Trinity House had the right to license mariners as Thames watermen; these were both older and fewer in number than the apprentices and freemen of the Company of Watermen and Lightermen. The one surviving register of Trinity House Watermen, covering 1829-1864, is available at the Guildhall Library (Ms 30335).

As with ships, the ownership of barges had to be registered. In this case they had to be registered (from 1795 to 1871) with the Clerk of the Peace, so the records should be sought in the County Record Office. Some material is to be found amongst the records of the Thames Watermen and Lightermen's Company, at the Guildhall Library. Later material does exist also: for example that for the Grand Union Canal, Brentford (1913-1938) is at Chiswick Library. Much material related to boats on canals in the north-west of England (from as early as 1795 in a few cases) is at the Ellesmere Port Boat Museum.

Newspapers

Mention has already been made of *Lloyd's List* and the way it may be used to trace ships' movements. In most major ports, one will usually find that there is a newspaper published to cater for the interests of shipowners and merchants. Examples of such newspapers, from Tyneside, are the *Shields Gazette and Shipping Telegraph* (published daily from 1855) and the *Port of Tyne Pilot* (published since 1839). Even where a specialist paper does not exist, one would expect the main newspaper covering the area to have a column entitled 'Shipping News' or something similar. Thus from the *North and South Shields Gazette* we noted:

The use of newspapers, however, is not limited to simply tracing arrivals and departures of ships. One may learn from them details of the sale of ships, as the following passage, from *The Cumberland Pacquet and Ware's Whitehaven Advertiser,* illustrates:

VALUABLE SHARES OF SHIPS, GAS SHARES, AND SHARES IN THE SOLWAY IRON CO., FOR SALE

TO be SOLD by AUCTION, at the Globe Hotel in Duke Street, Whitehaven, on THURSDAY, the 29th day of June 1876 at Three o'clock in the Afternoon, the following SHARES of SHIPS, GAS and other SHARES, viz.:-

4-64th of the Barque 'PATNA', of Whitehaven, burthen per Register 321-12 Tons; Mr. W.R. Kelly, Managing Owner.

...

8-64th of the Brigantine 'KENSINGTON', of Whitehaven, burthen per Register 152 1/2 Tons; Captain Borrowdale, Managing Owner.

If an ancestor was involved in a disaster at sea, then the information obtainable from newspapers can be extensive even if tragic, as this example, from the Goole Times of Friday, August 24th, 1894, illustrates:

FEARFUL DISASTER IN THE OUSE.
TWO MEN DROWNED
A Steamship on Fire

On Monday evening, shortly after half-past eight, the s.s. J.M. Lennard of Middlesbrough, owned by Messrs. Lennard and Sons, of that port, left Goole for Jersey with a cargo of 500 tons of coal. The command of the vessel was entrusted to Captain P. Horne, who had the assistance of Captain Cook, of Hull, as the pilot. She was drawing 15 feet 6 inches of water as she steamed away, and it was noticed that she had some difficulty in stemming the strong tide that was running. Shortly after passing Bennett's Jetty the steering gear failed to operate properly, and the stern of the ship is reported to have caught the sand bank which has recently formed in close proximity to the right bank training wall. Directly this mishap occurred the force of the tide drove the fore part of the vessel with great violence on to the stone wall, and immediately after she was struck she heeled over and became almost submerged in the water. The sudden lurch of the vessel was such that one of the crew was thrown overboard, and he swam ashore. The other members of the crew, including the captain and pilot, were in great peril, for after clinging to the side of the ship, they were conveyed to the shore by boats. When the steamer heaved over on the starboard side, water rushed into the engine room, and in doing so the iron ladders were disarranged, which caused the means of escape less easy. The chief engineer had a desperate struggle for life. Owing to the ladder getting out of position he was thrown back two or three times, but eventually he succeeded in reaching the deck, to find that the readiest means had to be adopted for securing a footing on land. The second engineer, named Cater, and an elderly man Mulholland, a fireman, were not so fortunate, because the inrush of water and the derangement of the means of exit prevented them from reaching the deck, and consequently they were ingulfed in the water that flooded the machine-room. They were heard to cry for help but under the circumstances assistance could not be rendered. It is stated by those who were adjacent that one of the men was heard to hammer at the interior of the ship as a sign that he was alive and required relief, but this signal could not effectually be obeyed. The ingress of water at length filled the engine room and the two men were drowned.

...

Mulholland, who is an aged man, belonged to Goole, but for several years has been engaged in the colliery district, chiefly at Normanton. The man Cater belongs London, and he leaves a widow and two children to mourn his loss.

...

Several efforts have been made to rescue the body of Albert Cater, the second engineer, but up to the present success has not crowned the labours of the police and others who were engaged.

Certainly this information is much fuller than the brief accounts contained in the Wreck Register, Loss Book and Death Certificate already quoted.

Newspapers should be sought at the British Library Newspaper Library (Colindale), local Reference Libraries or exceptionally at the office of the newspaper itself[98]. The catalogue of the British Library Newspaper Library (Colindale) is available on-line at http://prodigi.bl.uk/nlcat/.

A useful specialist magazine, aimed both at old sea-dogs and just those with an interest in the sea is *Sea Breezes*. It regularly prints articles about ships and seafarers, but mostly those within living memory. A search of back-issues may yield useful information or an enquiry may result in a helpful reply.

Shipping Companies

The records of shipping companies may prove to be another fruitful source for the family historian. One would, of course, expect to find their details of the Company's fleet and its sailings. One might also expect to find details of its permanent employees, as well as perhaps master mariners. For example the P&O staff magazine *About Ourselves* contains Obituaries and Retirements for land and sea based staff; the issue of March 1959 (Vol. 4 No. 28) includes details on our father's retirement, namely:

T.B. Watts

Mr. Watts who is to retire at the end of March at the age of 63, has been with the N&E Department since 1923. Prior to that he had served an apprenticeship with the Northumberland Shipbuilding Company but this was interrupted in 1914 when he promptly joined the Northumberland Fusiliers. He was recalled for shipyard work in 1916, resumed his apprenticeship on the Tyne, later joining Swan Hunters in their design office.

Transferring to the P&O he was to spend much of his time at shipyards where our tonnage was building, ships like the *Corfu, Carthage* and *Canton*.

During the second World War he was with the Sea Transport Division at Liverpool. Returning to P&O he had much to do with the reconditioning of ships after war service and of building of the first post-war cargo liners.

It is somewhat doubtful though whether information would have been retained about ordinary seamen. Certainly most companies ought at one time to have had copies of the Agreements and Crew Lists, but these are likely to have been considered ephemeral and discarded.

A survey of extant material is contained in *Shipping: A Survey of Historical Records*[99]. Many of the records are now at the National Maritime Museum (Greenwich), Merseyside Maritime Museum (Liverpool)[100] or at a County Record Office. The location of material related to some of the more significant shipping companies, for whom staff records survive, is listed below. It should be noted that any dates given are covering dates and there may be gaps in both the time periods and categories of individual for whom records are held.

Company	Location of records	Comments
Bibby Line	MMM Liverpool	Records of engineers and officers, c.1860-1955
Blue Funnel Line	MMM Liverpool	
Booth Line	Liverpool RO	
British and African Steam Navigation Co.	MMM Liverpool	Agreements, crew lists and log books 1869-1907
British India Steam Navigation Co.	NMM Greenwich	BIS
Thomas & John Brocklebank Ltd	MMM Liverpool	Staff records, some as early as 1797; includes some lists of apprenticeship records - Whitehaven (1809-1840) and Liverpool (1820-1897).
Cunard Steamship Co. Ltd	MMM Liverpool Liverpool University Archives	Does not include staff records. Staff registers, 1880-1922. Good collection of ship's plans
Elder Dempster & Co. (and successors)	MMM Liverpool	Staff records from 1897
Ellerman Lines	MMM Liverpool	Staff records 1918-1962
Glen and Shire Line	MMM Liverpool	Staff records, some from 1890
Hall Line	MMM Liverpool	Staff records, some from 1867
Lamport & Holt Line	MMM Liverpool	Staff records 1871-1897; apprenticeship indentures 1912-1918
Leyland Line	MMM Liverpool	A small holding that includes two volumes of Captain's Reports on Officers c.1875-1930 (DX/863).
Ocean Steamship Co. (and its successor)	MMM Liverpool	from 1868
P&O Steam Navigation Co. Ltd	NMM Greenwich	
Pacific Steam Navigation Co.	MMM Liverpool	Crew books and lists, 1916-1973 with gaps. Some sea staff records, 1920-1930
Papayanni Line	MMM Liverpool	Masters and mates 1918-1962
Tyne Tees Shipping Co. Ltd.	Cleveland Archives Office	U/TTS
White Star Line	MMM Liverpool	Most material probably destroyed after merger with Cunard

Insurance Companies

Insurance of ships and their cargoes has traditionally been associated in most people's minds with Lloyd's. Certainly it is true that they were the major underwriters, and their records should always be searched first for this sort of information. However there are other companies that have undertaken various forms of insurance associated with the marine trade. These should not be overlooked, if the records of Lloyd's do not yield the required information.

Some of the records of insurance companies have been deposited in record offices, but much still remains with the companies themselves. A survey of the extant archives of British Insurance Companies was carried out and published in 1976 by H.A. Cockerell and Edwin Green in *The British Insurance Business 1547-1970*[101], which should be consulted for details of what is available and where for each company. For example Section 1, The Archives of British Insurance Companies, includes the following companies associated with marine and similar business:

Company	Type of Business	Estab	Location
Alliance Marine Assurance	Marine Insurance	1824	Ghall
Britannia Steam Ship Insurance Association Ltd.	Protection & indemnity club for shipowners	1855	Co.
British & Foreign Marine Insurance Co. Ltd.	Marine Insurance (Liverpool)	1863	Co.
City Fire Office	Fire & Marine Reinsurance	1909	Co.
Cornhill Insurance Co. Ltd.	incl. Marine Insurance	1905	Co.
Elders Insurance Co. Ltd.	Marine Insurance (originally for Elder Dempster SS Co.) (Liverpool)	1921	Co.
English & Scottish Maritime Insurance Co. Ltd.	incl. Marine Insurance	1903	Co.
Indemnity Marine Insurance Co Ltd	incl. Marine Ins. (London)	1824	Ghall
International Marine Insurance Co. Ltd.	incl. Marine Ins. (London; offices in Manchester & Glasgow)	1879	Co.
London Assurance Corporation	incl. Marine Insurance	1720	Ghall
Marine & General Mutual Life Assurance Society	Mutual Life Assurance for sailors until 1886	1852	Co.
Marine Assurance Co. Ltd.	London Marine Insurance with overseas agencies	1836	NMM/Co.
Mercantile Marine Insurance Co.	Marine hull insurance	1863	Co.
Merchants Marine Insurance Co Ltd	London Marine Insurance	1871	Co.
Newcastle Commercial Insurance Co	Marine Insurance (Newcastle)	1863	Co.
Northern Maritime Ins. Co. Ltd.	Marine Insurance (Newcastle)	1863	Co.
Ocean Marine Insurance Co. Ltd.	London Marine Insurance	1859	Ghall
Royal Exchange	incl. Marine Insurance	1720	Ghall
Sea Insurance Co. Ltd.	Liverpool Marine Insurance	1875	LRO/Co.
Standard Marine Insurance Co Ltd	Marine Insurance (Liverpool)	1871	LRO/Co.
Thames & Mersey Marine Ins Co Ltd	Marine Insurance	1860	LRO/Co.
Ulster Marine Insurance Co. Ltd.	Marine Insurance (Belfast)	1867	PRONI
Union Marine & General Ins Co Ltd	Liverpool and London Marine Insurance	1863	NMM/MMM/Co.
World Marine & General Ins Co Ltd	London Marine Insurance	1894	Ghall/Co.

Many of the records are still with the insurance company, or its successors *(Co.)*; their addresses are given in Cockerell and Green's book. However a number are in record offices and libraries, namely: Guildhall Library *(Ghall)*, National Maritime Museum *(NMM)*, Liverpool Record Office formerly Liverpool City Library *(LRO)*, Public Record Office of Northern Ireland *(PRONI)* or Merseyside Maritime Museum *(MMM)*. Additionally Section 2 contains a list of Marine Insurance Underwriters for whom Risk Books survive; covering dates and places of deposit are given.

The Merseyside Maritime Museum holds some Shipping Insurance Ledgers, 1847-1962. Individual documents related to other marine insurers may sometime be found in private hands.

Trades Unions, Guilds and Employers' Associations

The rise of Trade Unionism amongst seamen is a subject in its own right. For those interested in that aspect there are a number of interesting articles[102]. All we wish to do here is to draw the researcher's attention to the existence of such material. In particular, the branch records of such unions may mention individuals for a variety of reasons, such as Payment of Dues, Receipt of Relief, 'Scabbing in a Strike', or for being a Union Official.

The Modern Records Centre of the University of Warwick is active in collecting such material. It has the national records of the National Union of Seamen (from 1911) and some of the branch records of the British Seafarers' Union (from 1911). They have published a useful booklet and guide[103] that briefly surveys the location and availability of such records. Another good collection of Trades Union records is held at the University of Hull[104]. It should be remembered though that much material related to local branch activities will probably still need to be sought from the current branch secretary, although much is finding its way into County Record Offices.

A lecture given by Richard Storey, and reprinted in the *Genealogists' Magazine*[105], describes more fully the type of information that may be found.

There is a London livery company, the Honourable Company of Master Mariners, that may possibly retains records of its activities. Members would presumably have been eligible for freedom of the city of London and so might be found amongst those records at the Corporation of London Records Office. Records of freedom of other cities should be sought locally.

Records of the Newcastle Guild of Master Mariners, originally deposited with the Newcastle Society of Antiquaries, are with the Northumberland Record Office. These include apprenticeship registers (1648-1882), admissions (1606-1929) and apprenticeship indentures (1694-1830; indexed).

Much material from Employers Associations is to be found in County Record Offices.

APPENDIX 1
ABBREVIATIONS, CODES AND FORMS
used by the Registrar General of Shipping and Seamen

Forms

A wide variety of forms were used by the Registrar-General of Shipping and Seamen to collect data on merchant seamen. As time went by new forms were introduced and existing ones were modified, so variants of them are bound to be found. It would be a momentous task to discover them all and such a list would be of limited value for our purposes. Here, though, we will list the most common ones where we believe that knowledge of them may assist your research in some way.

Five major schedules are to be found amongst the *Agreements and Crew Lists (BT 98)* between 1835 and 1858, namely:

Schedule	Type	Filing requirements
A	*Agreement (Foreign Trade)*	Within 24 hours of return to a UK port.
B	*Agreement (Home Trade)*	Within 30 days after the end of each half year (30th June and 31st December).
C	*List of Crew (Foreign Trade)*	Within 24/48 hours of return to a UK port.
D	*Account of Voyages and Crew (Home Trade)*	Within 21 days after the end of each half year.
G	*Names and Register Tickets of Crew (Foreign Trade)*	On sailing from the UK.

Pertinent information was annotated on these Schedules and entered, in an encoded form, into the relevant registers of service described in an earlier chapter; the system used is summarised there too.

With time, additional lists were introduced; the most common being:

Schedule or List ††	Type	Remarks
A	*Agreement (Foreign Trade)*	Covers a single foreign-trade voyage
AC	*Half-yearly Agreement (Foreign Trade)*	Covers a 6-month period in the foreign trade
A3	*Agreement and Crew List of a yacht*	Up to 40 men
B	*Agreement (Home Trade)*	Covers a 6-month period in the home trade
B&D1	*Births and Deaths*	
C	*List of Crew (Foreign Trade)*	Covers a single foreign-trade voyage
D	*Account of Voyages and Crew (Home Trade)*	Covers a 6-month period in the home trade
List C&D	*Casualty and Deaths List*	Filed by the owner of a vessel lost at sea.
D&O7	*Official Log and Crew List*	For ship of less than 80 tons registered employed on the coasts of the UK and Irish Free State
List D	*List of Crew of a Fishing boat (up to 15 men)*	Includes casualties and deaths on fishing vessels
Eng. 1	*Agreement and list of crew of a foreign-going ship or sea-going home-trade ship of 200 tons or more*	Supersedes AC, A and M
Eng. 2	*Account of changes of crew of a foreign-going ship or sea-going home-trade ship of 200 tons or more before final departure from UK*	
Eng. 4	*Agreement and list of crew of a sea-going home-trade ship of 200 tons or more*	
Eng. 5 & Eng. 6a	*Special half-yearly account of voyages and crews of home trade ships when the crew were employed on several vessels belonging to the same owners. employed on several vessels belonging to the same owners.*	

---

†† The term 'schedule', 'list' or simply the relevant alphabetical character(s) may be used to describe these forms. Whilst it is possible that there may be subtle differences between these they can, for our purposes, be considered the same.

Schedule or List ††	Type	Remarks
Eng. 6	*Half-yearly agreement, list of crew and official log book (Home Trade)*	Supersedes B and D
Eng. 7a	*Agreement and Account of Voyages and Crew of Fishing Boat of 25 tons engaged in the sea fishing trade,*	
Eng. 7b	*Running Agreement and Account of Voyages and Crew of Fishing Boat of 25 tons engaged in the sea fishing trade,*	
Eng. 11a	*Application for Exemption from certain provisions of the Merchant Shipping (Fishing Boats) Act 1883*	
Eng. 11b	*Form of Exemption from certain provisions of the Merchant Shipping (Fishing Boats) Act 1883 granted by a superintendent of a mercantile marine office*	
Eng. 11c	*Monthly List of Hands Employed on a fishing boat of 25 tons registered or upwards absent from port for less than seven days*	
Eng. 19	*Form of Agreement by the Minister of War Transport for the Purposes of Defence Regulation 47AA*	Believed to be used during World War 2 for merchant vessels being used by the Ministry of War Transport.
I	*Ordinary Apprentice's Indenture*	
M	*Release at the Termination of a Voyage*	Found after *c.*1850. Release by the crew of the master and owner in respect of wages etc., and vice versa
N	*Report of Character, giving Names and Ticket Numbers of Seamen*	Found after *c.*1850. Contains assessments of each crew member's Ability in Seamanship and Conduct
O	*Ship's Official Log*	
O8	*Official Log Book for Home Trade ship*	
O9	*Official Log Book*	
S9	*Running Agreement, list of crew and official log book of a fishing boat of 25 tons or upward.*	

†† The term 'schedule', 'list' or simply the relevant alphabetical character(s) may be used to describe these forms. Whilst it is possible that there may be subtle differences between these they can, for our purposes, be considered the same.

Codes

Port Rotation Numbers
Until the introduction of ship's official numbers (in 1857), a ship was often identified by a Port Rotation Number; at certain periods the ship's name was omitted and only the Port Rotation Number used. Whilst it seems to uniquely identify a ship, within its Port of Registry, no key to Port Rotation Numbers has yet been discovered. Thus, whilst it does confirm that the correct schedules have been found, it cannot now be used as an effective finding aid.

If it is necessary to know a ship's name, but only the Port Rotation Number is known, then a search may be shortened by assuming that the numbers were initially allocated from an alphabetical list of ships registered at that port, with further ones being allocated as further ships were registered - however a full understanding of how these numbers were allocated still eludes us.

Port Numbers
From 1835 to 1844, Port Numbers were used as shorthand for a ship's Port of Registry; numbers 1 to 108 were used during this period. Ships, with other home ports in the UK, were in fact registered at a nearby one of these 108 ports, and thus the crew lists for them will be found under that port of registry (e.g. Shields-based ships were registered at Newcastle until 1844).

After 1845, new UK ports of registry were gradually introduced, and Port Numbers 109 to 130 and 147 to 152 apply to these.

Port Numbers were also used, from 1845, to designate the port at which the various Schedules were filed and all the numbers 1 to 152 were used for this purpose.

In various other places in the records of the RGSS, Port Numbers were used as shorthand for the name of the port - all the numbers in Table 2 apply.

Table 2 contains a list of Port Numbers for all UK Ports of Registry, together with those currently known for other ports. This list includes information passed to us in personal communications from Mr. E.R. Zenthon and Mr. G. Somner which we duly acknowledge.

Table 2: Port Numbers

Colonial Ports

200	Halifax, Nova Scotia		259	Cape Town
201	Liverpool, Nova Scotia		260	Cochin, India
202	Pictou, Nova Scotia		261	
203	Yarmouth, Nova Scotia		262	Madras
204 - 206			263	Melbourne
207	Sydney, New South Wales		264 - 270	
208	Hobart Town		271	Gaspé, New Brunswick
209 - 210			272	Windsor, Nova Scotia
211	Launceston, Van Diemen's Land		273	St. Stephen, NB
212	Sydney, Cape Breton Island		274	Digby, Nova Scotia
213 - 216			275	Hong Kong
217	Kingston, Jamaica		276	New Glasgow (Pictou), NS
218	St. Lucia (see 223, 231)		277	Moulmein, Burma
219	Montego Bay, Jamaica		278	Lunenburg, Nova Scotia
220 - 221			279	Parrsboro, Nova Scotia
223	St. Lucia (see 218, 231)		280	Freemantle, Western Australia
224	Malta (plus Gibraltar ?)		281	Grand Island, Cape Breton Island
225	Louis, Mauritius		282	Weymouth, Nova Scotia
226 - 227			283 - 286	
228	Miramichi Bay, New Brunswick		287	Antigua
229	Prince Edward Island		288	Cape of Good Hope
230	St. John, NB (see 243)		289	Medway, Nova Scotia
231	St. John's, Nfld. (see 244) St. Lucia (see 218, 223)		290	Port Wallace, Nova Scotia
232	Kingstown, St. Vincent, WI		291	(Ganpboro??), Nova Scotia
233 - 235			292	
236	Bathurst, River Gambia		293	Richibucto, New Brunswick
237	Sierra Leone		294	Geelong
238 - 241			295	St. Mary's, Newfoundland
242	St. Andrews, Newfoundland		296	Stanley, Falkland Islands
243	St. John, NB (see 230)		297 - 299	
244	St. John's, Nfld. (see 231)			
245	St. Johns, Antigua			
246 - 249				
250	Bermuda			
251	Arichat, Cape Breton Island			
252	Montreal			
253	Quebec			
254	Demerara, Guiana			
255 - 256				
257	Bombay			
258	Calcutta			

Abbreviations:
NB = New Brunswick
Nfld. = Newfoundland
NS = Nova Scotia
WI = Windward Islands

Prefixes used with Dis.A. numbers
Most seamen's discharge book numbers (Dis. A) are prefixed by letters indicating the nationality or origin of the seaman, e.g.:

(no prefix)	Various, mainly British	K/O	India or Pakistan
A	India and Pakistan	M or Malta	Malta
BAR	Barbados	Mau	Mauritius
BG	British Guyana	Nig	Nigeria
B/HT	British, born in India	R	British seamen
C/O	Bangladesh citizens	S	Various, mainly British
C or CAN	Canadian	SA	South Africa
E	Eire	SE	Western Isles and Northern Ireland
F	Falkland Islands	SEY	Seychelles
G	Ghana	SI	Singapore
HK or Hong Kong	Hong Kong	SL	Sierra Leone
I, Ind or India	Indian nationality	St L	St. Lucia
J or Jam	Jamaica	T & T	Trinidad and Tobago
K	Tanganyika	Z or Zan	Zanzibar

Abbreviations
Rank, rating or certificate type
A number of other abbreviations were used in the Registers of Seamen's and Officers Service, usually to designate the rank or rating of a seaman or to denote the type of certificate held. Those commonly found are:

1M	First Mate	DH	Deck Hand
2E	Second Engineer	E	Engineer
2M	Second Mate	EC	Extra Captain
3M	Third Mate	EDH	Extra-Ordinary Deck Hand
A	Apprentice	F	Fireman
AB	Able Seaman	HTPS	Home Trade Passenger Ship
BB	Black Book (reference to disciplinary proceedings)	M	Mate
		OC	Ordinary Captain
Boat^n	Boatswain	OS	Ordinary Seaman
C	Captain	P	Purser
CC	Certificate of Competency	PN	Previous number
Cf M	Chief Mate	S	Seaman
Ck	Cook	S^{1}M^r	Sailmaker
Cr	Carpenter	Stoke	Stoker
CS	Certificate of Service		

Destinations
In both the records of the RGSS (especially the certificate registers for masters and mates) and *Lloyd's Captains Register* a number of abbreviations are used to indicate the destination or voyage of a vessel:

A	West Coast of Africa and adjacent islands
Aust	Australia, Tasmania, New Zealand
B	Baltic, Norway, White Sea, Gulf of Finland and Cattegat
C	China, Japan and oriental archipelago
Cp	Cape colonies, Ascension, St Helena, Natal, Algoa Bay
Ct	Coasting trade, including Holland, Belgium, France, from River Elbe to Brest
EI	East Indies, Burma, Mauritius, Red Sea
FPS	France, (South of Brest), Portugal, Spain (outside Straits of Gibraltar), Azores
M	Mediterranean, Black Sea, Sea of Azoff, Adriatic
NA	British North America, Greenland, Iceland
NP	North Pacific and West Coast of North America
NS	West Coast of Denmark
SA	Brazils, River Plate
SP	South Pacific and West Coast of South America
US	United States (East Coast and Gulf ports)
WI	West Indies and Gulf of Mexico

APPENDIX 2
RECORD REPOSITORIES AND THEIR HOLDINGS

Introduction

This Appendix contains the names and addresses of record repositories referred to elsewhere in the booklet. Included under each is a summary of the key records that may assist in tracing a merchant seaman. The difficulty facing anybody new to this area is deciding which records to turn to first. Naturally this depends rather on the specifics of the research problem. However we have attempted to give each a 'Which?' rating as to usefulness for researching into Ship Owners (Own), Masters (Mast), Other Ship's Officers (Off.), Ordinary Seamen (Sea.) or Ships themselves. The classification system we have used is:

**** These records are a primary source of information for that type of research.
*** These records should contain useful information, but considerable searching may be necessary to locate the required references.
** Whilst these records do include references to this type of individual, it is pure chance that they will refer to the specific individual being researched.
* A source of background information, or helpful as a finding aid in locating material in other records.

Where appropriate, each entry has been annotated where it is known that all or part of that record series has been microfilmed. Such records may possibly therefore be available elsewhere. Much of the microfilmed material is available through the Family History Library of the Church of Jesus Christ of Latter-Day Saints (LDS); this will be listed in their Family History Library Catalog available as a CD-ROM and on-line at http://www.familysearch.org

Researchers overseas might seek these records as follows:

USA In the Library of Congress or in other major State or Historical Society Libraries.

Canada In the National Archives of Canada in Ottawa, or with the Maritime History Archive, Memorial University of Newfoundland.

Australia Microfilms of much PRO material are available in the National Library in Canberra and at the Mitchell Library in Sydney. The *Handbook of the Australian Joint Copying Project*, published by the National Library of Australia[106], gives details of British public records available on microfilm in Australian libraries.

Under the heading 'On Film' we have indicated that the records are known to have been filmed in whole (μμ) or in part (μ).

When visiting a record office or library do bear in mind that some items may possibly be out-housed so do enquire about the availability of the material that you wish to consult well in advance.

British Isles

Public Record Office
Ruskin Avenue, Kew, Richmond, Surrey TW9 4DU.
020 8392 5200   enquiries@pro.gov.uk   http://www.pro.gov.uk

The PRO produce a wide range of leaflets describing their holdings, and their complete catalogue is available on-line; both are accessible via the website address given above. Two other published guides may also assist the researcher[107].

Where records have been described as in the process of transfer to the PRO then it is essential that you enquire before making a visit since the transfer process may take some considerable time during which the material will be unavailable.

On Film	Series reference	Title	Covering Dates	See Page	Own	Mast	Off.	Sea.	Ship
	ADM 1 code 85	Admiralty: Navy Department: Correspondence and Papers: gallantry awards	World Wars 1 & 2	82-83		***	***	***	
	ADM 2 /1319-1325	Admiralty Out Letters contain letters relating to Mediterranean Passes	1730-1816	13		**			**
	ADM 6 /134	Trinity House - Letters	1704-1797	133					
	ADM 7	Admiralty Miscellanea - includes:	1563-1953						
μ	/317-332, 649	- Registers of Letters of Marque	1777-1815	12	*	**	*		**
μ	/363-400	- Register of Protection from being Pressed	1702-1828	15				**	
μμ	/73-164	- Mediterranean Pass Registers and Indexes	1662-1850	13		**			**
	ADM 12	Admiralty: Digests and Indexes	1741-1897	82	**	**			**
	ADM 23 /71-75 and 194-199	Admiralty pensions granted to coastguards	1884-1926	132	Relevant to Coastguards				
	ADM 23 /170	Admiralty pensions granted to RNR ratings	1922-1925	96				**	
	ADM 28	Sea Fencibles: Pay Lists	1798-1810			***	***	***	
	ADM 30 /22-25	Navy Board: Navy Pay Office: Various Registers – Repatriation of shipwrecked mariners	1729-1826	15		**			**
μ	ADM 68 /194-219	Greenwich Hospital, Various Accounts and Ledgers: Receiver of Sixpences Accounts (London)	1725-1830	14		****			****
	ADM 104 /127-139	Naval War Deaths	1939-1948	110	Relevant to Royal Navy				
	ADM 116 code 85	Admiralty Secretariat Cases: gallantry awards	World Wars 1 & 2	82		***	***	***	
	ADM 119	Coastguard and Revenue Cruisers: Ships' Musters	1824-1857	132	Relevant to Coastguards				
	ADM 131 /109-118	Reports of sinking of allied merchant vessels by submarine	1916-1918	71					***
	ADM 137	War of 1914-1918: Admiralty Historic Section: Packs and Miscellaneous Record.	1860-1933	71		***	***	***	**
μμ	ADM 171	Admiralty: Navy Department: Medal Rolls	1793-1972	81-84		***	***	***	
μμ	ADM 175	Coastguard Records of Service	1816-1947	132	Relevant to Coastguards				
	ADM 177	Navy Lists Confidential Editions	1914-1945	76		**	**		
μμ	ADM 196	Admiralty: Officers' Service Records	1756-1954	76		**	**		

On Film	Series reference	Title	Covering Dates	See Page	Own	Mast	Off.	Sea.	Ship
	ADM 199 /80-84 and 2130-2148	Reports of interviews with masters and survivors of merchant ships lost by enemy action	World War 2	74		**	**	**	**
	ADM 237	incl. Convoy records	World War 2	74					**
	ADM 240	Royal Naval Reserve: Records of Service of Officers	1862-1960	76-77		****	****		
	ADM 242	Admiralty: Naval Casualties	1914-1923	110	Relevant to Royal Navy				
	ADM 267 /133	Allied merchant vessels sunk or damaged by torpedo, mine or bomb	1942-1947	73					***
μμ	ADM 339	Royal Naval Division: Records of Service	1914-1919	76		***	***	***	
(μ)	AIR 2 Code 30	Air Ministry: Registered Files: Flying	1887-1985	81-82					
μμ	BH	Hudson's Bay Company archives (microfilm copy)	1751-1870	128		**	**	**	**
μ	BT 6	Miscellanea (1697-1850) incl: Shipping Returns for:							
	/186	- Jamaica	1781	6	***	***			***
	/188	- St. Vincent Island	1784-1788	6	***	***			***
	/188	- Norfolk, Virginia	1801	6	***	***			***
	/190	- Quebec	1887-1894	6	***	***			***
	/191-193	Papers relating to Ship's Registers	1786-1793	124	***	***			***
	/218-219	Masters & Mates: List of Certificates	1845-1850	38		***	***		
	BT 97	Albert Medal Register	1866-1913	81		****	****	****	**
μμ	BT 98	Agreements and Crew Lists: Series I, Muster Rolls and Agreements	1747-1860	50-55	***	***	***	***	****
	BT 99	Agreements and Crew Lists: Series II, 10% sample of Agreements	1861-1994	55-63	***	***	***	***	****
μ	BT 100	Agreements and Crew Lists: Series III, Celebrated Ships	1835-1980	55-63	**	**	**	**	**
μ	BT 107	Transcripts and Transactions, Series I	1786-1854	120-121	***	***		**	****
	BT 108	Transcripts and Transactions, Series II, Transcripts	1855-1889	124-125	***	***		**	****
	BT 109	Transcripts and Transactions, Series III, Transactions	1855-1892	124-125	***	***		**	****
	BT 110	Transcripts and Transactions, Series IV, Closed Registries	1891-1994	125	***	***		**	****
μμ	BT 111	Transcripts and Transactions, Index to Ships' Registries	1786-1907	124					****
μμ	BT 112	Register of Seamen, Series II	1835-1844	20-24			****	****	
μμ	BT 113	Registers of Seamen's Tickets	1845-1854	24-27			****	****	
μμ	BT 114	Alphabetical Register of Seamen's Tickets	1845-1854	24-27			****	****	

On Film	Series reference	Title	Covering Dates	See Page	Own	Mast	Off.	Sea.	Ship
μμ	BT 115	Alphabetical Register of Masters	1845-1854	36		****			
μμ	BT 116	Register of Seamen, Series III	1853-1857	28			****	****	
μμ	BT 119	Alphabetical Index of Seamen	1835-1844	20-24			****	****	
μμ	BT 120	Register of Seamen, Series I	1835-1836	20			****	****	
μμ	BT 122	Registers of Certificates of Competency, Masters and Mates, Foreign Trade	1845-1900	38-44		****	****		
μμ	BT 123	Registers of Certificates of Competency, Masters and Mates of Steamships, Foreign Trade	1881-1921	38-44		****	****		
μμ	BT 124	Registers of Certificates of Service, Masters and Mates, Foreign Trade	1850-1925	38-44		****	****		
μμ	BT 125	Registers of Certificates of Competency, Masters and Mates, Home Trade	1854-1888	38-44		****	****		
μμ	BT 126	Registers of Certificates of Service, Masters and Mates, Home Trade	1854-1888	38-44		****	****		
μμ	BT 127	Index to Registers of Certificates of Competency and Service, Masters and Mates, Home and Foreign Trade	1845-1894	38-44		****	****		
μμ	BT 128	Registers of Certificates of Competency, Masters and Mates, Colonial	1870-1921	38-44		****	****		
μμ	BT 129	Registers of Certificates of Competency, Skippers and Mates of Fishing Boats	1880-1921	38-44		****	****		
μμ	BT 130	Registers of Certificates of Service, Skippers and Mates of Fishing Boats	1883-1917	38-44		****	****		
μμ	BT 138	Index to Registers of Certificates of Competency and Service, Skippers and Mates of Fishing Boats	1880-1917	38-44		****	****		
μμ	BT 139	Registers of Certificates of Competency, Engineers	1861-1921	38-44			****		
μμ	BT 140	Registers of Certificates of Competency, Engineers, Colonial	1870-1921	38-44			****		
μμ	BT 141	Index to Registers of Certificates of Competency and Service, Engineers	1861-1921	38-44			****		
μμ	BT 142	Registers of Certificates of Service, Engineers	1862-1921	38-44			****		
μμ	BT 143	Registers of Certificates of Competency and Service, Miscellaneous	1845-1849	37-38, 41		****	****		

On Film	Series reference	Title	Covering Dates	See Page	Own	Mast	Off.	Sea.	Ship
	BT 144	Agreements and Crew Lists: Series IV, Fishing Agreements	1884-1929	55-60	***	***	***	***	****
	BT 145	Returns of Fishing Boats	1887-1938	-	***				****
	BT 150	Index of Apprentices	1824-1953	85				****	
	BT 151	Apprentices' Indentures (only every 5th year preserved)	1845-1950	85-86			** ****		
	BT 152	Apprentices Indentured for Fishing (only every 5th year preserved)	1895-1935	85-86			** ****		
	BT 153	Registers of Wages and Effects of Deceased Seamen	1852-1881 1888-1889	98-100			****	****	
	BT 154	Index to Seamen's Names (in BT 153)	1853-1889	98-100			****	****	
	BT 155	Index to Ship's Names (in BT 153)	1855-1889	98-100					****
	BT 156	Monthly Lists of Deaths of Seamen	1886-1889	98-100			****	****	
	BT 157	Register of Seamen's Deaths, classified by Cause	1882-1888	98-100			*	*	
μμ	BT 158	Registers of Births, Deaths and Marriages of Passengers at Sea	1854-1890	100-101					*
μμ	BT 159	Registers of Deaths at Sea of British Nationals	1875-1888	100-101			****	****	
μμ	BT 160	Registers of Birth at Sea of British Nationals	1875-1890	100-101			****	****	
μμ	BT 162	Annual Lists of Ships Registered	1786-1955	-					****
	BT 163	Quinquennial Lists of Ships Registered	1905-1955	-					****
	BT 164	Royal Naval Reserve - Representative Records of Service	1860-1913	77-78				***	
	BT 165	Ships' Official Logs	1857-1972	54-64	**	**	**	**	***
	BT 167	Precedent Books, Establishment Papers etc. incl:	1702-1950						
	/33-37	- Black Books	1851-1893	49		**	**		
	/38-52	- Receiver of Sixpences accounts (Exeter)	1800-1820 1832-1851	15	****				****
	/103	- Colchester: Register of Apprentice seamen's indentures	1704-1757 1804-1844	86				****	
	BT 238	Marine Crews: Registered Correspondence	1929-1992	82		***	***	***	
	BT 261	Gallantry at Sea Awards	1856-1981	81-82		****	****	****	**
	BT 317	Registers of Masters and Mates Certificates Passings and Renewal	1917-1977	47-48		***	***		
	BT 318 (in process of transfer)	Registers of Examinations for Certificates of Masters, Mates and Engineers, Returns of Passings and Failures	1928-1981	47-48		***	***		

On Film	Series reference	Title	Covering Dates	See Page	Own	Mast	Off.	Sea.	Ship
	BT 319	Indexes to Registers of Cooks Certificates of Competence and Service	1913-1956	49			****		
	BT 320 (in process of transfer)	Registers of Engineers Passings and Renewal	1913-1935	47-48			***		
	BT 334	Registers and Indexes of Births, Marriages and Deaths of Passengers and Seamen at Sea	1891-1972	101-102	****	****	****	**	
	BT 336	Register of Changes of Master	1893-1948	36	***				***
	BT 339	Registrar General of Shipping and Seamen: Rolls of Honour, Wars of 1914-1918 and 1939-1945	World War 2	81-82	***	***	***	***	
	BT 340	Transcripts and Transactions, Registries open as at 21 March 1994	1994	125					****
	BT 341	Inquiries into Deaths at Sea, Papers and Reports	1939-1946 1964	107	***	***	***	***	
μ	BT 347	Daily Casualty Registers and Index of Ships, War of 1939-1945	1940-1945	73, 117					****
μμ	BT 348	Registrar General of Shipping and Seamen: Register of Seamen, Central Index, Numerical Series (CR 2)	1921-1941	30			****	****	**
μμ	BT 349	Registrar General of Shipping and Seamen: Register of Seamen, Central Index, Alphabetical Series (CR 1)	1921-1941	29-30			****	****	**
μμ	BT 350	Registrar General of Shipping and Seamen: Register of Seamen, Special Index, Alphabetical Series (CR 10)	1918-1921	29, 31		****	****	****	**
μμ	BT 351	British War Medal and Mercantile Marine	World War 1	83	****	****	****		
μμ	BT 352	Index to Certificates of Competency, Masters, Mates, Engineers and Fishing Officers, Home and Foreign Trade	1910-1930 (and probably much later)	47	****	****			
μμ	BT 364	Registrar General of Shipping and Seamen: Register of Seamen, Combined Numerical Index (CR 1, CR 2 and CR 10)	1921-1941	30		**	**	**	**
	BT 368 (in process of transfer)	Shanghai Registry: Papers related to Registry of Ships		125					****
	BT 369	Shipping Casualty Investigation Papers	1910-1968	72-73, 117	**	**	**	**	***

On Film	Series reference	Title	Covering Dates	See Page	Own	Mast	Off.	Sea.	Ship
	BT 372	Central Register of Seamen: Seamen's Records (pouches)	1941-1972	35			****	****	
	BT 373	Merchant Seamen Prisoner of War Records	1939-1945	80		****	****	****	**
	BT 374	Registers of Changes of Names of Ships	1959-1993	125					****
μμ	BT 377	Royal Naval Reserve: Records of Service, Ratings	1914-1958	78, 83				****	
	BT 380	War of 1939-1945: Log Books, crew agreements and associated records	1949-1950	62	***	***	***	***	****
	BT 381 (in process of transfer)	World War II: log books, crew lists	1939-1946	62	***	***	***	***	****
	BT 382	Central Register of Seamen: CRS 10 docket books	1941-1972	32-34			****	****	
	BT 385	Index to WW2 Ships Logbooks and Crew Agreements [Voyage Record Cards]	1939-1946	125-126					****
	CHAR	Records of the Charity Commissioners		89					
	CO 5 to CO 317	Board of Trade Shipping Returns for:		5-7					
μ	CO 5 /508-511	America - Carolina, South	1716-1765	5	***	***			***
μ	/573	- Florida, East	1765-1769	5	***	***			***
μ	/709-710	- Georgia	1764-1767	5	***	***			***
μ	/749-750	- Maryland	1689-1765	5	***	***			***
μ	/848-851	- Massachusetts	1686-1762	5	***	***			***
μ	/967-969	- New Hampshire	1723-1769	5	***	***			***
μ	/1035-1036	- New Jersey	1722-1764	5	***	***			***
μ	/1222-1229	- New York	1713-1799	5	***	***			***
μ	/1441-1450	- Virginia	1699-1770	5	***	***			***
	CO 10/ 2	Antigua and Montserrat (see CO 157/1 for 1704-1720)	1784-1814	5	***	***			***
μμ	CO 27 /12-15	Bahamas	1721-1815	5	***	***			***
μμ	CO 33 /13-26	Barbados	1678-1819	5	***	***			***
μμ	CO 41 / 6-12	Bermuda	1715-1820	5	***	***			***
	CO 47	Upper Canada - Quebec	1786-1814	5	***	***			***
	/80-83	- St. John's	1786-1795	5	***	***			***
	CO 66/4	Curacao	1808-1818	6	***	***			***
μμ	CO 76 /4-8	Dominica	1763-1819	6	***	***			***
	CO 95/ 1-2	Gibraltar	1804-1806 & 1825	6	***	***			***
μμ	CO 106/1-8	Grenada	1764-1816	6	***	***			***
	CO 110 /23-24	Guadeloupe	1810-1812	6	***	***			***

On Film	Series reference	Title	Covering Dates	See Page	Own	Mast	Off.	Sea.	Ship
	CO 116/17	Guiana, British (Demerara)	1808-1809	6	***	***			***
	CO 128/ 1	Honduras, British	1807-1812	6	***	***			***
μμ	CO 142 /13-29	Jamaica	1680-1818	6	***	***			***
μμ	CO 157/ 1	Leeward Islands (incl. Montserrat)	1683-1787	6	***	***			***
	CO 166/6-7	Martinique	1809-1814	6	***	***			***
μμ	CO 187/1-2	Nevis (see CO 157/1 for 1683-1715)	1704-1729	6	***	***			***
	CO 193/1-2	New Brunswick	1786-1815	6	***	***			***
	CO 221 /28-33	Nova Scotia	1730-1820	6	***	***			***
	CO 221 /34-35	Cape Breton	1785-1815	6	***	***			***
	CO 231/2	Prince Edward Island	1807-1809	6	***	***			***
μμ	CO 243/1	St. Christopher (see CO 157/1 for 1685-1787)	1704-1787	6	***	***			***
	CO 259/1	St. Thomas	1808-1815	6	***	***			***
μμ	CO 265/1-2	St. Vincent	1763-1812	6	***	***			***
	CO 278/7-9	Surinam	1804-1816	6	***	***			***
μμ	CO 290/1-3	Tobago	1766-1825	6	***	***			***
	CO 317/1	Virgin Islands	1784-1786	6	***	***			***
	CO 386 /169-172	Registers of deaths of emigrants at sea	1847-1869	108					
	CO 693 /5 & 9	Incl. list of Merchant Seaman and Fishermen Prisoners of War	1917-1918	79	***	***	***	***	***
	CO 820/62	Military Department: Honours and Awards – awards to merchant seamen	1947-1949	83			**	**	
	CUST 18	Establishments, Series I	1675-1813	8	Relevant to Customs Officers				
	CUST 19	Establishments, Series II	1814-1829	8	Relevant to Customs Officers				
	CUST 20	Salary Books and Establishments (Ireland)	1682-1826	8	Relevant to Customs Officers				
	CUST 21	Miscellaneous Books(include Establishments at Bermuda, British Guiana and West Indies c.1806)	1715-1857	8	Relevant to Customs Officers				
	CUST 39	Establishment: Staff Lists	1671-1922	8	Relevant to Customs Officers				
	CUST 40	Establishment: General	1818-1926	8	Relevant to Customs Officers				
μ	CUST 50 to CUST 102	Outport Records for ports in England and Wales Outport records incl.:	late 17th to mid 20th centuries	9	*	**	*	*	**
	CUST 52 /112	Register of Apprentice Indentures for Ramsgate	1893-1908	9, 86				** / ****	
	CUST 56 /89	Register of Apprentice Indentures for Newhaven	1893-1908	9, 86				** / ****	
	CUST 57 /28	Register of Apprentice Indentures for Littlehampton	1856-1897	9, 86				** / ****	
	CUST 64 /205	Register of Apprentice Indentures for Teignmouth	1853-1893	9, 86				** / ****	

On Film	Series reference	Title	Covering Dates	See Page	Own	Mast	Off.	Sea.	Ship
	CUST 66 /227	Ships' Muster Books for Plymouth	1776-1780	50	***	***	**	**	***
	CUST 67 /74	Register of deaths and births at sea first reported at Falmouth	1892-1918	102		****	****	****	
	CUST 67 /81	Register of Apprentice Indentures for Fowey	1825-1925	9, 86				** ****	
	CUST 68 /185	Register of Apprentice Indentures for Scilly Isles	1857-1878	9, 86				** ****	
	CUST 69 /224	Register of Apprentice Indentures for Bideford	1857-1880	9, 86				** ****	
	CUST 91 /111-112	Ships' Muster Books for Scarborough	1747-1765	50	***	***	**	**	***
	CUST 91 /121	Register of Apprentice Indentures for Scarborough	1884-1894	9, 86				** ****	
	CUST 104	Outport Records, Isle of Man	1820-1970	9	*	**	*	*	**
	CUST 105	Outport Records, Channel Is.	1806-1965	9	*	**	*	*	**
	CUST 113	Outport Records, Ireland	1679-1849	9	*	**	*	*	**
	DEL 1	High Court of Delegates: Processes	1609-1834	18	**	**			**
	DEL 2	Delegates Cause Papers (incl. some Letters of Marque, Bonds)	c.1600-1834	12, 18	**	**	**		**
	DEL 7	High Court of Delegates: Bound Volumes of Printed Appeal Cases	1796-1834	18	**	**			**
	DEL 8	High Court of Delegates: Miscellanea	1536-1866	18	**	**			**
	DEL 9	High Court of Delegates: Muniment Books	1652-1859	18	**	**			**
	DEL 10	High Court of Delegates: Testamentary Exhibits	1636-1857	18	**	**			**
	DEL 11	High Court of Delegates: Miscellaneous Lists and Indexes	19th cent	18	**	**			**
	E 122	Customs Accounts	Edw.I (1272) to 1565	4-5		***			***
μ	E 190	Port Books (*Note:* Port Books for London, 1696 - 1795, have been destroyed)	1565-1798	4-5		***			***
	E 209	Coast Bonds	Eliz.I (1558) to Geo.III (1820)	4-5		***			***
	FO 371	Foreign Office Correspondence: Political	1906-1966	80	**	**	**	**	**
	FO 383 /352 file 4651	Incl. list of Merchant Seaman and Fishermen Prisoners of War	1917	79	***	***	***	***	***
	HCA 1	Admiralty Court: Oyer and Terminer Records	1535-1834	17	**	**			**

On Film	Series reference	Title	Covering Dates	See Page	Own	Mast	Off.	Sea.	Ship
	HCA 3	High Court of Admiralty: Instance Court: Acts	1524-1786	17	**	**			**
	HCA 13	Examinations (Prize)	1536-1826	17-18	**	**			**
	HCA 15	Instance Papers, Early	1629-1778	17	**	**			**
	HCA 16	Instance Papers, Series I	1772-1806	17	**	**			**
	HCA 17	Instance Papers, Series II	1807-1839	17	**	**			**
	HCA 18	Instance Papers, Series III	1840-1859	17	**	**			**
	HCA 19	Instance Papers, Series IV	1860-1876	17	**	**			**
	HCA 20	Instance Papers, Series V	1875-1943	17	**	**			**
	HCA 24	Libels etc	1519-1814	17	**	**			**
	HCA 25	Letters of Marque, Bonds etc.	1549-1815	12	**	**	**		**
	HCA 26	Letters of Marque, Declarations	1689-1814	12	**	**	**		**
	HCA 27	Minute Books (Instance)	1860-1924	17	**	**			**
	HCA 30	Miscellanea	1531-1948	17-18	**	**			**
	HCA 31	Monitions (Prize)	1664-1815	18	**	**			**
	HCA 32	Prize Papers	1661-1855	17	**	**			**
μ	HO 3	Aliens Act, 1836: Returns and Papers	1836-1869	66		**		**	
μ	HO 45	Home Office Registered Papers	1839-1979	67	*	*	*	*	*
μμ	HO 76	Naval Officers' returns - Vessels cleared inwards and outwards at Colonial Ports	1791-1797	6	***	***			***
μ	HO 144	Home Office Registered Papers, Supplementary	1868-1959	67	*	*	*	*	*
μμ	IR 1	Board of Stamps: Apprenticeship Books	1710-1811	86	**	**		**	**
	J 96 /112-142, 191-192	Supreme Court of Judicature, High Court, Queen's Bench Division, Orders in Appeals and other papers [against Pensions Appeal Tribunals]	1947-1979 1943-1968	96		**	**	**	
	MT 4	Ministry of Transport: Marine Out-Letters	1851-1939	94-95		**	**	**	
	MT 5	Index to Out-Letters and Registers of Correspondence	1864-1918	94-95		**	**	**	
	MT 9	Ministry of Transport: Marine Correspondence and Papers	1854-1969	49	**	**	**	**	**
	code 6	- medals		81-82					
	code 106	- prisoners of war		79-80					
	MT 25	Ministry of Shipping: Correspondence and Papers	1917-1928	71	**	**	**	**	***
	MT 26	Local Marine Boards	1850-1953	125	**				
	NDO 7 /49-50	National Debt Office, Correspondence	1871-1897 1871-1942	96					
	NDO 14	Pensions Commutation Board Minutes	1869-1970 (75 year closure)	96					

On Film	Series reference	Title	Covering Dates	See Page	Own	Mast	Off.	Sea.	Ship
	PC 5	Plantation Books (include Warrants for Letters of Marque)	1678-1806	12	**	**			**
	PIN 15	War Pensions	1901-1983	96		**	**	**	
	PIN 22	Ministry of Pensions and National Insurance: Registered Files, MA and MA(X) series	1912-1974	96		**	**	**	
	PMG 23	Coastguards: Civil Pensions	1855-1935	132	Relevant to Coastguards				
	PMG 56	Naval Establishment, Warlike Operations: Pensions etc.	1914-1928	96		**	**	**	
	PMG 70	Greenwich Hospital Pensions and Civil Superannuation Allowances	1866-1928	132	Relevant to Coastguards				
	PREM 2	Prime Minister's Office: Honours List and Papers	1915-1967	82		**	**	**	
μ	PROB 1-50	Records of the Prerogative Court of Canterbury	1383-1858	109-110	**	**	**	**	*
	RAIL 113 /53	Crew Lists of Ferries owned by Railway companies		66	**	**	**	**	**
	RAIL 227 /190, 488-489			66	**	**	**	**	**
	RAIL 491 /1057, 1137-1138			66	**	**	**	**	**
	RAIL 1057 /3556-3568			66	**	**	**	**	**
μμ	RG 32	Miscellaneous Foreign Returns	1831-1951	107-108		**	**	**	
μμ	RG 33	Foreign Registers and Returns	1627-1958	107-108		**	**	**	
μμ	RG 34	Foreign Marriages	1826-1921	107-108		**	**	**	
μμ	RG 35	Foreign Deaths	1830-1921	107-108		**	**	**	
μμ	RG 36	Registers and Returns of Birth, Marriage and Death in the Protectorates etc of Africa and Asia	1895-1950	107-108		**	**	**	
μμ	RG 43	Miscellaneous Foreign Returns of Birth, Marriage and Death: Indexes	1627-1947	107-108		**	**	**	
μ	SP series	State Papers, Henry VIII - George III	1509-1820	10-11	**	**		**	**
μμ	SP 14	State Papers, Domestic , James I	1603-1625	11	**	**		**	**
μμ	SP 15	State Papers Domestic, Addenda, Edward VI to James I	1547-1625	10	**	**			**
μμ	SP 16	State Papers, Domestic, Charles I [see also large docs in SP 17]	7 Hen. VIII - 1665	11	**	**		**	**

On Film	Series reference	Title	Covering Dates	See Page	Own	Mast	Off.	Sea.	Ship
μμ	SP 35	State Papers Domestic, George I	1714-1727	10	**	**			**
μμ	SP 36	State Papers Domestic, George II	1727-1760	10	**	**			**
	T 1	Treasury Board Papers include:	1557-1920	6					
μμ	/430	Shipping Lists - Nova Scotia	1764	6	***	***			***
μμ	/435	Shipping Lists - Annapolis, Maryland	1764	6	***	***			***
μμ	/512	Naval Office Shipping Returns for Antigua, St. Christopher, Nevis and Montserrat	1774-1775	6	***	***			***
μμ	/523	Customs & Excise Returns of ships arriving from and leaving for North America	1775-1776	6	***	***			***
	Various	Correspondence with Pension Commutation Board	1869 -	96					
	T 2	Treasury: Register of Papers (index to T 1)	1777-1920	96					
μ	T 64	Treasury Miscellanea, Various include: Ships entered and cleared	1547-1930	7					
	/47-50	- Barbados	1710-1829	7	***	***			***
	/82	- St John's, Newfoundland	1770	7	***	***			***
	/84	- Halifax, Nova Scotia	1749-1753	7	***	***			***
	/182	Vessels registered in Irish Ports	1787-1796	7	***	***			***
	/251-252	Shipping Returns - Scotland	1771-1785	7	***	***			***
	/273-289	Colonies (incl. Shipping & Trade Returns)	1680-1867	7	***	***			***
	T 108	Treasury: Subject Registers (index to T 1)	1852-1909	96					
	TS 15	HM Proctor General: Assignation Books	1827-1878	18	**	**			**
	WO 4 /752-754	Out Letters, Secretary at War: Merchant Seamen	1851-1856	95		**	**		**
	WO 22	Royal Hospital Chelsea Pension Returns	1842-1883	95		**	**	**	
	WO 32 code 91	War Office Registered Files [re Merchant seamen prisoners of war]	World War 2	80		**	**	**	**
	WO 193 /343-359	Directorate of Military Operations Collation Files	World War 2	80		**	**	**	**
	WO 208 /3242-3566	Military Intelligence (MI9) files: Escape & evasion reports	World War 2	80		**	**	**	**
μ	ZJ 1	*London Gazette*	1665-1986	Var.		***	***		
μμ	--	*Parliamentary Papers*, with index on CD-ROM	1801-1998	Var.	**	**	**	**	**

National Archives of Scotland
HM General Register Office, Edinburgh EH1 3YY.
0131 535 1314   research@nas.gov.uk   http://www.nas.gov.uk

The NAS (formerly known as the Scottish Record Office) website contains useful information about its holdings.

On Film	Series reference	Title	Covering Dates	See Page	Own	Mast	Off.	Sea.	Ship
	AC.7, AC.8, AC.9, AC.10, AC.15 and	High Court of Admiralty: Decreets and Processes	Up to 1830	18	**	**			**
	AC.16		1705-1830	18		**	**	**	**
	BT.3	Agreements and crew lists relating to Scottish ships (a small number)	1867-1913	59	***	***	***	***	****
μ	CC and SC	Testamentary records from Commissary and Sheriff's courts		-					
	CE.3 and CE.12	Establishment Books, Scottish Board of Customs	1707-1829	8	Relevant to Customs Officers				
	CE.11	HM Customs and Excise: Shipping Registers for some Scottish ports		121					****
	E.71	Customs Accounts	up to 1640	5		***			***
	E.72	Customs Accounts	1661-1696	5		***			***
	E.502	Customs cash accounts	1750-1825	8, 10	**	**		**	**
	E.504	Customs Accounts	1742-1830	5		***			***
	E.508	Vouchers for bounties: whale and herring-fishing	1750-1825	10	***	***		***	***
	GD.1/372/1 RH.2/8/102	Customs officers on the establishment	1752 1755	8	Relevant to Customs Officers				
	GD.226	Trinity House, Leith	from mid 17th cent.	91		**	**	**	

Family Records Centre
1 Myddelton Street, London EC1R 1UW.
020 8392 5300   enquiries@pro.gov.uk   http://www.pro.gov.uk
0870-237788   certificate.services@ons.gov.uk   http://www.stastics.gov/registration

The FRC is a facility jointly operated by the Public Record Office and the General Register Office for England and Wales (part of the Office for National Statistics). The holdings of the two sections are described below:

Public Record Office
The whole of the censuses of England, Wales and the Channel Islands for 1841, 1851, 1861, 1871, 1881, and 1891 (Record series HO 107, RG 9, RG 10, RG 11 and RG 12) may be seen in microform here. The specific index to those on board ships in the 1861 census (of England and Wales) and the 1881 census index on CD-ROM are available both there and at the PRO at Kew. Microfilm copies, of some or all of these returns, are available at many other locations in the UK (but not at the PRO at Kew) as well as overseas. For local holdings in the UK see the latest edition of *Census Returns on Microfilm (1841-1891)* by Jeremy Gibson, published by the Federation of Family History Societies. The Census Returns for 1901 are available on the web at the FRC and at www.census.pro.gov.uk and on microfiche (RG13) at the PRO, Kew.

Indexes (on paper and in series PROB 12), Administration Act Books (PROB 6) and Register Copy Wills (PROB 11) from the Prerogative Court of Canterbury are available on film both at the FRC and the PRO at Kew. Copies of many of these are available elsewhere.

The following miscellaneous returns are available here and at the PRO at Kew:

On Film	Series reference	Title	Covering Dates	See Page	Own	Mast	Off.	Sea.	Ship
µµ	RG 32	Miscellaneous Foreign Returns	1831-1951	107-108	**	**	**		
µµ	RG 33	Foreign Registers and Returns	1627-1958	107-108	**	**	**		
µµ	RG 34	Foreign Marriages	1826-1921	107-108	**	**	**		
µµ	RG 35	Foreign Deaths	1830-1921	107-108	**	**	**		
µµ	RG 36	Registers and Returns of Birth, Marriage and Death in the Protectorates etc of Africa and Asia	1895-1950	107-108	**	**	**		
µµ	RG 43	Miscellaneous Foreign Returns of Birth, Marriage and Death: Indexes	1627-1947	107-108	**	**	**		

General Register Office
The GRO holds the indexes to Births, Marriages and Deaths, registered in England and Wales since 1 July 1837. Copies of these indexes (until 1992) are available in microform at many locations world-wide; a microfiche copy is available at the PRO at Kew. In addition a range of indexes to miscellaneous registers (overseas, military etc) are held here; these include those to Births and Deaths at sea since 1837. Copies of the Marine Births and Marine Deaths indexes are available, on microfiche, at many locations world-wide including (up to 1965) at the PRO at Kew.

Information about individual events located in the indexes can only be obtained by purchasing a certificate from the General Register Office. Postal request for certificates from the GRO should be directed to Office for National Statistics, Smedley Hydro, Trafalgar Road, Southport, Merseyside, PR8 2HH.

Access is available, at a fee, to on-line indexes to births, marriage and deaths registered in Scotland since 1 January 1855.

National Maritime Museum
Greenwich, London SE10 9NF.
020 8312 6673   library@nmm.ac.uk   http://www.nmm.ac.uk
020 8312 6669/6691   manuscripts@nmm.ac.uk
[Research enquires to: 020 8312 6712   lxveri@nmm.ac.uk]

The NMM produce a wide range of useful Research Guides; these are available both on-line (found under 'PORT' from the homepage given above, namely http://www.port.nmm.ac.uk/research/) or by postal request. The library catalogue is already on-line and the manuscript catalogue is in the process of being put on-line; both may be accessed from the homepage address given above under 'Centre for Maritime Research'. A published guide may also assist the researcher[108].

Some documents are outhoused at Woolwich and need to be ordered up to one week in advance.

On Film	Series reference	Title	Covering Dates	See Page	Own	Mast	Off.	Sea.	Ship
		Agreements and Crew Lists	1861,1862, 1865,1875, 1885,1895, 1905,1915, 1925,1935, 1955,1965, 1975,1985	55-63	***	***	***	***	***
		Crew lists for ships without official numbers and those of some companies (e.g. Mersey Docks and Harbour Board, Great Western Railways)	1861-1913	55-61	***	***	***	***	***
		Fishing Agreements	1884-1914	55-61	***	***	***	***	***
		Casualty & Death (C&D) Lists	1920-1933	66, 106		****	****	****	***
		Birth & Death (B&D) Lists	1914-1919 1939-1964	106-107		****	****	****	***
		Card index to deaths of merchant seamen during World War 2 (up to 1948)	World War 2 (to 1948)	107		****	****	****	
		Office copies of certificates, with applications, for Masters', Mates', Engineers' and Fishing Boat Officers.	1845-1928; a few to 1940	44-47		****	****		
		Certificates of Pilotage, Ports: A-W	1859-1897	46		***	***	***	
		Registers of Cooks Certificates of Competence and Service	1915-1958	49			****		
		Apprenticeship registers [sample]	1845-1856	87	**	**		***	**
		Voyage Record Cards (under arrangement)	c1928-1980 [not 1939-1946]	125-126					****
		Lloyd's Register	1764-	111-112	***	***	(**)	*	****
		Mercantile Navy List	1857-	113	***	****	(**)	*	****
		Lloyd's List	1741-	114-115		***		*	****
μ		Index to Lloyd's List	1838-	114-115		***		*	****
		Wreck Registers	1855-1898	118		**		*	**
		Lloyd's Wreck Reports	1900-1968	118					
		Lloyd's Ships' Surveys (from 1870, include Plans)	c1830-1914	118-119				*	****
	LLY/IND	Lloyd's Ships' Surveys, Index	1839-1914	118-119				*	****
	MS88/006	Percy Smith Collection		131					
		Frank C. Bowen Collection of notes and newspaper cuttings	1880-1940	-	**	**		*	**
		Collection of details of monuments to people connected with the sea		-					

On Film	Series reference	Title	Covering Dates	See Page	Own	Mast	Off.	Sea.	Ship
		Transcripts of Ship Registers	1786-	121	***	***		**	****
		Many deposited Shipping Company records	various	137-138		**	**	**	****
		HMS Worcester (Thames Nautical Training College), Greenhithe, Kent – minutes, financial records and news cuttings	1861-1968	88					
		Some material on training ship HMS Worcester at London	1863-1972	88					
μ	MSY	Records of the Marine Society include:	1756-	92				**	
μμ	MSY/H /1-2	Registers of boys recruited for the Royal Navy	7 Years War	92					
	MSY/H /3-4	Boys returned to Marine Society at end of 7 years war		92				**	
	MSY/J	Marine Society: miscellaneous volumes and papers		92				**	
	MSY/K	Registers of boys received and discharged from the Marine Society's ship	1786-1874	92					****
μ	MSY/L	Register of admissions	1854-1958	92					****
	MSY/O	Registers of boys entered as servants in the King's ships	1770-1873	92					**
	MSY/Q	Registers of apprentices sent to merchant ships	1772-1950	92					****
μμ	MSY/S/1	Registers of men recruited for the Royal Navy	7 Years War	92					
μ	MSY/T	Register of girl apprentices under Hickes Trust	1772-1978	92					
	DSH	Dreadnought Seamen's Hospital: including:							
	DSH/1	Admissions	1826-1977	92-93		**	**	**	
	DSH/101	Index to Admissions		92-93		**	**	**	
	DSH/201	Outpatients	1857-1964	92-93		**	**	**	
	DSH/401	Nurses and records of training	1895-1968	92-93					

Guildhall Library

Aldermanbury, London EC2P 2EJ.

020 7332 1862/3   manuscripts.guildhall@ms.corpoflondon.gov.uk

printedbooks.guildhall@ms.corpoflondon.gov.uk

http://www.ihrinfo.ac.uk/gh/

The Guildhall Library produce a wide range of useful leaflets; these are available both in the library and on-line. A published guide to Lloyd's Marine Collection may also assist the researcher[109].

Most of the material listed below may be found in the Manuscripts section but some will be in the adjacent Printed Books section of the library.

On Film	Series reference	Title	Covering Dates	See Page	Own	Mast	Off.	Sea.	Ship
μ	Ms 10926	'International Memoranda' of baptisms, marriages and burials overseas	1816-1924	108		**	**	**	
	Ms10926C /1-2	Indexes to International Memoranda	1816-1924	108		**	**	**	
	Ms 11531	List of certificates of marriage on board HM ships (Refers to Ms 10926)	1843-1879	109					
	Ms 11817	Certificates of baptism on British vessels (Indexed in Ms 15061/1-2 under 'Sea')	1955-1961	109		**	**	**	
	Ms 11827	Certificates of miscellaneous baptism and burial at sea	1894-1952	109		**	**	**	
	Ms 14932	Lloyd's Loss & Casualty Books	1837-1972	72-74, 117	***	***		*	**
	Ms 14933	Index to Lloyd's Loss & Casualty Books	Incl. 1878-1934 1936-1972	72-74	***	***		*	**
	Ms 14934	Lloyd's War Casualty Books	1914-1922	72	***	***		*	**
	Ms 14934A	Lloyd's First World War Loss Books	1914-1918	72	***	***		*	**
	Ms 14935	Index to Lloyd's War Casualty Books	1914-1922	72	***	***		*	**
	--	Lloyd's Marine Loss Cards	1939-1972	74					***
	Printed book	Lloyd's War Losses: the Second World War	1939-1945	74					***
μμ	Ms 18567 - Ms 18571	Lloyd's Captains' Register	1869-1947	115-116		****	****		**
		Lloyd's Marine Loss Records	1939-1970	-	***	***		*	**
		Some records of the Marine Society	1762-1869	92				**	
	Ms 23,607 indexed in Ms 23607A	Bishop of Gibraltar: memorandum book of miscellaneous baptisms	1921-1969	108					
	Ms 30055	Register of Pensionable staff	Born 1870-1931	133	Lighthouse keepers, crews of light vessels and Trinity House cutters				
	Ms 30121	Register of Staff Appointed	1914-1972	133					
	Ms 30122	Station book, listing keepers and crew	1941-1955	133					
	Ms 30182	Trinity House: Registers of exemption certificates	1850-1957	38	***	***			
	Ms 30184	Trinity House: Registers of masters' and mates' examinations	1864-1986	38		***	***		
	Ms 30218	Trinity House: Registers of almspeople and pensioners	1729-1946	90		**	**	**	

On Film	Series reference	Title	Covering Dates	See Page	Own	Mast	Off.	Sea.	Ship
μμ	Ms 30218 A & B	Trinity House Petitions	1787-1854	90		**	**	**	
	Ms 30219	Trinity House: Registers of almspeople	1845-1971	90		**	**	**	
	Ms 30335	Trinity House: Register of watermen	1829-1864	134		**	**	**	
	Ms 30338	Christ's Hospital Mathematical School: ships' apprentices	1816-1857	88		***	***	***	**
	Ms 31372	Register of shipping - listing of EIC vessels arrived at English ports.	1799-1809	131					
	Ms 31373	Jerusalem Coffee House	1785-1833	131					
		Annual lists of ships in the service of the EIC.	1757 1759-1762 1801-1873	131					
	Ms 31374	Register of sailings (EIC) from England.	1813-1828	131					
	Ms 31376	Society of EIC Commanders – memorandum book.	1774-1828	131					
μμ	Various	Records of the Thames Watermen and Lightermen's Company	1700-1942	134	Relevant to Thames Watermen				
	Various	Records of the Shipwrights' Company	1428-1930	131	Relevant to Shipwrights				
μμ		Wills proved in Commissary Court of London (London Division)	-1858	109		**	**		**
		Lloyd's Register	1764-1970	111-112	***	***	(**)	*	****
		Mercantile Navy List	1857-1970	113	***	****	(**)	*	****
μ		Lloyd's List	1740-1970	114-115		***		*	****
μ		Index to Lloyd's List	1838-	114-115		***		*	****
		Lloyd's Missing Vessels Books	1873-1954	117	***	***		*	**
		Lloyd's Voyage Supplement (late Voyage Record)	1946-1970	114					****
		Lloyd's Weekly Shipping Index	1880-1917	-					****
		Lloyd's Voyage Record Cards (advance notice needed)	1927-c1975	114					****
		Board of Trade Enquiries	1908-1965	-		**			**
		Board of Trade Casualty Returns	1873-1918	118					**
		Lloyd's Register Wreck Returns	1900-1970	118					**
		Lloyd's Calendar (formerly Lloyd's Seaman's Almanac)	1898-1975 1893-1897	82		**	**	**	**
μ		*London Gazette*	Var.			***	***		
μμ		*Parliamentary Papers*, with index on CD-ROM	Var.		**	**	**	**	**
		Records of several marine insurance companies	various	139					

167

General Register Office
England and Wales
See Family Records Centre

General Register Office for Scotland
New Register House, Edinburgh EH1 3YT.
0131 334 0380 records@gro-scotland.gov.uk http://www.gro-scotland.gov.uk

The Scottish GRO holds records, beginning 1 January 1855, relating to births and deaths at sea of British nationals normally resident in Scotland. Held there also are the census returns for Scotland for 1841, 1851, 1861, 1871, 1881, 1891 and 1901. Indexes are available for a fee, on-line, to the registers of birth, marriage and death and to the census returns for 1881, 1891 and 1901 at http://www.origins.net/gro

General Register Office (Northern Ireland)
Oxford House, 49-55 Chichester Street, Belfast BT1 4HL.
01232 252021   http://www.nics.gov.uk/nisra/gro/
General Register Office of Ireland
8-11 Lombard Street East, Dublin 2, Republic of Ireland.
+353 (0)1 6711000 http://homepage.tinet.ie/~seanjmurphy/gro/index.htm

The General Register Offices have similar records to those for England and Wales relating to Births and Deaths at Sea of British nationals normally resident in Ireland. The records start on 1 January 1864. Those in Dublin are for the whole of Ireland up to 31 December 1921, and thereafter for the Irish Republic. The records in Belfast are for Northern Ireland after 1 January 1922.

Merseyside Maritime Museum
Albert Dock, Liverpool L3 4AA
0151 207 0001   http://www.merseyworld.com/museums/maritime.htm

There is a published guide to part of the holdings of the Merseyside Maritime Museum[110] but it is not easy to locate material in it, as it has no index and the table of contents lacks page numbers.

On Film	Series reference	Title	Covering Dates	See Page	Own	Mast	Off.	Sea.	Ship
	C/EX/L/2	Wool Act Register	1739-1792	121	***	***			***
μμ	C/EX/L/3	Plantation Registers	1743-1784	121	***	***			***
	D/CON 12	HMS Conway: Indexes to Registers of Cadets	1859-1972	87-88		***	***		

On Film	Series reference	Title	Covering Dates	See Page	Own	Mast	Off.	Sea.	Ship
D/CON 13		HMS Conway: Registers of boys	1859-1971	87-88		***	***		
D/CON 14		*The Cadet* - magazine of HMS Conway	1889-1974	87-88		***	***		
D/LH		Liverpool Sailor's Home: minutes	1838-1963	89				**	
D/SO		Royal Liverpool Seamen's Orphan Institution archives	1869-c.1970,	89				**	
		Liverpool Seamen's Pension Fund	1909-1917	96					
		Many deposited Shipping Company records	various	137-138		**	**	**	****
		Some records of Marine Insurance companies	various	137-140					
		Liverpool Pilotage Service	from 18th century	133					

Southampton Archives Service
Civic Centre, Southampton SO14 7LY
01703 832251   city.archives@southampton.gov.uk
          http://www.southampton.gov.uk/education/libraries/arch.htm

On Film	Series reference	Title	Covering Dates	See Page	Own	Mast	Off.	Sea.	Ship
μμ	CR 1 cards	Registrar General of Shipping and Seamen: Register of Seamen, Central Index, Alphabetical Series (CR 1)	1921-1941	29-30					
μμ	CR 2 cards	Registrar General of Shipping and Seamen: Register of Seamen, Central Index, Numerical Series (CR 2)	1921-1941	30					
μμ	CR 10 cards	Registrar General of Shipping and Seamen: Register of Seamen, Special Index, Alphabetical Series (CR 10)	1918-1921	29-30					
μμ	Mixed series	Registrar General of Shipping and Seamen: Register of Seamen, Combined Numerical Index (CR 1, CR 2 and CR 10)	1921-1941	30					

These records are the originals for which the Public Record Office holds
microfiche copies as series BT 348, BT 349, BT 350 and BT 364.

County Record Offices
Addresses are to be found in *Record Repositories in Great Britain* (HMSO), *Record Offices: How to find them* (FFHS) or any good genealogical book.

Some County Record Offices hold the following:

On Film	Series reference	Title	Covering Dates	See Page	Own	Mast	Off.	Sea.	Ship
		Agreements and Crew Lists (from PRO series BT 99, relating to ships registered at ports in their area)	1863-1913	55-60	***	***	***	***	****
		Shipping Registers	1786-	120-125	***	***		**	****
		Registration of Barges	1795-1871	134					
		Apprenticeship Registers	late 1800s	85-87				**	

In addition records of local trades union branches and employers' associations, shipbuilders and repairers may often be found in County Record Offices.

National Register of Archives
Royal Commission on Historical Manuscripts, Quality House, Quality Court, Chancery Lane, London WC2A 1HP.
020 7242 1198   nra@hmc.gov.uk   http://www.hmc.gov.uk/

The RCHM is a clearing house for information about the nature and location of historical documents that are not public records. The National Register of Archives, as well as the Manorial Document Register, is available in its search room and on the web. Searches here may well reveal information about holdings at County Record Offices, Libraries or in private hands that could assist.

National Register of Archives (Scotland)
West Register House, Charlotte Street, Edinburgh EH2 2DF.
0131 535 1314   research @nas.gov.uk   http://www.nas.gov.uk

The National Archives of Scotland maintain the National Register of Archives for Scotland.

Registry of Shipping and Seamen

P.O. Box 165, Cardiff CF14 5FU

Anchor House, Cheviot Close, Parc-Ty-Glas, Llanishen, Cardiff CF4 5JA.

029 20 768 227   rss@mcga.gov.uk   http://www.mcagency.org.uk

The Registry of Shipping and Seamen, now part of the Maritime and Coastguard Agency, holds records related primarily to its current administrative tasks related to shipping and seamen. The vast majority of historical records have been transferred already, or are in the process of transfer, to appropriate archives. Those remaining with the RSS include:

On Film	Series reference	Title	Covering Dates	See Page	Own	Mast	Off.	Sea.	Ship
		Register of Merchant Seamen - UK series	1973-	35		****	****	****	
		Register of Officers' Certificates	1966-	49		****	****	****	
		Appropriation books	1855-1994						****
		Log books and Crew Agreements [Held pending transfer to the PRO]	1939-1946	61-62	***	***	***	***	****
		Records of issue of medals	World War 2 and later	84		***	***	***	
		Log books and Crew Agreements	1995-	64	***	***	***	***	****
		Ships' registration details	1994-	-					****
		Registers of births and deaths at sea	1965-	102		**	**	**	**

Society of Genealogists

14 Charterhouse Buildings, Goswell Road, London EC1M 7BA

020 7250 0291   library@sog.org.uk   http://www.sog.org.uk

On Film	Series reference	Title	Covering Dates	See Page	Own	Mast	Off.	Sea.	Ship
μμ		Trinity House Petitions	1787-1854	90		**	**	**	
μμ		Trinity House Apprenticeship Indentures	1780, 1818-1845	90		**	**	**	
μμ		Lloyd's Captains Register	1869	115-116		****	****		
		Crisp's Indentures	1845-c.1861	85		**	**	**	
μμ		Tax on Apprentices [transcript/index to part of PRO series IR 1]	1710-1774	86	**	**		**	**

Relevant material is listed in their booklet: *Library Sources No. 10*[111].
The Society of Genealogists also has a copy of the complete LDS International Genealogical Index, including the part for events 'At Sea'. Certain material is available on line via http://www.sog.org.uk/

Principal Probate Registry
Personal searchers: Probate Search Room, Principal Registry of the Family Division, First Avenue House, 42-49 High Holborn, London WC1V 6NP.
Postal enquiries: The Court Service, York Probate Sub-Registry, Duncombe Place, York YO1 2EA.

The Principal Registry holds copies of all Wills proved, and Letters of Administration (admons) granted, in England and Wales since 12 January 1858. The indexes have been microfilmed down to 1957, and are available in this form in the LDS Library; microfiche copies are available at the Family Records Centre and at the PRO down to 1943. Original indexes are available at some District Probate Registries, or nearby Record Offices, in England and Wales; see *A Simplified Guide to Probate Jurisdictions: Where to Look for Wills* (FFHS) for more details. Indexes to later wills and admons may be consulted at the Probate Search Room or at any District Probate Registry.

Wills may be seen at the Probate Search Room, or copies ordered by post from the York Probate Sub-Registry.

British Library, Newspaper Library
Colindale Avenue, London NW9 5HE.

020 7412 7353 newspaper@mail.bl.uk

http://www.bl.uk/collections/newspaper/

The British Library has a unique newspaper collection that includes Lloyd's List and most local newspapers of interest to the shipping community. The catalogue is on-line at http://prodigi.bl.uk/nlcat/

Oriental and India Office Collections
British Library, Orbit House, 96 Euston Road, London NW1 2DB.

020 7412 7873 oioc-enquiries@bl.uk

http://www.bl.uk/collections/oriental/records/

On Film	Series reference	Title	Covering Dates	See Page	Own	Mast	Off.	Sea.	Ship
	L/MAR/A	Ships Logs of East Indiamen	1605-1701	129-131					
	L/MAR/B	Ships Logs of East Indiamen (often contain muster lists of officers, crew, passengers and deaths that occurred on the voyage)	1702-1834	129-131					
	L/MAR/C /644	EIC merchant marine appointments	1736-1810	129-131					
	L/MAR/C /650-651	EIC merchant marine officers' services	1737-1832	129-131					
	L/MAR/C /652-666	EIC merchant marine services	1771-1833	129-131					
	L/MAR/C /667	EIC merchant marine pensions	1828-1834	129-131					
	L/MAR/C /668	EIC merchant marine register of masters/mates of extra ships	1790-1825	129-131					
	L/MAR/C /669-670	EIC marine officer's certificates of baptism etc.	c.1780-1820	129-131					
	L/MAR/C /671 and 687	EIC midshipmen's certificates of baptism and competence	1820-1840	129-131					
	L/MAR/C /680-681	EIC officers and men aboard ships (arranged by ship)	1766-1837	129-131					
	L/MAR/C /774-777	EIC masters and mates for extra ships,	1796-1833	129-131					
	L/MAR/C /779-780	EIC marine petitions for relief	1795-1798 & 1801-1873	129-131					

Overseas

Maritime History Archive
Memorial University of Newfoundland, St. John's, Newfoundland, Canada A1C 5S7.   +1 709 737 8428/9
mha@morgan.ucs.mun.ca   http://www.mun.ca/mha/
The Maritime History Archive holds a wide range of material, both in printed and microfilm form, about shipping and seamen, much of which is related to the Maritime Provinces of Canada. Details may be found on their website or in their guide[112].

The following original material is of particular note:

On Film	Series reference	Title	Covering Dates	See Page	Own	Mast	Off.	Sea.	Ship
		Agreements and Crew Lists:							
		- 70% from PRO series BT 99	1863-1912	60	***	***	***	***	****
		- 80% from PRO series BT 99	1913-1938	60-61	***	***	***	***	****
		- 80% from PRO series BT 99	1951-1976	63	***	***	***	***	****
		Agreements and Crew Lists: - Commissioned Chartered Ships (T124)	1914-1920	61	***	***	***	***	****
		Name (research) files of Keith Matthews	1650-1930	-	**	**	**	**	**
		Board of Trade Wreck Registers – Index for ships registered in Atlantic Canada	1855-1858	118					
μ		Index to Lloyd's List	1838-	114	***			*	****

Prof. Matthews has published *A Who Was Who of Families engaged in the Fishery and Settlement of Newfoundland, 1660-1840*; a copy is available in the library of the Society of Genealogists.

National Archives of Canada
395 Wellington Street, Ottawa, Ontario K1A 0N3, Canada
+1 613-996-7458   http://www.archives.ca/
Holds material related to Canadian seaman, applications for officers' certificates and has a card index of Canadian-registered ships that includes transaction data and copies of Hudson's Bay Company archives.

Society of Australian Genealogists

Richmond Villa, 120 Kent Street, Sydney, New South Wales 2000, Australia.

+61 (0)2 9247 3953   info@sag.org.au   http://www.sag.org.au/

On Film	Series reference	Title	Covering Dates	See Page	Own	Mast	Off.	Sea.	Ship
		Sea Captains' Index	1834, 1836, 1848 and 1852	37		****			
		Index to Ships Musters (NSW departures)	1816-1825	-		**	**	**	**	**

State Records, New South Wales

2 Globe Street, Sydney, New South Wales 2000, Australia.
http://www.records.nsw.gov.au/

State Records, New South Wales has significant material, much of which comes from the Shipping Master's Office, this includes:

- Arrivals and departures of vessels at Sydney, Newcastle, Wollongong and various outports, 1799-1978;
- Crew List for Sydney and Newcastle, 1794-1922;
- Certificates of Competency and Service for Masters, Mates and Engineers, 1872-1936;
- Certificates of Competency, Marine Ship Surveyors and Compass Adjusters, 1899-1960;
- Registration of vessels and shipwrecks.

This is more fully described in their guide[113].

A useful work, compiled primarily from the *NSW Government Gazette* and *NSW Police Gazette* listing Ships' Deserters is the book by Jim Melton[114].

Public Record Office of Victoria

PO Box 2100, North Melbourne, Victoria 3051, Australia.

The following, primarily from the Mercantile Marine Office, Melbourne may be of use:

On Film	Series reference	Title	Covering Dates	See Page	Own	Mast	Off.	Sea.	Ship
μμ as VPRS 3503	VPRS 13	Inward Shipping Index (alphabetical)	1839-1900						
	VPRS 22	Miscellaneous shipping registers	c.1840- c.1890						
	VPRS 38	Inward Ship's reports	1843-1885						
	VPRS 945	Release Books of Ships' Crew	1857-1922						
μμ as VPRS 2144	VPRS 946	Registers of Discharged Seamen and Deserters (indexed)	1852-1925						
	VPRS 952	Reports of Vessels cleared	1888-1905						
μμ as VPRS 3504	VPRS 953	Index to Inward Shipping	1880-1924						
	VPRS 954	Registers of Inward Shipping	1869-1924						
	VPRS 955	Registers of Outward Passenger Ships							
μμ	VPRS 4320	Register of Seamen held at Pentridge – Index	1853-1856 1869-1885						

State Records of South Australia
PO Box 40, Enfield Plaza, South Australia 5085.

The State Records of South Australia hold material related to shipping, seamen and passengers in South Australia. This is more fully described in their guide[115] and in the book by Andrew Peake[116]. Another book[117] by that author includes sources listing deserters from ships at all states in Australia.

National Archives of Australia
ref@naa.gov.au   http://www.naa.gov.au/

A summary of the holdings of the several regional offices of the Australian Archives are given in section 1.2 (Shipping) of *Relations in records: A guide to family history in the Australian Archives*, (Canberra: AGPS) 1998.

Department of Trade (Australia)
Marine Operations Division, DTC House, Dickson, ACT 2602, Australia

On Film	Series reference	Title	Covering Dates	See Page	Own	Mast	Off.	Sea.	Ship
		Records of Australian Seamen	1968 -			****	****	****	
		Records of Discharges	1872-1965			***	***	***	***
		Register of Deserters, Sydney	1924-1965			***	***	***	***

National Archives of New Zealand
P.O. Box 6148, Wellington, New Zealand

The National Archives holds material related to shipping and seamen that may assist:

- Passenger lists that often list crew members, from 1883;
- Logs, articles of agreement and crew lists, mostly from 1945 onwards;
- Index cards, and certificates, for masters, mates, engineers, pilots, compass adjusters and some cooks for those born before 1920;
- Shipping reports and ships surveys.

National Archives and Records Administration (US)
Washington, DC 20408, USA   http://www.nara.gov/

The scope of this book is limited, primarily, to records that will enable researchers to trace information about merchant seamen from Britain and its colonies. Whilst it is true that America fell into that category at one time, it ceased to be a colony long before comprehensive records began to be maintained about seamen. Hence most of the records that are available, in the US, are relevant to tracing American rather than British seamen. The prime records are to be found in the National Archives, in Washington and its various out-repositories across the country; a good starting point to discovering what is available is their guide[118]. Much additional material, especially about the colonial period, will be found in the various State Archives and at state historical societies.

Two sets of material that may be of specific interest are the *List or Manifest of Aliens Employed on the Vessel as Members of Crew* (and the lists of any changes that had taken place prior to departure) and the *Alien Seamen's Identification Cards* – both date from 1917-18 – *see page 32*.

Miscellaneous

Address	Records referred to:	See Page
Chiswick Library Dukes Avenue, London W4 2AB.	Owners of barges on the Grand Union Canal, Brentford (1913-1938).	134
Cleveland Archives Office Teeside Archives, Exchange House, 6 Malton Road, Middlesbrough TS1 1DB ☎ 01642 248 321	Records of the Tyne Tees Shipping Co. Ltd.	138
Commonwealth War Graves Commission (CWGC) http://www.cwgc.org,	Merchant seamen buried in graves and war cemeteries worldwide; those with no known grave commemorated on the Tower Hill and Halifax the Memorials.	109
R.J. Cottrell 19 Bellevue Road, Bexleyheath, Kent DA6 8ND http://members.aol.com/_ht_a/rjcindex/TRUEFLARE.html	Thames Watermen & Lightermen's index	134
Cumbria Record Office Scotch Street, Whitehaven, Cumbria CA28 7BJ ☎ 01946 852 920 whrec@dial.pipex.com	Apprenticeship registers for Workington (1859-1892).	85
Devon Record Office Castle Street, Exeter EX4 3PU. ☎ 01392 384 253 http://www.devon-cc.gov.uk/dcc/services/dro/homepage.html	Register of Barges and numbers of men raised by the county for service in Navy" (1795) and "Enrolment of men for Navy, North Division" (c.1800).	132
Dundee City Archives and Records Centre 1 Shore Terrace, Dundee. (Correspondence to: Department of Support Service, 21 City Square, Dundee DD1 3BY) ☎ 01382 434 494 http://www.dundeecity.gov.uk/archives/main.htm	Records of Trinity House, Dundee	91
Museum in Docklands Units C 14/16, Poplar Business Park, 10 Prestons Road, London E14 9RL ☎ 0207 515 1162	Records of the Port of London Authority	133
The Boat Museum South Pier Road, Ellesmere Port, Cheshire CH65 4FW ☎ 0151 355 5017 archives@boatmuseum.org.uk http://www.boatmuseum.org.uk/archive.htm	Records of barges and boats on canals in the north-west of England.	134

Address	Records referred to:	See Page
Gwent Record Office County Hall, Cwmbrân NP44 2XH ☎ 01633 644 886 gwent.records@torfaen.gov.uk http://www.llgc.org.uk/cac/cac0004.htm	Records of Newport Pilotage Authority	133
Ellis Island on-line database www.ellisislandrecords.org	Passenger manifests (1892-1924) and lists of alien seamen (1917-1924) arriving through the Port of New York and Ellis Island.	32
Hudson's Bay Company Archives Provincial Archives of Manitoba 200 Vaughan Street, Winnipeg, Manitoba, Canada R3C 1T5 ☎ (204) 945 4949	Archives of the Hudson's Bay Company.	128
Hull University, Brynmor Library Cottingham Road, Hull HU6 7RX ☎ 01482 465 265 archives@lib.hull.ac.uk http://www.hull.ac.uk/lib/archives/	Records of Trinity House, Hull	91
Hydrographic Department Ministry of Defence, Taunton ☎ 01823 337 900	Records of World War 1 and World War 2 wrecks.	118
John Rylands Library Manchester University, 150 Deansgate, Manchester M3 3EH ☎ 0161 834 5343 jhodgson@man.ac.uk http://rylibweb.man.ac.uk	Some material related to East India Company.	131
Lloyd's Manager's Secretarial Department, Lime Street, London EC3M 7HL	Citations for Lloyd's medals	82
Liverpool Record Office & Local History Service Central Library, William Brown Street, Liverpool L3 8EW ☎ 0151 225 5417 RO@lvpublib.demon.co.uk http://www.liverpool.gov.uk/	Records of some marine insurance companies.	139
Liverpool University Archives PO Box 123, Liverpool L69 3DA ☎ 0151 794 2696 archives@liv.ac.uk	Cunard Shipping Company: • Staff registers, 1880-1922 • Good collection of ship's plans	138
Corporation of London Records Office PO Box 270, Guildhall, London EC2P 2EJ ☎ 020 7332 1251 http://www.corpoflondon.gov.uk/	Records of Freedom of City of London	140
Pepys Library, **Magdalene College**, Cambridge.	The Duke of Buckingham's Survey of Mariners and Ships, 1619 (Ref: PL 2122)	11

Address	Records referred to:	See Page
Master Mariners' Company The Clerk, Master Mariners' Hall, HQS 'Wellington', Temple Stairs, Victoria Embankment, London WC2R 2PN	Records of the Master Mariners' Company.	140
Medway Archives Office Civic Centre, Strood, Rochester, Kent ME2 4AU ☎ 01634 332714 archives@medway.gov.uk http://cityark.medway.gov.uk/centre.html	Records of Trinity House, River Thames Pilots Association	91
Merchant Navy Association Enquiries and Research, 131 Foxholes Lane, Callow Hill, near Redditch, B97 5YT		72, 74
Modern Records Centre University of Warwick Library, Coventry CV4 7AL. ☎ 01203 524 219 archives@warwick.ac.uk http://www.warwick.ac.uk/services/library/mrc/	The Modern Records Centre has a good collection of Trade Union Records[119] that include the national records of the National Union of Seamen (from 1911) and some of the branch records of the British Seafarer's Union (from 1911).	140
Norfolk Record Office Gildengate House, Anglia Square, Upper Green Lane, Norwich NR3 1AX ☎ 01603 761349 norfrec.nro@norfolk.gov.uk http://www.norfolk.gov.uk/council/departments/nro/nroindex.htm	Records of Yarmouth Port and Haven Commissioners	132
North East Lincolnshire Archives Town Hall. Town Hall Square, Grimsby DN31 1HX john.wilson@nelincs.gov.uk	Registers of those apprenticed to the fishing industry in Grimsby, 1879-1937	85
Northumberland Record Office Melton Park, North Gosforth, Newcastle-upon-Tyne NE3 5QX	Records of the Newcastle Guild of Master Mariners	140
P&O Art Collection P&O Corporate Affairs, 207 The Chambers, Chelsea Harbour, London SW10 0XF		126
Public Record Office of Northern Ireland 66 Balmoral Avenue, Belfast BT 9 6NY ☎ 028 90 251 318 proni@doeni.gov.uk	Records of some marine insurance companies; Agreements and Crew Lists for ports in Northern Ireland (1863-1938)	59, 61
International Committee of the Red Cross Archives Division, Public Information Centre, 19 avenue de la Paix, CH 1202 Genève, Switzerland. ☎ +41 (22) 734 60 01 archives.gva@icrc.org http://www.icrc.org	Prisoner of War records	79

Address	Records referred to:	See Page
Royal National Lifeboat Institution RNLI Headquarters West Quay Road, Poole, Dorset BH15 1HZ	[Enquirers might consider offering a donation.]	135
UK Shipwreck Computer Index Longstone Heritage Centre, St. Mary's, Isle of Scilly TR21 0NW, Cornwall. Attn: Richard Larn ☎ 01720 22924	Shipwrecks around the coast of the British Isles mainly concentrating on the 12th to 19th centuries.	118
Shaftesbury Homes and Arethusa The Chapel, Royal Victoria Patriotic Building, Trinity Road, London SW18 3SX. Attn: Edward Hardman ☎ 020 8875 1555 The *Arethusa* Old Boys Association (Hon. Sec., John Bruce, 13 Park Terrace, Crimchard, Chard, Somerset TA20 1LA) have a website at www.users.zetnet.co.uk/arethusa/history.htm	Records of the training ship *Arethusa*. [Enquirers might consider offering a donation].	87
Société Jersiaise The Secretary, 7 Pier Road, St. Helier, Jersey, Channel Islands. www.societe-jeriaise.org	Records of Jersey Merchant Seamen's Benefit Society.	93-94
Southampton University Library Highfield, Southampton SO17 1BJ. ☎ 01703 593724/592721 archives@soton.ac.uk http://www.archives.lib.soton.ac.uk/guide/	Applications for pensions to the 1st Duke of Wellington, Master of Trinity House, 1829-1852 (reference MS 61).	91
Mrs Eileen Stage 150 Fulwell Park Avenue, Twickenham, Middlesex TW2 5HB	Coastguards' Index	132
Suffolk Record Office, Ipswich Branch Gatacre Road, Ipswich IP1 2LQ ☎ 01473 584 541 pauline.taylor@libher.suffolkcc.gov.uk http://www.suffolkcc.gov.uk/ libraries_and_heritage/sro/	Records of Trinity House, Ipswich	91
Sunderland City Library 28/30 Fawcett Street, Sunderland SR1 1RE ☎ 0191 514 8439	Photocopy of register of Trafalgar Square Aged Seamen's Homes	93
East Sussex Record Office The Maltings, Castle Precinct, Lewes BN7 1YT ☎ 01273 482 349 http://www.eastsussexcc.gov.uk/archives/ main_page.htm	Records of Trinity House, Newhaven and district	91
Tower Hamlet's Local History Library and Archive Bancroft Library, 277 Bancroft Road, London E1 4DQ ☎ 020 8980 4366	Good collection of Lloyd's Register (1842/43 – 1978/79) and Mercantile Navy List (1934-1957)	111-112

Address	Records referred to:	See Page
Tyne & Wear Archives Blandford House, Blandford Square, Newcastle upon Tyne NE1 4JA ☎ 0191 232 6789 Ext. 407 twas@dial.pipex.com www.thenortheast.com/archives/	Newcastle Admiralty Court Trinity House, Newcastle Trinity House, South Shields Sunderland and Tyne Pilotage Authorities	16 91 91 133
Whitby Museum Pannett Park, Whitby, North Yorkshire YO21 1RE ☎ 01947 602 908 graham@durain.demon.co.uk http://www.durain.demon.co.uk	Muster Books of Whitby ships: 1708-1805; 1835-1838	50
Great Yarmouth Maritime Museum 4 South Quay, Great Yarmouth, Norfolk NR 30 2QH	Records of Great Yarmouth Shipwrecked Sailors Home.	93
North Yorkshire County Record Office Malpas Road, Northallerton (Correspondence to: County Hall, Northallerton, DL7 8AF) ☎ 01609 777 585	Records of Trinity House and Merchant Seamen's Hospital, Scarborough.	91

APPENDIX 3
REFERENCES AND BIBLIOGRAPHY

General Reading

- Thomas L. Ainsley, *A Guide Book to the Local Marine Board Examination* (South Shields: the author) 1856 [later editions published until at least the 49th edn, 1891].

- Amanda Bevan (ed.), *Tracing your Ancestors in the Public Record Office*, (PRO), 5th edn. 1999

- Joseph Blunt, *The Shipmaster's Assistant and Commercial Digest* (E. & G.W. Blunt, New York) 1837; reprinted (Macdonald and Jane's, London) 1974.

- Michael Bouquet, *South Eastern Sail - Merchant Shipping from the Medway to the Solent 1840-1940* (Newton Abbot: David & Charles)

- Peter Box, *All at sea: the nautical experiences of Edwardians and Victorians along the Thames coast from Great Yarmouth to Dover* (Lowestoft: Rushmere Publishing), 1992.

- Frank T. Bullen, *The Men of the Merchant Service* (London) 1900.

- R.J. Cornewall-Jones, *The British Merchant Service* (London) 1898.

- Capt. A.G. Course, *The Merchant Navy: A Social History* (Fredk Muller Ltd) 1963.

- David Dobson, *Scottish Maritime Records, 1600-1850: a guide for family historians* (St. Andrews, Fife) 1996.

- Aled Eames, *Ships and Seamen of Gwynedd* (Gwynedd Archives Service), 1976.

- Tim Flannery (ed*), Life and Adventures, John Nicol, Mariner, 1776-1801*, (Melbourne) 1997.

- Alec Gill, *Lost Trawlers of Hull, 1835-1987,* (Beverley: Hutton Press), 1989.

- Basil Greenhill, *The Ship: The life and death of the Merchant Sailing Ship, 1815-1965,* (London: HMSO) 1980.

- Basil Greenhill, *The Ship: The century before steam: The development of the Sailing Ship , 1700-1820,* (London: HMSO) 1980.

- A.A.C. Hedges, *History in Camera: East Coast Shipping,* (Haverfordwest: Shire) 2nd edn 1989.

- Charles Hocking, *Dictionary of Disasters at Sea during the age of steam* (London) 1969.

- Peter L. Hogg, *Basic Facts about...Using Merchant Ship Records for Family Historians,* (Birmingham: FFHS), 1997.

- Archibald Hurd, *History of the Great War: The Merchant Navy* (London) 1921.

- Susan Campbell Jones, *Welsh Sail,* (Gomer Press), 1976.

- Frank Knight, *The Clipper Ship* (Collins) 1973.

- Tony Lane, *Grey Dawn Breaking: British Merchant Seafarers in the late twentieth century,* (Manchester University Press) 1986.

- Tony Lane, *The Merchant Seamen's War* (Manchester University Press) 1990.

- Richard Larn and Clive Carter, *Cornish Shipwrecks: The South Coast* (Pan).

- Richard Larn, *Devon Shipwrecks* (Pan) 1974.

- Lew Lind, *Sea Jargon: A Dictionary of the unwritten language of the sea*, (Cambridge: Patrick Stephens), 1982.

- Christopher Lloyd, *The British Seaman, 1200-1860, a social survey*, (London: Collins). 1969.

- David Marcombe, *The Victorian Sailor* (Haverfordwest), Shire Album 131, 1985.

- Michael Mason, Basil Greenhill and Robin Craig, *The British Seafarer* (Hutchinson/BBC in association with NMM) 1980.

- Alison McLeay, *The World of the Onedin Line*, (Newton Abbot: David & Charles), 1977.

- Ronald Parsons, *Trying to find a seafaring ancestor* (Gumeracha, SA: Gould Books), 1988.

- David R. MacGregor, *Square Rigged Sailing Ships* (Argus Books) 1977.

- Robert Simper, *Britain's Maritime Heritage*, (Newton Abbot: David & Charles) 1982.

- Robert Simper, *East Coast Sail - Working Sail 1850-*(Newton Abbot: David & Charles).

- Robert Simper, *North East Sail - Berwick to King's Lynn* (Newton Abbot: David & Charles) 1975.

- Robert Simper, *Scottish Sail - A Forgotten* (Newton Abbot: David & Charles).

- A. Hassell Smith (ed.) *A Case of Piracy in the Sixteenth Century*, (Norwich) 1983.

- David Starkey (ed.) *Sources for a new maritime history of Devon*, (University of Exeter) 1987.

- A.J.Tennent, *British Merchant Ships Sunk by U-boats in the 1914-1918 War* (Starling Press) 1990.

- Grant Uden, *British Ships and Seamen, Book One: The Ships*, (MacMillan St. Martin's Press) 1969.

- Grant Uden, *British Ships and Seamen, Book Two: The Seamen*, (MacMillan St. Martin's Press) 1969.

- Simon P. Ville, *English shipowning during the Industrial Revolution: Michael Henley and son, London shipowners, 1770-1830* (Manchester University Press), 1987.

- Milton H. Watson, *Disasters at Sea* (Cambridge: Patrick Stephens Ltd 1988.

- *Mariner's Mirror* (Society for Nautical Research) published quarterly since 1911.

- *Sea Breezes: the magazine of ships and the sea*; published (Liverpool) monthly since 1919.

- *Maritime History* published (Newton Abbot: David & Charles) half-yearly from 1971.

- *Maritime History Newsletter* (Maritime History Group, Memorial University of Newfoundland) 1976 –

- *Newsletter of the Maritime Economic History Group* (Maritime Studies Research Unit, Memorial University of Newfoundland) published half-yearly since March 1988.

ENDNOTES

Introduction

1. N.A.M. Rodger, *Naval Records for Genealogists* (PRO Handbook No. 22) 1998.

2. G. Charles, *India and the Far East: A Genealogists Guide*, (Society of Genealogists) in press 2002.

3. T.V.H. Fitzhugh, East India Company Ancestry, *Genealogists' Magazine*, 1984, **21** (5) 150-4, and references cited therein.

4. I.A. Baxter, India Office Library and Records: A Brief Guide to Biographical Sources, 1959

5. Commissioned Sea Officers of the Royal Navy 1660-1815 (National Maritime Museum) 1954

Trade and Taxation

6. Public Record Office, Descriptive List of Exchequer, Queen's Remembrancer Port Books, Part 1, 1565-1700, 1960. {E190}

7. To E 190:
   Exchequer K.R. Port Books 1701-1798, Part I East Coast: Berwick to Yarmouth, *List and Index Society*, 1970, **58**.
   Exchequer K.R. Port Books 1701-1798, Part II South-East South and South-West Coasts: Ipswich to Barnstaple, *List and Index Society*, 1971, **66**.
   Exchequer K.R. Port Books 1701-1798, Part III South-West and West Coasts: Plymouth to Carlisle, *List and Index Society*, 1972, **80**.

   To E 122:
   Exchequer K.R. Customs Accounts (E 122), Vol. I Aldborough to Lyme Regis, *List and Index Society*, 1969, **43**
   Exchequer K.R. Customs Accounts (E 122), Vol. II Lymington to York with Associated Ports and Addenda, *List and Index Society*, 1970, **60**.

8.   B. Foster (ed.), *Port Books of Southampton 1435-36* (Univ. of Southampton) 1963.
B. Dietz (ed.), *Port and Trade of Early Elizabethan London: Documents* (London Record Society) 1972.
R.W.K. Hinton (ed.), *Port Books of Boston in Early Seventeenth Century* (Lincoln Record Society) 1956.
The Gloucester Port Books Database, 1575-1765 on CD-ROM (University of Wolverhampton) 1998

9.   J.C. Hotten, *Original Lists of Persons Emigrating to America, 1600-1700*, 1874.

10.   *Naval Officers Shipping Lists*, with introductions (Microfilm Academic Publishers):
East Florida, 1764-1769 {CO 5/570}
Georgia, 1752-1767 {CO 5/709-710}
Jamaica, 1683-1818 {CO 142/13-20}
Maryland, 1689-1754 {CO 5/749-750}
Massachusetts, 1686-1765 {CO 5/848-851}
New Hampshire, 1723-1769 {CO 5/967-969}
New Jersey, 1722-1764 {CO 5/1035-1036}
New York, 1713-1765 {CO 5/1222-1229}
Nova Scotia, 1730-1820 {CO 221/28-35; CO 217/44; T64/84; T 1/360, 369, 379, 387, 393, 411, 416, 424, 447 and HO 76/1}
South Carolina, 1716-1767 {CO 5/508-511}
Virginia, 1698-1769 {CO 5/1441-1450 and T 1/481-482, 484, 488, 494, 498, 506}
West Indies (excluding Jamaica), 1678-1825 {CO 27/14; CO 33/13, 15; CO 41/12; CO 76/4; CO 106/1, 3-5; CO 166/6; CO 259/2-3; CO 265/1; CO 278/7; CO 317/1}

11.   Edward Carson, *The Ancient and Rightful Customs: A History of the English Customs Service*, (Faber & Faber), 1972.

12.   R.C. Jarvis, Records of Customs and Excise Services, *Genealogists' Magazine,* 1948, **10** (7) 219ff.

13.   *List of the Records of the Board of Customs and Excise from 1697*, 1967, List and Index Society, **20**. {Covers CUST 1 to CUST 27 and CUST 45}

14. K.O. Kupperman, J.C. Appleby and M. Banton (ed), *Calendar of State Papers, Colonial, North America and West Indies 1574-1739* (London and New York) 2000. {CD-ROM}

15. Todd Gray, *Early-Stuart Mariners and Shipping: The Maritime Surveys of Devon and Cornwall, 1619-35*, Devon and Cornwall Record Society, New Series **33**, 1990.

Military Connections

16. *Letters of Marque – Declarations against France, Spain and the United Provinces, 1777-1783*, with introduction by W.E. Minchington and D. Starkey (Microfilm Academic Publishers). {Covers HCA 26/33-59}
Letters of Marque – Declarations against America, 1777-1783, with introduction by W.E. Minchington (Microfilm Academic Publishers). {Covers HCA 26/60-70}

17. Records of the High Court of Admiralty, 1967, *List and Index Society*, **27**. {Covers HCA 1 - HCA 15, HCA 20 - HCA 32/500}

18. *Mediterranean Passes (1662-1784)* with introduction by D. Richards (Microfilm Academic Publishers). {Covers ADM 7/75-103, 630}.

19. N.A.M. Rodger, Some Practical Problems Arising from the Study of the Receiver of Sixpences Ledgers, *The Mariner's Mirror*, 1976, **lxii**, 223-4; *idem.*, The Receiver of Sixpences Ledgers, *ibid*, 270.

20. Ralph Davis, Seamen's Sixpences: An Index of Commercial Activity, 1697-1828, *Economica*, Nov 1956, 328-42.

21. Christopher Lloyd, *The British Seaman, 1200-1860, a social survey*, (London: Collins). 1969, page 158.

Legal Disputes

22. H. Horowitz, *Chancery Equity Records and Proceedings: 1600-1800* (PRO Handbook No. 27), 1995.

23. R.E.F. Garrett, *Chancery and other Legal Proceedings* (Pinhorns) 1968.

24. Peter Wilson Coldham, Genealogical Resources in Chancery Records, *Genealogists' Magazine*, 1979, **19** (10) 345-9.

25. Mark H. Hughes, Notes on some Finding Aids to Chancery Proceedings in the Library of the Society of Genealogists, *Genealogists' Magazine*, 1975, **18** (3) 129-31.

26. Records of the High Court of Admiralty, *List and Index Society*, 1967, **27**. {Covers HCA 1 - HCA 15, HCA 20 - HCA 32/500}
     Oyer and Terminer Records - Descriptive List: 1535-1834, *List and Index Society*, 1969, **45**. {Covers part of HCA 1}
     Oyer and Terminer Records - Descriptive List: 1535-1834, *List and Index Society*, 1969, **46**. {Covers part of HCA 1}
     High Court of Admiralty, Index to Prize Papers of the War 1739-1748, *List and Index Society*, 1973, **93**. {Covers HCA 32/94 - /160.}
     High Court of Admiralty, Index to Prize Papers of the Seven Years War 1756-1763, *List and Index Society*, 1975, **112**. {Covers HCA 32/161 - /259.}
     High Court of Admiralty Prize Papers, Index 1776-1786, *List and Index Society*, 1982, **183**. {Covers HCA 32/260 - /493.} {This Volume duplicates the last 165 pages of vol. 27.}
     High Court of Admiralty Prize Papers, Index 1793-1803, *List and Index Society*, 1982, **184**. {Covers HCA 32/494 - /930.}
     High Court of Admiralty Prize Papers, Index 1803-1817, *List and Index Society*, 1983, **194**. {Covers HCA 32/931 - /1345.}

27. Tracing Your Scottish Ancestors (Scottish Record Office) 1990, sections 11.31-11.34 and 12.18. – Cecil Sinclair, *Tracing your Scottish Ancestors: A Guide to Ancestry Research in the Scottish Record Office* (Edinburgh, 2nd ed., 1997).

Registration of Merchant Seamen

28. Leonard Harris, *London General Shipowners' Society, 1811-1961*. A private publication produced for the 150th anniversary of the society.

29. Nicholas Cox, The Records of the Registrar General of Shipping and Seamen, *Maritime History*, 1972, **2** (2) 168-88.

30. A.R. Archibald, *Alien Seamen*, US Immigration and Naturalization Service Lecture No 26 (Washington) 1934.

Certificates for Sea Officers

31. Charles Hardy, *A Register of Ships employed in the Service of the East India Company from the year 1760*, 1835.

32. John Jean, *Jersey Sailing Ships* (Chichester) 1982.
A.G.E. Jones, *Ships Employed in the South Sea Trade, 1775-1861*, 1986.
J.S. Cumpson, *Shipping Arrivals and Departures, Sydney, 1788-1825*, 1964.
Rhys Richards and Joceyln Chisholm, *Bay of Islands Shipping Arrivals and Departures, 1803-1840*.
H.A. Woods, *Our Master Mariners: a Selected Biographical Dictionary of Sea Captains who sailed in Australian waters over 150 years from 1789-1938* (Sydney: privately published), 1992.
[Note: Lists 127 master mariners; documentation on which this work is based has been donated to the Mitchell Library, Sydney]

Agreements, Crew Lists and Log Books

33. Jon Press, The Collapse of a Contributory Pension Scheme: The Merchant Seamen's Fund, 1747-1851, *Journal of Transport History*, 1979, **5** (2) 91-104.

34. *A Guide to the Crew Agreements and Official Logbooks, 1863-1913, held at the County Record Offices of the British Isles* (Maritime History Archive).
Record Offices and Libraries holding Crew Lists and Agreements for 1863-1913, Crew List Index Project (CLIP), Information Sheet No. 3 (2000).
Personal enquires to some record offices.

35. For example: *Ships' Crew Lists: A Handlist of Records in the Devon Record Office*, (Exeter: Devon RO) 1987.

36. David Alexander and Keith Matthews, *An Index to the Crew Lists and Agreements of the British Empire 1863-1913,* 1977. {A leaflet}

37. *A Guide to Agreements and Crew Lists: Series II (BT 99), 1863-1912* (Maritime History Archive), 1992. In two parts covering 1861-1890 and 1891-1912.

38. A.A. and B.M. Austin, *Bristol Merchant Seamen. An alphabetical index to the crew lists for the year 1863.* This covers those crew lists held at the Bristol Record Office. It is available as BRISTARS.RTF in CompuServe on-line library; a printed copy is available at the PRO. Belfast mariners at http://www.standard.net.au/~jwilliams/mariners.htm Cardiff Master Mariners at http://www.angelfire.com/de/BobSanders/CREWIN.html

    Somerset crew lists at: http://www.somerset.gov.uk/archives/database/crewlist.htm Mariners and ships is Australian waters at http://sites.archivenet.gov.au/Mariners/

39. *Ships and Seafarers of Atlantic Canada* (Maritime History Archive) 1998. {CD-ROM}

40. *A Guide to Agreements and Crew Lists: Series II (BT 99), 1913-1938* (Maritime History Archive), 1987.

41. Edward Higgs, *Making Sense of the Census*, (PRO Handbook No. 23) 1989

42. *Report for the Select Committee on Manufactures, Commerce, and Shipping*, House of Commons 19 August 1833.

43. J.P. Press, *Economic and Social Conditions of the Merchant Seamen of England 1815-1854*, Ph.D. Thesis (Bristol University) 1978.

44. Sir Walter Runciman, *Collier Brigs and their Sailors*, reprinted (Conway Maritime Press) 1971.

45. David Marcombe, *The Victorian Sailor*, 1985, Shire Press Album No 131.

46. Basil Greenhill and Denis Stonham, *Seafaring under Sail: The life of the merchant seaman* (Patrick Stephens Ltd) 1981.

47. J.P. Press, *Economic and Social Conditions of the Merchant Seamen of England 1815-1854*, Ph.D. Thesis (Bristol University) 1978.

War Service and Medals

48. Kelvin Smith, Christopher T. Watts and Michael J. Watts, *Records of Merchant Shipping and Seamen* (PRO Readers' Guide No. 20), 1998 reprinted with addendum 2002.

49. D.T. Barriskill, , *A Guide to the Lloyd's Marine Collection at Guildhall Library* (2nd edition, London) 1994.

50. Kelvin Smith, Christopher T. Watts and Michael J. Watts, *Records of Merchant Shipping and Seamen* (PRO Readers' Guide No. 20), 1998 reprinted with addendum 2002.

51. *The Second World War: A Guide to Documents in the Public Record Office* (PRO Handbook No 15); 1993, revised edition 1998.

52. D.T. Barriskill, *A Guide to the Lloyd's Marine Collection at Guildhall Library* (2nd edition, London) 1994.

53. N.A.M. Rodger, *Naval Records for Genealogists* (PRO Handbook No. 22) 1998.

54. Jim Gawler, *Lloyd's Medals 1836-1989: a history of medals awarded by the Corporation of Lloyd's*, (Ontario: Hart Publishing) 1989.

Apprenticeship, Charities and Pensions

55. J.P. Press, *Economic and Social Conditions of the Merchant Seamen of England 1815-1854*, Ph.D. Thesis (Bristol University) 1978.

56. E.P. Stapleton, Trinity House Petitions, *Genealogists' Magazine*, 1934, **6** (11) 490-2.

57. *Trinity House Petitions*, 1987, Society of Genealogists

58. M.E. Duggan, Trinity House Apprenticeships, *Genealogists' Magazine*, 1970, **16** (8) 427-30.

59. Roland Pietsch, A Boyhood at Sea: The records of the Marine Society at the National Maritime Museum, *Genealogists' Magazine*, 2001, **27**, 3-8.

60. A.G. McBride, *The History of Dreadnought Seamens Hospital at Greenwich*, (Greenwich) 1979

61. Sunderland Seamen on the 19th Century, *The Journal of the Northumberland & Durham Family History Society*, 1994 **19** (1) 20-22.

62. Trafalgar Square Sunderland Aged Seamen's Homes, 1839-56 (Northumberland & Durham Family History Society), 1994 on microfiche.

63. History of the Aged Merchant Seamen's Homes, *Antiquities of Sunderland Vol. IV* (1903) (Sunderland Antiquarian Society*).*

64. Marie-Louise Backhurst, *Family History in Jersey*, (Jersey: Channel Isles Family History Society) 1991.

65. Rosemary Oliver, War Office District Pension Returns, *Genealogists' Magazine* 1984 **21** (6) 196-9

Births, Marriages and Deaths at Sea

66. *The British Overseas*, Guildhall Library Research Guide 2 (Guildhall Library), 3rd edition, 1994 page 9 *et loc.cit.*

67. Pubic Record Office reference BT 334/117; letter written 12 December 1991

68. N.A.M. Rodger, *Naval Records for Genealogists* (PRO Handbook No. 22) 1998.

69. *The British Overseas*, Guildhall Library Research Guide 2 (Guildhall Library), 3rd edition, 1994.

70. *The Cross of Sacrifice, Volume 5, The Officers, men and women of the Merchant Navy and Merchant Fleet Auxiliary, 1914-1919* (Naval & Military Press).

71. Barbara Tomlinson, The National Maritime Museum Memorial Index, *Family Tree Magazine*, August 1997, 22.

72. Miriam Scott, *Prerogative Court of Canterbury Wills and Other Probate Records* (PRO Readers' Guide No. 15) 1997.

73. David Dobson, *Scottish Seafarers of the seventeenth century* (St. Andrews) 1992.
David Dobson, *Scottish Seafarers of the eighteenth century* (St. Andrews) 1996.

74. N.A.M. Rodger, *Naval Records for Genealogists* (PRO Handbook No. 22) 1998.

Lloyd's Marine Collection

75. D.T. Barriskill, *A Guide to the Lloyd's Marine Collection at Guildhall Library* (2nd edition, London) 1994.

76. F.W.D. Manders (ed.) *Bibliography of British Newspapers: Durham and Northumberland* (British Library) 1982. {Volumes also available on Kent and Wiltshire.}
Tercentenary Handlist of English and Welsh Newspapers, 1620-1920 (Times) 1920.

77. B.C. Stephenson, *Lloyd's Captains' Register* (Lloyds, London) 1869.

78. D.T. Barriskill, *A Guide to the Lloyd's Marine Collection at Guildhall Library* (2nd edition, London) 1994.

79. Admiralty Merchant Shipping (Losses), 1919, *House of Commons Paper* 199.

Registers of Shipping

80. Rupert C. Jarvis, Ship Registry - 1707-86, *Maritime History*, 1972, **2** (2) 151-67.

81. Robert Craig and Rupert Jarvis, *Liverpool Registry of Merchant Ships, 1967*, Chetham Society, 3rd series **xv**.

82. G. Farr, *The Ship Registers of the Port of Hayle* (National Maritime Museum) 1975, Maritime Monographs and Reports No 20.
Grahame Farr, Custom House Registers of the West Country, In H.E.S. Fisher (ed.), *The South-West and the Sea (Papers from a Seminar)* (University of Exeter) 1968.

83. Richard E. Keys, *Dictionary of Tyne Sailing Ships - A record of merchant sailing ships owned, registered and built in the Port of Tyne from 1830 to 1930* (Richard E. Keys, 99 St John's Road, High Cross, Benwell, Newcastle upon Tyne NE4 7TJ) 1998.

84. *Ships and Seafarers of Atlantic Canada* (Maritime History Archive) 1998. {CD-ROM}

85. P&O Art Collection, P&O Corporate Affairs, 207 The Chambers, Chelsea Harbour, London SW10 0XF.

86. Grahame Farr, *Shipbuilding in North Devon* (National Maritime Museum) 1976, Maritime Monographs and Reports No. 22. See also: Grahame Farr, *The Ships and Harbours of Exmoor* (Exmoor Press) 2nd edn. 1974.

87. J.F. Clarke, *Building ships on the North East coast, Part 1 (c.1640-1914), Part 2 (c.1914-c.1980)* (Berwick Press) 1997.
    See also: J.W. Smith & T.S. Holden, *Where ships are born Sunderland 1346-1946: A History of shipbuilding on the River Wear* (Sunderland: Thomas Reed & Co. Ltd) 1953 (first published 1946).

88. *Directory of Shipowners, Shipbuilders and Marine Engineers* published since 1952 by *Shipbuilding and Shipping Record* (Westminster)

89. L.A. Ritchie, ed., The Shipbuilding Industry. A guide to historical records (Manchester, 1992).

90. John Hailey (compiler), *Maritime Sources in the Library of the Society of Genealogists*, (London: Society of Genealogists) 1997.

91. G. Charles, *India and the Far East: A Genealogists Guide*, (Society of Genealogists) in press 2002.
    I.A. Baxter, *India Office Library and Records: A Brief Guide to Biographical Sources*, (London) 2nd ed.,1990.
    Martin Moir, *A general guide to the India Office Records*, (London: British Library) 1988.
    T.V.H. Fitzhugh, East India Company Ancestry, *Genealogists' Magazine*, 1984, **21** (5) 150-4, and references cited therein.

92. Anne Bulley, Country Ships and Free Mariners in Bombay, *Genealogists' Magazine*, 2001, **27** (1) 14-17.
    Anne Bulley, *The Bombay Country Ships, 1790-1833*, (Richmond: Curzon) 2000.
    Anne Bulley (ed.), *Free Mariner: John Adolphus Pope in the East Indies, 1786- 1821* (London: British Association for Cemeteries in South Asia), 1992.

93. Anthony Farrington, *A biographical index of East India Company Marine Service Officers, 1600-1834*, (London: British Library), 1999.
    Anthony Farrington, *Catalogue of East India Company ships' journals and logs, 1600-1834*, (London: British Library), 1999.

94. G. Charles, *India and the Far East: A Genealogists Guide*, (Society of Genealogists) in press 2002.

95. *City Livery Companies and related organisations*, (Guildhall Library Research Guide No. 3), 3rd edn., 1989.

96. *The Records of the Company of Shipwrights of Newcastle upon Tyne, 1622-1967*, Vol. I (1970), Vol. II (1971), Publications of the Surtees Society **181** (1966 {sic}).

97. *City Livery Companies and related organisations*, (Guildhall Library Research Guide No. 3), 3rd edn., 1989.

98. F.W.D. Manders (ed.) *Bibliography of British Newspapers: Durham and Northumberland* (London: British Library) 1982. {Volumes also available on Kent and Wiltshire.}
    Tercentenary Handlist of English and Welsh Newspapers, 1620-1920 (Times) 1920.
    R.S. Crane and F.B. Kaye, *Census of British Newspapers 1620-1800*, 1927.

99. Peter Mathias and A.W.H. Pearsall (ed.), *Shipping: A Survey of Historical Records* (Newton Abbot: David & Charles) 1971.

100. Gordon Reid and Michael Stammers (compilers*), Guide to the records of Merseyside Maritime Museum*, (St. John's Newfoundland) 1995.

101. H.A.L. Cockerell and Edwin Green, *The British Insurance Business 1547-1970 - An Introduction and Guide to Historical Records in the United Kingdom* (Heinemann) 1976.

102. Stephen Jones, Community and Organisation - Early Seamen's Trade Unionism on the North-East Coast, 1768-1844, *Maritime History*, 1973, **3** (1) 35-66.
    Norman McCord, The Seamen's Strike of 1815 in North-East England, *Economic History Review*, 1968 (21) 127-143.
    D.J. Rowe, A Trade Union of the North-East Coast Seamen in 1825, *Economic History Review*, 1972 (25) 81-98.

103. John Bennett *Trade Union and Related Records* (University of Warwick Library) 5th ed. 1988.
Richard Story and Janet Druker, *Guide to the Modern Records Centre* (University of Warwick Library), 1977.
Richard Story and Susan Edwards, *Supplement to the Guide to the Modern Records Centre* (University of Warwick Library), 1981.

104. John Saville and Brian Dyson, *The Labour archive at the University of Hull*, (Brynmore Jones Library) 1989.

105. R.A. Storey, Records of the Working Man, *Genealogists' Magazine*, 1980, **20** (1) 5-10.

Record repositories and their holdings

106. National Library of Australia, *The Handbook of the Australian Joint Copying Project*.

107. Kelvin Smith, Christopher T. Watts and Michael J. Watts, *Records of Merchant Shipping and Seamen*, (PRO Readers' Guide No. 20), 1998 reprinted with addendum 2002.
Amanda Bevan (ed.), *Tracing your Ancestors in the Public Record Office*, (PRO), 5th edn. 1999.

108. R.J.B. Knight, *Manuscripts in the National Maritime Museum*, (London: Mansell), 1980.

109. D.T. Barriskill, *A Guide to the Lloyd's Marine Collection at Guildhall Library* (2nd edition, London) 1994.

110. Gordon Reid and Michael Stammers (compilers*), Guide to the records of Merseyside Maritime Museum*, (St. John's Newfoundland) 1995.

111. John Hailey (compiler), *Maritime Sources in the Library of the Society of Genealogists*, (London: Society of Genealogists) 1997.

112. Roberta Thomas under the guidance of Keith Matthews (compilers) *Preliminary Inventory of Records held at the Maritime History Group* (Maritime History Group, Memorial University of New Foundland) 1978.

113. Guide to the State Archives of New South Wales No. 17, *Guide to Shipping and Free Passenger Records* (Sydney) 1984.

114. Jim Melton, *Ships' Deserters 1852-1900*, (Sydney: Library of Australian History), 1986.

115. *Ancestors in Archives: A guide to Family History Sources in the Official Records of South Australia* (Adelaide) 1991.

116. Andrew G. Peake, *Sources for South Australian History* (Dulwich, SA: Tudor Australia Press), 1987.

117. Andrew G. Peake, *National Register of Shipping Arrivals: Australia and New Zealand*, (Blackburn, Vic. AFFHO), 2nd edn 1989.

118. *Guide to Genealogical Research in the National Archives* (Washington), 1983.

119. John Bennett *Trade Union and Related Records* (University of Warwick Library) 5th ed. 1988.
Richard Story and Janet Druker, *Guide to the Modern Records Centre* (University of Warwick Library), 1977.
Richard Story and Susan Edwards, *Supplement to the Guide to the Modern Records Centre* (University of Warwick Library), 1981.

INDEX

Principal entries are shown in **bold**.